# Essay Index

REPOSSESSING AND RENEWING

Alfred Stieglitz
SPRING SHOWERS
1902
*From the collection of*
*the Museum of Modern Art*

*Sherman Paul*

# REPOSSESSING AND RENEWING

Essays in the
Green American Tradition

LOUISIANA STATE UNIVERSITY PRESS / BATON ROUGE

Designer: Dwight Agner
Type face: VIP Electra
Typesetter: The Composing Room of Michigan, Grand Rapids
Printer: Edwards Brothers, Inc., Ann Arbor, Michigan
Binder: Universal Bookbindery, San Antonio, Texas

LIBRARY OF CONGRESS CATALOGING IN PUBLICATION DATA

Paul, Sherman.
    Repossessing and renewing.
    Includes bibliographical references and index.
    1. American literature—History and criticism—Addresses, essays, lectures.
    2. Paul, Sherman. I. Title.
PS121.P316                      810'.9                      75-5351
ISBN 0-8071-0179-6

*In Memory of My Father*

"What is good in this book is given back."
BLACK ELK

Where does the drama get its material? From the "unending conversation" that is going on at that point in history when we are born.

KENNETH BURKE

Our present situation, in whatever sphere of life one looks, must be regarded as a field of creative possibility, or it is frankly intolerable.

PAUL GOODMAN

Affirmation of man's whole nature, embrace of all the earth bound up with it... is the American principle. Presently not only in the idea of the American democracy, but in all vigorous American thought, it must come to us out of the air, the soil, the climate as well as institutionally, since it is so deeply ingrained in us from birth. If there is a green American tradition, it is this. The dreams of all our moral authorities from Emerson to Randolph Bourne have embodied it. The grandest of our expressions, Lincoln and Whitman's of yesterday, Stieglitz's of today, have projected it. . . . There has been no major American life uninspired by it.

PAUL ROSENFELD

In the end, tradition is what makes a critic, the tradition he grows out of and the tradition he tries to re-establish independently, for its inherent meaning. And when there is a break in tradition—too injurious a sense of "strangeness"—the critic wants to restore consciousness of it.

ALFRED KAZIN

# CONTENTS

# PREFACE

THIS COLLECTION is an informal account of the Emersonian tradition and of some of the critics who have fostered it. It is also, in the commentary, an account of how (and why) I possessed it—an account of one scholar, in his time, finding a usable past, a vital tradition. The work itself is autobiographical, though not autobiographical work like the commentary, because one's vocation (lifework), as Emerson knew, is a fable of you and because it permitted me, as Thoreau said of his enterprise, to live in the ideas that contain the reason of my life. It is not necessary to rehearse these ideas now but only to note that I find that the value of my work resides in them and that they concern renewal: the reclamation of possibility by means of the imagination—of language, of art—and the continuity of human effort.

Ever since I came on the phrase in Paul Rosenfeld's *Men Seen*, my working title for the organic tradition treated here has been "the green American tradition." It yields now to the title, which tells of process, of the deep impelling force to which the work answers. But I retain it in the subtitle even at the risk of evoking the more promissory title of Charles Reich's recent book.

**Preface**    I owe this book to Austin Warren, its instigator and a sustaining presence in all the work gathered in it; to John Callahan and Richard Wentworth, who encouraged me to complete it; and to my wife, Jim, who, as always, shared in its making. The most immediate debt in a book such as this is to the editors who solicited my work and the publishers who granted permission to reprint it. I am grateful to them and would like to mention them here: E. F. Bozman of Everyman's; Gordon N. Ray and Henry Thoma of Houghton Mifflin Company; Gwynne Evans of the *Journal of English and German Philology*; Donald Jackson of the University of Illinois Press; Robert Hatch, Warren Miller, Helen Yglesias and Beverly Gross of *The Nation*; Hilton Kramer of *The New Leader*; Jeanne Sinnen and John Ervin, Jr., of the University of Minnesota Press; and Merle Brown of *The Iowa Review*. I would also like to acknowledge and remember other help: for Thoreau, the attentive listening of Harriet and Milton Stern and, after its publication, the criticism of Warner Berthoff; for Paul Rosenfeld, the reading by Edward Davidson and the letters provided by Lewis Mumford; and for Gary Snyder, discussion with Kim Merker and Douglas Wilson.

Harry Callahan and Art Sinsabaugh immediately answered my request for photographs, and John Szarkowski kindly procured the Stieglitz photograph for me.

These are the photographers about whom I have written and whose work has become part of my own. "Spring Showers," an early photograph by Stieglitz, is one of my favorites and seemed to me the appropriate frontispiece for this book. Callahan's "Detroit 1941" (from *Harry Callahan*, 1967) represents his sensitive art and is also, for me, rich in associations with Transcendentalism and Orientalism and the landscape of my summertime. Sinsabaugh's "Midwest Landscape #97" (from 6 *Mid-American Chants*/11 *Midwest Photographs*) depicts the environment with which long residence has made me familiar. I speak of my associations, but the photographs, of course, merit attention solely because they are profound images of the artists'

interaction with the world.

I thank the libraries of Yale University, Columbia University, the University of Illinois, and the University of Iowa for extending me their services, and the English Department, Research Council, and Graduate College of the University of Iowa for financial assistance.

What is reprinted here has sometimes been retouched but not appreciably revised. The essay on John Jay Chapman stands in the slightly modified version of a subsequent printing in *Transcendentalism and Its Legacy*. The essays on William Carlos Williams and Alfred Kazin have not been published before.

# ACKNOWLEDGMENTS

MUCH OF the material in this volume has appeared in other publications, some under slightly altered titles. Grateful acknowledgment for permission to reprint is made for "Emerson's *Essays*," from the book *Essays* by R. Waldo Emerson, Everyman's Library, published by E. P. Dutton and Company, Inc. in the United States and by J. M. Dent and Sons Ltd., in Great Britain; for "Thoreau's *Walden*," the introduction to the Riverside Edition of *Walden* published by Houghton Mifflin Company; for "Paul Rosenfeld," the introduction to *Port of New York*, University of Illinois Press; and for "The Identities of John Jay Chapman," *Journal of English and Germanic Philology* (1960), University of Illinois Press.

Under "Louis Sullivan and Organic Architecture" appear five book reviews from *The Nation*: "Architect of American Thought," CXCI (1960); "Architect of Society," CXCII (1961); "For Love of Chicago," CCII (1966); "Interior Order," CCIV (1967); and "No Loitering!" CCIX (1969). "Van Wyck Brooks's Ordeal and Pilgrimage," also a review, is reprinted with permission from *The New Leader*, XLVIII (1965) © The American Labor Conference on International Affairs, Inc. "Randolph Bourne" is from *Randolph Bourne*, University of Minnesota Press, Mpls. © 1966. "From Lookout to Ashram: The Way of Gary Snyder" appeared in *Iowa Review*, I (1970).

REPOSSESSING AND RENEWING

# EMERSON'S *ESSAYS*

EMERSON created a vocation and a form, both in response to the spirit of the times. In "New England Reformers," he said that the "disease with which the human mind now labors is want of faith"—want of faith in the force of the individual man, in the rectitude of his character, in the certainty of the moral law which sustains the universe, and which, as spirit, pervades man and his affairs. Having that faith abundantly, he became its leading spokesman; in a critical and experimental age bent on organized social reform, he remained detached, only to be free to be its prophet and to affirm again for New England the efficacy of individual moral regeneration. He himself had courageously come out of the church of his fathers; believing that forms without life are heavy yokes, he left all institutions behind: he set up as a "scholar." By scholar, he meant "intellectual." He meant the free spirits, the "genius" and the artist, whose stock-in-trade is in themselves and their perception of truth. The times called for apostles of Being, not defenders of Seeming; and against the manipulators of masses and matter, he put the man of ideas. He believed the truth—spiritual power—would prevail: not by itself, however, but through man, in his resolute heroism, in his daring to use ideas as weapons in the face of a deaf and hostile society. He expected 1 the scholar to lead his society, and he had every hope that society would be led, because he believed that at bottom all men reverence truth and find irresistible the sway of the great man who makes it luminous. His scholar, therefore, acquired the mantle of heroes; he was militant, steadfast, indomitable. "God offers to every mind its choice between truth and repose"— truth is action, its field is "the state of war" of public strife. "Beware," he exclaims with revolutionary ardor, "when God lets loose a thinker on this planet."

The former minister, then, became the lecturer and writer; he exchanged his pulpit for the far-flung Lyceum; his sermon became the lecture, and the lecture the essay. In this way, his new calling created its own form of expression, a form more available, lay and democratic. And it represented also a liberation of the moral conscience, a protestantism without a church, a spiritual communication launched in the open air for the ears of all. Thus, the essay, in which Emerson's beliefs were given their final form, was itself his message: chiefly about the ebb and flow of spirit, it proclaimed the democracy of spirit.

The *Essays, First Series* (1841) are for the most part reworkings of lectures Emerson gave in the years of his gathering fame, when, with his groundwork laid in *Nature* (1836), he forthrightly applied his doctrines to the reigning institutions of New England. In *The American Scholar* (1837), he had summoned the studious from their closets to the needed action of the day; in *The Divinity School Address* (1838), he had called for a clergy with a living faith to replace the "pale negations" of Unitarianism. Now, from the lecture series, *The Philosophy of History* (1836–1837), *Human Culture* (1837–1838), and *Human Life* (1838–1839), he gleaned for his *Essays* his thoughts on moral individualism. Here were his ethics of self-reliance, his most sustained examination of the prerogatives of individual genius and of the spirit that supplied his strength.

These essays, like his early sermons, show Emerson's preoccupation with character. Character, the necessity for virtue, adherence to duty—these were already ingrained New England traits. Emerson, however, identified them with individualism

2

and with the early nineteenth-century discovery of self. He planted character in the soil of individual uniqueness and obedience to the spirit within; his essays called for self-culture as man's first duty. In effect, he transformed the narrow notion of character as the limitation of self into the wider notion of personality as the expansive expression of self. He preached the divinity of man and his self-sufficiency, and only Whitman, taking his fire from Emerson, proclaimed more nakedly the pride of this assurance. Though this God-prompted individualism was not without an element of power, it was not the ruthless or rugged individualism with which we associate the word today. When he talked of the divinity of man, Emerson meant the completeness of man: "To us," he said in a sermon, "remains the work of forming *entire men.*" And one of his services to his generation was his reexamination of the nature of man and his insistence as supreme guides on his imaginative and spiritual faculties—those faculties whose workings are not so easily charted, whose joy is innerness, and whose agency is subliminal and sublime.

Perhaps what Emerson intended might be translated in the language of our time as authenticity. He exalted the man who could find his center, with perfect equanimity rest on himself and act from himself, the autonomous man "who has ventured to trust himself for a taskmaster." If he said in "Self-Reliance"—the spine of the essays and the one to which we give our deepest assent—"Whoso would be a man, must be a nonconformist," he meant nonconformist to the end of self-discovery, not puerile defiance. He knew that for nonconformity "the world whips you," and that, viewed from the vantage of self-culture, "Society everywhere is in conspiracy against the manhood of every one of its members." Still, it was a duty of the scholar to avoid that conspiracy; as he told the graduating class at Dartmouth College, the way to truth and selfhood was lonely, and one must take solitude for his bride. It was for this reason that Emerson had removed to Concord, and that his friends Thoreau and Alcott had found that distance from Boston sufficient for a life of independence. It was a way of life that

Emerson time and again defended, for it was an attempt to live sincerely and become the "genuine man" he had sketched long before in the notes of a sermon:

> Marks of the genuine man.
>
> 1. He believes in himself.
> 2. He speaks the truth.
> 3. He thinks the truth.
> 4. He acts the truth.

The belief in oneself prescribed here is not arrogant egoism; it is qualified by something larger than the self, by an active dedication to Truth. And to make this clear, Emerson added a final note: "Grandeur of this character and its identity with religious life."

Nothing shows better the moral sensibility of New England than this clustering of character, truth, and religious life by one who would enfranchise man. *Truth* and *Spirit* are the dominant words of the essays, and the horizon they extend before us fades into the Reality that alone promises man a true fulfillment. To find one's self, as Emerson had—and his whole work is a diary of this continuing discovery—is to find within oneself, in inner experience, the current of the Universal Being. It is to partake of spirit, to act with the power of God. For self-reliance, Emerson assures us, is nothing if it is not a dependence on and obedience to this overwhelming tide. The essay, therefore, that complements "Self-Reliance" is "The Over-Soul." And the trust that underlies his individualism—for he recognized the incompleteness of men and had known the paralysis of self-distrust—is expressed in "Compensation": in the vigilance of law in the universe, in the glorious fact that "all things are moral" and that by heeding the law the partial man can be made whole. Emerson's exaltation of man, therefore, is praise to the God in man, and the self he describes is the higher self whose paternity is divine. What he rhapsodizes in the essays are his occasions of spiritual enlargement.

A self-realization of this high order provides the thematic unity of the essays and gives them their electric and liberating effect. How high-handed this genial man can be with the sacred idols of his generation! History—the records of the past, the traditions that were so readily appealed to by the Unitarians; "history," he says, "is an impertinence and an injury if it be any thing more than a cheerful apologue or parable of my being and becoming." This is indeed a new way of seeing; and Emerson began with "History" because it was a convenient way of describing his challenging belief that all external circumstances must submit to the mind of man, that by assimilating fact as idea he was invincible. The primacy of mind, the reality of ideas, these are the heart of his Idealism; for ideas are the correlatives of the moral law, they are the content of the intuitive communion with the Over-Soul on which he built his faith. And since this communion was vouchsafed every man *now*, what need for the sanctions of the past and second-hand? Consciousness was the test of history: "It is all to be explained from individual experience." Rich in experience, a man might possess all the world, might be "an owner of the sphere." Having in this way nullified the authority of history, as he had in *Nature* the limitations of space and time, Emerson turned to its positive use; and this, like everything external to man, lay in its educative function. "The world exists for the education of each man," he said: history is valuable only when he can read the historical event as a psychological event that explains himself, when the panorama of the past is used as the symbol of his own development. And there was still an ultimate value: by taking this new point of view, man was able to perceive the radical identity of spirit beneath the flow of events. Far from being a record of diversity, history—and art and literature as well—would reveal the divine unity; it could be read, as Emerson believed everything should be read, as an expositor of the divine mind.

The enabling act of moral individualism is this transfer of point of view; and the rest of the essays are perspectival reports of Emerson's insights into the mysteries of the Over-Soul. "Self-Reliance" is his metaphysics of self-trust and his account of the revolution it works in the relations of man to religion, education, art, and society. It is also the thinly disguised manifesto of a man who would get *his* work done and *his* truths said; nowhere else is the first person so conspicuous. "Compensation," his favorite doctrine, shows his need for faith in the invulnerability of virtue. "If I am true," he wrote in his Journal, "the theory [Compensation] is, the very want of action, my very impotency, shall become a greater excelling than all skill and toil." In "Spiritual Laws," he explains this faith: "The good soul [Over-Soul] nourishes me and unlocks new magazines of power and enjoyment to me every day." He deals tenderly with marital life (the only institution he allows) in "Love," and, following Plato, advances from sensuous to intellectual love, expressing again the unsatisfied spiritual longing of man. Love is a means; but friendship, a purer relationship that excites his imagination more, is the consummation of virtue, "an absolute running of two souls into one." In "Friendship," he describes its austerities and occasions; and since it is another form of intellectual ecstasy, conversation—how characteristically Emersonian—is its mode. (His neighbor, Bronson Alcott, said that his idea of heaven was a conversation; and Margaret Fuller, another member of his circle, instead of lecturing, held public "conversations.") To balance these essays on higher duties, Emerson returns to the "lower observances" of everyday life in "Prudence." The Yankee, practical virtues, the attention to "trifles" he once deplored, here find their praise; for law operates on the level of sense as well as the level of spirit, and is an exacting teacher of character. "Heroism," however, is a more kindling theme, anticipated in "Self-Reliance" and "Spiritual Laws." For the hero acts as a law to himself, negligent of prudential risks— he is all that Emerson wished to be, daring, active, good-humored, hospitable, militantly stoical. He is the man of will and energy; and perhaps to amend this description of the defiant self, he recognized again in "The Over-Soul" the first duty of dependence and abdication of the will. "Circles" is an intellectual geometry of spirit, a celebration of the dynamics of Idealism; vibrant with the excitement of possibility, it describes a universe in process, where limitations are temporary and merely the platform of higher advances. And "Intellect" and "Art" are its

6

companion pieces, the one on the receptive and constructive
phases of mind—the expanding and empowering, and the
form-making—and the other, a further testimony to the fact
that in the hands of the genius art is not artifice, but "the action
of the soul on the world." It concludes with the self-reliant man
at his proper work, a creator in the finite, an agent of God.

The *Essays, First Series* are characterized by expansiveness;
only "Prudence" and "Circles" acknowledge limitation. The
*Essays, Second Series* (1844), however, speak with a growing
knowledge and experience of the limiting conditions of life. The
first series is alive with the assurance of inspiration and power
that Emerson called health; the second series confronts the facts
of ebbing power and decay. And where the earlier essays speak
out of eternity, from the timeless unity of ecstasy, the later essays
recognize, in the conception of a process world, the element of
time, the fact that in nature wholeness is achieved through
succession. "You have not got rid of parts," Emerson now
writes, "by denying them." Here, the lover of unity shows his
respect for facts, particulars, diversity, surface—all the limitations his metaphysics was intended to transcend. At last Emerson shows us the skepticism from which his optimism was
struck. He wrote in "Experience," "I have set my heart on
honesty in this chapter."

The central essays are "The Poet," "Experience," "Nature,"
and "Nominalist and Realist." All of the remaining essays consider the problems of character, only now in closer connection
with actual life—they are Emerson's oblique tribute to society.
"Character" is another description of "manly force"—a rework-
ing of the themes of "Self-Reliance," "Heroism," and "Friendship"; such men of character compose his good society in
"Manners." "Politics" also turns on the aboriginal force in
character: institutions are the lengthened shadows of men, their
origin and end is character. One of Emerson's fine sketches of
his age, "New England Reformers," puts his case for private
inner reform, the indispensability of character. And "Gifts,"
with its high demand for "a portion of thyself," is Emerson's
confession of social defenselessness. The central essays explain

7

the growth of thought that brought about this transition. "The
Poet," for example, should be compared with "The American
Scholar" or "Heroism." There the great man is a doer. The poet,
who now embodies Emerson's experience and replaces the
scholar as his ideal, is a sayer. "We call the poet inactive," he
had complained in "Spiritual Laws"; and from that height he
had asked, "Why should we be cowed by the name of Action? . . . The rich mind lies in the sun and sleeps, and is
Nature. To think is to act." To see and to report is enough; and
although the man of affairs never loses his fascination, Emerson
extols the poet as the most complete man. In "Experience," his
finest essay on the psychology of spirit, Emerson records, as
nowhere else, his failure to conquer the world by perception.
Fully aware now of a nature other than himself, a *flowing* nature
that uses everything to its ends rather than man's and that fulfills
its purposes in time—the vast, prodigal, terrifying, living energy
he describes in "Nature"—aware of this movement, his vasta-
tion comes from finding it too difficult to grasp Reality, the
abiding permanence of things. Reality, nevertheless, can be
found by sounding the depths of one's skepticism, by accepting
one's servitude to mood and succession and surface, by the
decisive action of taking up actual life. "Life is not dialectics," he
writes; there are positive goods in "the potluck of the day." For
the goods of life are incalculable, and at one end life opens into
novelty—there are spontaneous moments when the veil is removed and Being again works its miracle. Emerson now admits
his helplessness: it is not for him to summon inspiration, but
await it faithfully; faith is not faith but faithfulness, affirmation
encloses skepticism. This deeper knowledge also informs the
essay, "Nominalist and Realist." "I loved the centre," he says,
"but doated on the superficies." If evolutionary nature is prolific
of particulars and "will not remain robed in a thought," he will
learn to use the many as a transitory symbol of the one. If there is
no end in nature, as he said in "Circles," then he will be the
"endless seeker" of more adequate images for his thought.

To be an endless seeker of Truth, to stand ready to perceive it
anew regardless of consistency—this is the liberating freshness

8

of Emerson, the test of his sincerity, and the end to which he put his essays. Edmund Wilson has spoken of their "uninviting literary form," and Henry James has said that Emerson "is a striking exception to the general rule that writings live in the last resort by their form." Emerson, however, was not indifferent to the value of form. Although most of the essays follow the topical development of his earlier sermons and, in their way, preach from a text and illustrate it by examples, their form embodies his central idea that Truth is the larger generalization that encloses the seeming contradictoriness of things. The form itself is a way of seeing. The key to his literary method is his determination to see all sides and to reconcile them ("Nominalist and Realist" is an excellent example): to state the case on the prudential level and again on the level of spirit. His form thereby instructs the reader in this essential lesson: "The soul's scale is one, the scale of the senses and the understanding another." The end of the conduct of life, the end of art, is to accommodate the duality of experience—to transcend the lower and partial by rising to the higher and whole. All good is in seeing this difference; and the essays, especially the more dialectical ones, "Art" and "Experience," are the means to this perception. No one put more reliance on perception, so that, armed with it, "the value of life lay in its inscrutable possibilities"; no one, not even James, was so intent on making form the instrument of this experience. Because Emerson put the essays to these dynamic uses, he knew that they might be perplexing. But he also knew that the essays were quick with the inspiration he had known, that their tone was the proof of the genuineness of his experience. His essays had caught and conveyed the fleeting Reality. Their power to certify this for us now is the measure of Emerson's achievement.

**Emerson's Essays**

For me, Emerson was an origin. Discovering him in Cambridge after the war was liberation.

Four years in the air force made me ready. But my preparation began earlier with those teachers in high school (in Lakewood, Ohio) and college (in Iowa City) who were legatees of New England. I do not remember reading Emerson with

*Author's Note*

9

any of them, but when I recall them I feel the presence and appeal of their dedication to New England plain living and high thinking. My teachers at the University of Iowa were New Humanists and New Critics: disciplined, spiritual men. I found this congenial; it accorded with my Jewish heritage. Much later and for different reasons New Critics would be called talmudists, but as Austin Warren, who did most to confirm me in the vocation of literature, used to say, we were seminarians trying to make ourselves worthy of the literary priesthood, and some of the priests, as he said of himself, were apostles to the Midwest.

In 1938, when I came to Iowa, the School of Letters, directed by Norman Foerster, was a center of New Humanism and of the New Criticism that did not supplant so much as extend it. The university was small then, and undergraduates sometimes attended the lively meetings of the Humanities Society and Sunday evenings at Professor Foerster's house—he used them to read drafts of his own learned papers. For undergraduates like myself, these high literary events were merely part of the wonderfully indiscriminate excitement of college life that included rallies on the steps of Old Capitol for the Abraham Lincoln Brigade and productions of *Johnny Johnson* and *Waiting for Lefty*. Perhaps the university theater, so famous then, countervailed the equally famous School of Letters. I learned later that E. C. Mabie, its director, had helped to found the Federal Theater—and Mabie's theater, where I studied community theater for a while, was the reason I had come to Iowa in the first place. My father's desperate checks were all the reminder of social realities and the luxury of literary pursuits I needed. They did service for the courses in economics and sociology I never took. So did my roommate from New York, who worked for meals in a greasy spoon and had to leave school for financial reasons, and who became a Communist not only because his existence was harsh but because he had been moved by the idealism that prompted him to copy out the text of *Democratic Vistas* he had chanced on in the
Union browsing room.

That I did not find my experience especially discordant may
be explained by the fact that it was exhilarating and neither my
deprivation nor class consciousness was acute. I lived in a
rooming house and partly worked my way, but my clothes were
good—my mother saw to that. I knew the lore of immigrants
in a strange land, but I felt less an outsider than I do now. My
rearing had been in a WASP suburb where nothing had been
closed to me, and I had not yet deeply felt its sting. I recognized the excellence of my teachers, not their gentility; and
because I was able to go elsewhere for graduate work, I did not
feel as fully as I should have the enormity of Foerster's discreet
advice that I not continue.

This was not wound enough to propel my bow, though
much later it provided whatever ground of pleasure I found in
Foerster's rejection of my view of Emerson as a reconciler of
man and nature. None of the major writers about whom I have
written, not even Emerson or Thoreau, had been wholly acceptable to the New Humanists and New Critics. For all of
them were indebted to romantic and democratic thought and
belonged to the tradition of resurgence in American literature.
Of this tradition I learned nothing at college; I had to find it for
myself. And what compelled me was not hostility to my
teachers' views, though I was vaguely dissatisfied with their
neglect of history and American literature, but the milieu itself, one that had made me keenly responsive to America and
eager to follow writers like Thomas Wolfe who were again
discovering it.

My American education began during the war. Besides af-
fording me time for reading big books like *Moby-Dick* and the
Beards' *The Rise of American Civilization,* the army was my
school of geography and politics, acquainting me with some of
the continent and some of the world and thoroughly teaching
me the nature of "system." I did not object to the war but to
bureaucracy and incompetent authority. The army riled me,
but at the same time as it challenged my democratic faith, it
stirred my desire to study out the land, its idioms and its men.
What strike me now on looking back are the intensity of that

11

desire and the incredible energy, unused and stored up by years of army life, that was ready to back it at war's end.

When I was released in 1946, I did not continue the graduate work in English I had begun at Lehigh University. Aided by the GI bill, I began again at Harvard, where I took a doctorate in the history of American Civilization. Harvard had figured in my imagination in much the way Boston had in Howells', but I found it admissive, a democracy of intellect. A great institution, its greatness was institutional. Its busy teachers, almost without exception, were first-rate, not only on their own account, but because they were sustained, as I felt I was, by the tradition and atmosphere of the place.

Of my teachers, the most influential was Perry Miller. At Iowa my training had been in New Criticism, and at Lehigh it had been in philology. Now, because of Miller, it was in intellectual history. His enthusiasm for ideas and the brilliant drama he made of them overwhelmed me. He introduced me to Emerson and the Transcendentalists and to his own concern with epistemology. I wrote my thesis on Emerson under his supervision—he read and approved it during a year's absence in Europe—and it was published because he recommended it to the Harvard University Press. And it may be that I began with Emerson because the way in which Miller had begun his work suggested to me that I find for myself an appropriate beginning.

Yet for all I owe Miller—and such debts are incalculable—I did not owe him the spirit in which I undertook my work. Miller, I felt, was too intellectual an intellectual historian: too much concerned with ideas in themselves (Lionel Trilling calls them "pellets of intellection") and too little concerned with the men who had held them and the conditions of life in which they had been entertained. He lacked the moral passion for ideas one finds in Irving Babbitt, Paul Elmer More, and Vernon Parrington, in Edmund Wilson, F. O. Matthiessen, and Trilling. His delight was in intellectual system, in the play (game: exegesis) of ideas; and this, I found, even though he was not attentive to the formal elements of literary texts, was in a

12

way New Critical. Our intellectual differences were profoundly personal; they became clearer when we became colleagues. But my Emerson reflects them as well as the heady
period after the war when we lived in Brookline, Cambridge,
and the Concord countryside, and I was free and glad to be
pursuing my vocation.

This introduction is one of two on Emerson I did for Everyman's Library. I wrote it in Urbana, Illinois, where we had
gone after Cambridge, in a little red house, holed up during
the fall following an automobile accident that summer. It took
all my energy for two months to write it, but the lassitude of
shock, I think, is not detectable. A by-product of my work on
Emerson, it represents here *Emerson's Angle of Vision: Man
and Nature in American Experience,* which was published in
1952.

How much of oneself is in a first book! Rereading it now, I
fall in with familiar cadences and recognize early contours of
thought—and wish that it were less thickly written, more co-
gent and sophisticated. The preponderance of quotations is
owing to Miller, who was adept at building exposition with
them, and to Kenneth Burke, from whom I had learned to
"cluster" them; the "admirative" approach and the tendency of
the history of ideas to become biographical and phenomenological are my own. I am happily surprised by the way my intui-
tion of Emerson's "imagination" drives through the book and
outlines his "world." And surprised too by how much the Emerson in it is a psychologist. I did not have a psychology then, but
clearly it should have been that developed by Perls, Hefferline,
and Goodman in *Gestalt Therapy,* which, with a kind of concurrence that startles me, was published in 1951. Emerson was
my scholar-hero then, and remains one, because, as Jonathan
Bishop and William Bridges have recently shown so well, he
taught us how to reattach ourselves to life and to renew ourselves in vital experience. Because he refused to make the universe a blind alley and was willing to let new generations speak
their truths, it was easy for me to identify with him.

# THOREAU'S *WALDEN*

LIFE—the "irrepressible satisfaction with the gift of life"—is the single theme of Thoreau's writing, all of which is biographical, the record of an aspiring soul's exploration of reality. "I . . . require of every writer," Thoreau said in explaining the "I," the subjective center of *Walden*, "a simple and sincere account of his own life." From first to last, all his work was devoted to telling not only how he had lived but how alive he had been, how much life he had got. But founded as it was on actual firsthand experience, it was never the immediate report of his experiment on life. Instead, it was the fruit of a slow growth, ripened by recollection, deeply colored by the hues of his mind, and "folded many times thick" by the seasons through which it matured. Place the day-to-day entries in his *Journals* against their final appropriation in his finished work, and the imaginative alchemy—the symbolization of his materials—becomes apparent. For he discovered early that "what is actually present and transpiring is commonly perceived by the common sense and understanding only, is bare and bald, without halo or the blue enamel of intervening air," but that "let it be past . . . and it is at once idealized." Then, he said, "it is a deed ripe and with the bloom on it. It is not simply the understanding now, but the imagination that takes cognizance of it."

Now, this is true of *Walden*, which, for all of its riches of common sense and actual things, was the "flower and fruit of a man," a deed ripe with the bloom on it, full of fragrance. According to Thoreau's intention, *Walden* was not to lead men to strict economies, not even to a life in the woods. In a letter to his "disciple" Harrison Blake, telling of his first encounter with Daniel Ricketson (a spiritual seeker who having read *Walden* turned to Thoreau for guidance), he reported that Ricketson wanted him, "having common sense," to "write in plain English always" in order to "*teach* men in detail how to live a simpler life." But, Thoreau told Blake, "I have no scheme about it,—no designs on men at all; and, if I had, my mode would be to tempt them with the fruit, and not with the manure." Give man, he added, changing the metaphor, "the bread of life compared with which *that* is bran," let him "only taste these loaves, and he becomes a skillful economist at once. He'll not waste much time in earning those." Unfortunately, like Ricketson, the reviewers and readers misunderstood Thoreau's intention: the symbolism—or *extra-vagant* expression, as he called it—they thought only extravagance ("namby-pamby," "stuff," "mystical," Ricketson claimed); they did not see that "the words which express our faith and piety are not definite" but "significant and fragrant like frankincense"; and even Thoreau's warning that words have several meanings, a "volatile truth," went unheeded. He did not intend, of course, to "level downward to our dullest perception always, and praise that as common sense"; and he had adopted symbolism because he had seen his universe symbolically and because it was the only way to truly communicate his valuable experience, to speak "like a man in a waking moment, to men in their waking moments." If the "commonest sense is the sense of men asleep, which they express by snoring," nothing less would awaken them or cure their "brain-rot." Indeed, to get men to see their universe symbolically, to read beyond its lessons of matter-of-fact, was one of the most liberating things Thoreau had to offer.

Having misunderstood his method, however, these literalists of common sense also misunderstood what he had to say. They read *Walden* only as an account of Thoreau's life in the woods; they took the "residual statement," the factual record of his life at the pond, for the whole story, once more forgetting Thoreau's instructions—that the heavier element, the narrative fact, was required to float the lighter or spiritual fact. Seizing upon the dramatic act of his withdrawal from society, they thought him uncivil and, like Emerson who provided his Walden acres but did not approve of the experiment, branded him a hermit. As Holmes later remarked, giving the judgment of his generation, Thoreau was "the nullifier of civilization, who insisted on nibbling his asparagus at the wrong end." And perhaps to heal the sting of his remarks on economy, they saw in this simple means of dodging the pressures of society an end they considered worthless. Did this crank (and there were cranks aplenty in New England preaching the salvation of fresh air and water, of graham flour, of going without money) expect them, so happily satisfied with the luxurious benefits of civilization, to listen to his exultation over a needless belt-tightening? At best, as American society compounded the evils Thoreau had avoided, *Walden* was read as a social gospel—and *Walden* today is most often associated with his doctrine of simplicity, with escape from the burdens of complicated urban existence. That escape, however, is usually associated with the woods, with a return to a long-lost pastoralism; and even in Thoreau's time the identification of his experiment with the woods, as if only the woods promised fulfillment, forced him to clarify his intention by dropping the subtitle, *Life in the Woods*. If *Walden* needed any subtitle, it should have been *Life*; and to this end he offered, and continues to offer, not an escape, but the greatest discovery and gift: an open universe, forever novel, alive, and full of life, forever awaiting and sustaining the untried enterprises of man.

This was the discovery he made when he went to Walden in the spring of 1845, a discovery that certified the transcendental faith he had learned from Emerson and that, in the years of "decay" following Walden, he cherished and maintained by writing his book. Only after the fact, when he was powerless to perform the deed again, did he relive it in words, and then he more poignantly and fully realized its significance. With the trials and losses of these years, those glorious years of achievement climaxing the endeavors of his youth were subtly transformed into a testament of prospective hope, and *Walden* affirmed his faith in "the unquestionable ability of man to elevate his life by a conscious endeavor." The ecstasy of his former life in the Elysian fields—as he called Walden then— was magnificently reported because it was now colored by his resolution; and the season of joy was given its natural place among the other seasons he had known in such a way that joy was not only the gift of youth but the reward of a mature remaking of one's life.

That one does not readily separate these chronological strands, however, was due in part to Thoreau himself. He knew the artistic value of his narrative facts, that his "fable" had to have a firm foundation, and he minimized all that time had wrought by speaking of *Walden* as the record of his residence at the pond in 1845–1847, claiming that only a few details had been added. And because he believed that the hero hides his struggles and that one should not communicate his dyspepsia but his joy, he did not "propose to write an ode to dejection, but to brag as lustily as chanticleer in the morning." His spiritual history, nevertheless, was woven into the texture of *Walden*. The resolute tone, if nothing else, proclaims it; and the chapter on "Higher Laws," full of his later determination of discipline and purity, and indeed the very structure of the book, with its culmination in rebirth, disclose it. To read *Walden*, then, as the account of only the Walden years—and it has been read in this way because it has long been assumed that he wrote the book at the pond—is to miss the tremendous struggle that makes *Walden* so glorious. It is to overlook the obstacles and evils that transcendentalists, like all human kind, have known, to make the faith that Thoreau enacted easy, when he himself knew the abyss beneath unity and the horrors of spiritual emptiness, and confessed during the years he was writing *Walden* that "a ticket to Heaven must include tickets to Limbo, Purgatory and Hell." And it is to disregard the fact that the years at Walden yielded two books, that there he wrote A *Week on the Concord and Merrimack Rivers* and infused it with the new found joys of his adventure. For *Walden* was his second book and his second attempt to find a form that would express his life; it was primarily the spiritual history of the years from 1845 to 1854, just as the *Week* was the spiritual history of the years from 1839 to 1849. Companion volumes, they cover the course of his quest for an organic life in Nature, the easy, available communion of his youth and the hard-won, intellectual communion of his manhood; taken together, they are the American equivalent of Wordsworth's *Prelude*; they are the richest account we have of American transcendental experience.

## II

One would have to know more of Thoreau's life than he provides in *Walden* in order to explain the "private business" he referred to when he said that "my purpose in going to Walden Pond was not to live cheaply nor to live dearly there, but to transact some private business with the fewest obstacles." For his private business was a concern of long standing, a matter long delayed that he preferred to speak of in whimsy and allegory. When he told of how he had desired to spend his life in years past, he said that he had been anxious "to stand on the meeting of two eternities, the past and the future, which is precisely the present moment," that he had been eager "to anticipate, not the sunrise and the dawn merely, but, if possible, Nature herself," and that he wanted "to hear what was in the wind, to hear and carry it express!" He told how in trying to achieve these ends—to live in the moment or eternal now, to know the laws of Nature so well that in her every phenomenon his mood would find its correspondence, and to participate in spirit and express it for all mankind—he had kept a journal "of no very wide circulation," had been the "self-appointed inspector" and warden of Nature and the wild, and had "woven a kind of basket of a delicate texture [the *Week*]" which no one would buy. His townsmen, he said, would not "make my place a sinecure with a moderate

18

allowance," and his accounts—he punned—had never been "audited." And so he turned "more exclusively than ever to the woods"—for these reasons, and for other losses darkly hinted at in the hound, bay horse, and turtle-dove that he said he had lost long ago. Not one to postpone his life, he went to the pond, built a hut (his "small counting house"), and, entering the business without any capital but his own self-reliance, began his trade with the "Celestial Empire."

It was an unusual trade, and "a labor to task the faculties of a man"—certainly one that he had not been trained for at Harvard College, although there he had first been stirred by a nascent transcendentalism to follow it. Already dedicated to Truth and Principle, and hungry for the superiority and public influence he believed were the warrants of a devotion to Reason (as his college essays clearly show), he was one of those young men who illustrated, according to Henry James, the "queer search" of the New England character for "something to expend itself upon." He was one of the "young men of the fairest promise," whom Emerson addressed in "The American Scholar" on the occasion of the commencement of Thoreau's class: young men "who begin life upon our shores, inflated by the mountain winds, shined upon by all the stars of God" but who "find the earth below not in unison with these" and "are hindered from action by the disgust which the principles on which business is managed inspire." "The American Scholar" and the Emerson who represented him were, of course, a challenging alternative to the professions of expediency; especially since Emerson had wrapped about the scholar the mantle of greatness and had made his work "the study and the communication of principles" and "the conversion of the world" at the same time that he united this public end with individual fulfillment—with the "peculiar fruit . . . each man was created to bear." The scholar, he said at Dartmouth College in the following year, "is the favorite of Heaven and earth, the excellency of his country, the happiest of men. . . . His successes are occasions of the purest joy to all men."

The way to that vocation, however, was difficult because it required self-reliance—the repudiation of the traditional, social institutions of culture—because one's vocation was unique, ultimately one's own character, and even the calling Emerson had created for himself would not afford, as both Alcott and Thoreau were to learn, a sufficient model for others. Like many ideas Emerson announced in his early years with the expectation of immediate enactment, that of the scholar was slow in being fulfilled. Do what he would to instruct the youth who answered his summons, he found—and most painfully in the case of his "brave Henry," in whom he saw the promise of an executive genius and the active powers to engineer for all America that would complement his own passivity—that if the young men "do not wish to go into trade" and "reject all the ways of living of other men," as he told Carlyle in 1842, still they "have none to offer in their stead."

The problem of vocation troubled Thoreau all his life—not that he was without one, but that his was not covered by any respectable label. It was not proper for a youth educated at Harvard, and at great sacrifice on the part of his family, to walk idly in the woods; and while all his classmates were "choosing their profession, or eager to begin some lucrative employment... it required rare decision," Emerson admitted in his funeral tribute, "to refuse all the accustomed paths and keep his solitary freedom at the cost of disappointing the natural expectations of his family and friends." Disappoint them he did, even Emerson who in "Self-Reliance" had approved of Thoreau's determination to follow his genius: "He walks abreast with his days and feels no shame in not 'studying a profession,' for he does not postpone his life, but lives already."

It was easier, perhaps, to walk abreast of the day in the years immediately following his graduation, when schoolteaching put off the expectations of his friends and he was free to begin his apprenticeship as a writer—for that was the vocation he had chosen. He could even delay long enough to get the graduate training Emerson provided him during his stay at the Emersons

in 1841–1843. Apprenticeships, however, have their term and
even Emerson's benign help had its obligations: when
Thoreau's lectures before the Concord Lyceum and his poems
and essays in *The Dial* (which he edited with Emerson) showed
that he was ready, Emerson shipped him off to Staten Island, to
his brother William, as a tutor, with the understanding that this
scholar and poet "as full of buds of promise as a young apple
tree" should have the time and place to continue his work,
"pending the time when he shall procure for himself literary
labor from some quarter in New York." Unfortunately,
Thoreau did not carry his seige against the literary capital; he
could not write "companionable" articles, and what he could
and did write the Knickerbockers would not pay for. He returned
home, having paid his debt to Emerson with failure, and having, meanwhile, acquired other debts, which he paid off in the
following year in his father's pencil factory. Once more an
Apollo enslaved to Admetus, as he frequently lamented his
condition, he simply wrote in his biographical record of the year
before he went to Walden Pond, "Made pencils in 1844."

Thoreau had chosen writing because to be socially useful the
transcendental life had to be expressed and because writing
permitted him to live the transcendental life that was "agreeable
to his imagination." Success in the literary marketplace would
have made this possible: then the very life he had chosen to live
would have paid its way with its own fruit. But having failed to
sell his "baskets," his vocation set him another problem, that of
getting his living without losing his life, that of mingling in the
world where "trade curses everything" without impoverishing
those inspirations and perceptions for which he lived. "If we live
truly," Emerson had posed the problem in "Self-Reliance," "we
shall see truly." To be self-reliant was to live an organic life, to
cut the bonds of artificial social life and remake one's relations
according to the primary laws of Nature; it was self-culture,
nothing less than making one's life one's vocation, tending it as
one would a plant or as a poet shapes a poem. Thoreau never
fully achieved this goal, though at the end of his life, as he

recounted it in "Wild Apples," he was proud of his hardy, long-matured, and spicy fruit, sure that his determination to grow wild had been a good thing even though it had left him dwarfed and stunted and encrusted with thorns. That was the price he had paid to go his own way: the wild apple tree that "emulates man's independence and enterprise" had been browsed on by fate, by the coercions and importunities of society and friends, by the pencil-making and surveying which were, for the rest of his life, in spite of his continued efforts to succeed as a lecturer and writer, the servitudes by which he earned his freedom.

Even by the time he went to Walden, and especially afterwards, his problem was not so much finding a vocation as finding the conditions that would make the one he had never postponed possible; and then the success he sought became the moments of ecstatic communion with Nature, the perceptions and the insights that were *life* and that, by radiating him, vindicated his endeavor to live truly. Everything he wrote from the "Natural History of Massachusetts" to "Walking" was an attempt to define this vocation, from the sympathetic way of beholding "facts" by the "finer organization" of his senses, by an "Indian wisdom," to the sauntering that enabled him by long association with his environment to make the fact "flower in a truth." The bravery this life demanded, and which was one of its attractions for Thoreau, had been proclaimed as early as his lecture on "Society," in his youthful testament, *The Service: Qualities of the Recruit*, where the military imagery that figures in his work was first made explicit, and in "A Winter Walk"; and the leisure it required, and the richer experience it offered, which the pace and tone as well as the actual narrative of his writing always conveyed, were already in his earliest excursions, "A Winter Walk" and "A Walk to Wachusett."

In this early work, however, he defined his vocation only to announce it; from the *Week* on, with growing insistence, he defined it to defend it. For his vocation was defined or focused by the life he lived, by his deepening awareness of the struggle to

22

wrest meaning from Nature and so make his life significant, and
by a widening awareness of the uses of Nature. Indeed, the definition which took the final form of the saunterer—though walking had always been the mode of his life—was that of the student of environment. The loss of the private ecstasy of his youth, when his own delight in Nature had been sufficient, had transformed him into a student of human culture. Though life remained the heart of his vision, his vision had become public, scanning wide reaches of human history, even turning to close scientific scrutiny, that he might learn the essential lessons of man's interaction with the organic world. This was a greater "fruit" than the wild apple, simply because it opened to all men the possibility of self-culture that Thoreau's own life dramatized. And perhaps it was the greatest fruit of transcendentalism as well: for though the function of the organic environment in human culture no longer rests on the transcendental philosophy of Nature—as one sees in Benton MacKaye's *The New Exploration*, a landmark in regional planning directly inspired by Thoreau, "the philosopher of environment"—the transcendental view had led Thoreau to the first American exploration of that relationship. Here, in fact, Thoreau had gone beyond Emerson's *Nature*, which had been the manual of his vocation and his introduction to the uses of Nature, and, unrecognized by his teacher, had engineered for all America.

Although Emerson's treatise, which Thoreau had read during his college years, had awakened him to the new vistas of a life in Nature, he did not at first associate this life with the woods. When he left college, Nature for him was a rather indefinite concept, a "prospect" of untried fields for heroism, a new way of seeing the possibilities of life. It answered his desire, as he wrote in his commencement part on "The Commercial Spirit," for a manly and independent life. Repudiating the "blind and unmanly love of wealth," he would be a "Lord of Creation" rather than a "slave of matter"; he would live in "this curious world which . . . is more wonderful than it is convenient; more beautiful than it is useful; . . . more to be admired and enjoyed than used." To do this, moreover, he would reverse the order of things—a promise he carried out in the *Week* and *Walden*, where vocation became vacation; for "the seventh should be man's day of toil," he said, "and the other six his Sabbath of the affections and the soul,—in which to range this widespread garden, and drink in the soft influences and sublime revelations of Nature."

Such was the life that was agreeable to his imagination, one that he felt was guaranteed by the stimulating assurances of Emerson's *Nature*. There he had learned not only that Nature was beneficent, that it supplied the needs of spirit as well as commodity, but that by means of the wonderful correspondence of man and Nature he could "enjoy an original relation to the universe"—share the currents of Being and thereby become a "creator in the finite." Armed with the idealistic philosophy Emerson had reclaimed for his generation, a philosophy in which ideas were sovereign, he felt that he could "walk even with the Builder of the Universe" and put the foundations under the castles he had built in the air. For Nature, Emerson had shown, was not mechanical but organic, the continuing hand-iwork of God; the life in Nature was the ever-present spirit of God, and her phenomena "the present expositor of the divine mind." Man, therefore, had "access to the entire mind of the Creator" because the ideas he had in his communion with Nature were Ideas, the constitutive Reality of the universe as well as the reality of his mind.

In this organically spiritualized idealism, every fact of Nature answered to a fact of consciousness in the human mind, and because of this correspondence the life of consciousness could best be pursued in Nature. Everything in Nature, the entire external world, could be taken possession of by the mind: the brute fact transformed in this experience into value, fused with the inner and subjective and given its human-spiritual sig-nificance. Seized in this way the fact flowered in a truth; or rather projected in this way—since Emerson in going beyond "Idealism" to "Spirit" had internalized the whole process and

24

had made Nature, the facts themselves, the issue of spirit—
every mood of the mind found its objective expression. As
Thoreau described his youthful confidence in this subjective
idealism in "The Inward Morning,"

> Packed in my mind lie all the clothes
> Which outward nature wears,
> And in its fashion's hourly change
> It all things else repairs.
>
> In vain I look for change abroad,
> And can no difference find,
> Til some new ray of peace uncalled
> Illumes my inmost mind.

The inward morning, the wakefulness he sought later on, was,
of course, the influx of inspiration without which Nature, as he
found, was barren. Then his universe was indeed broken in two,
the galvanic ecstasy gone. But rather than disown the faith in
which he had invested his life, he accepted the implication of
Emerson's statement that to see truly one must live truly: "The
ruin or the blank that we see when we look at nature, is in our
own eye." He found the fault, not in the Emersonian theory,
but in his own unworthiness: he acknowledged the guilt of
impurity. And where once, in his youth, he had all uncon-
sciously had a perfect communion, he now determined, with a
heroism he never dreamed he would be called on to show, to
rebuild his universe and his faith. He tried to bring the poles of
the Emersonian universe together by purifying the channels of
perception, by living a disciplined and ascetic life, and by
studying Nature more objectively. By the one he hoped to renew
his worthiness, by the other to know Nature so intimately that he
could anticipate her moods—together, he hoped, he would
once more complete the circuit of inspiration. But if this conscious endeavor had its rewards in the richer symbolic readings
of Nature of his mature writing, it did not bring with it the
fullness of ecstasy, the flow of inspiration through him. "The
unconsciousness of man," he said in the *Week*, where he
criticized Goethe for being too consciously the artist, "is the   25

consciousness of God." By conscious means he could not retrieve the unconsciousness of his youth, that glorious passivity
he recalled in *Walden*, when he spent his life lavishly "dreaming
awake," "floating over its [the pond's] surface as the zephyr
willed." This was the personal tragedy that humanized the
youth who had had eternity in his eye; this rooted him and
socialized his vision; but it was also the struggle that the hero
tried to hide.

When he first read *Nature* he was hardly aware that the
mountain by which he symbolized his transcendent aspirations
would be so steep. He had been dazzled by the American
scholar who had personally set him to work journalizing and
who later sheltered him—the Emerson in whose world "every
man would be a poet, Love would reign, Beauty would take
place, Man and Nature harmonize." He had been stirred more
deeply than anyone else in his generation by the power of
Emersonian perception in the conduct of life, by the possibility
of making life an art. For *Nature* affirmed that man was no
longer the slave of matter but the shaper of the external circumstances of his life. These he could build around him with the
same organic fitness with which the bark fits the tree, as a
function of the idea that controlled his life, in the very way the
Creator—the Supreme Artist—"put forth" the organic world as
the expression of His Ideas. Man's life would grow out of him in
the way a tree springs from the seed, puts forth leaves, flowers,
and fruit, assimilating and transforming all that Nature provides
for its nurture into a resplendent ripeness. Man would be the
poem of his own creation, or the statue, as Thoreau said, that he
would carve out of the elements about him. And even more
grandly, he would make his own world, the landscape would
radiate from him; he would have, as Thoreau had at Walden,
"my own sun and moon and stars, and a little world all to
myself." This was the exhilarating prospect Emerson had
opened: "'Nature is not fixed but fluid,'" he said. "'Spirit alters,
moulds, makes it. The immobility or bruteness of nature is the
absence of spirit; to pure spirit it is fluid, it is volatile, it is

obedient. Every spirit builds itself a house, and beyond its house
a world, and beyond its world a heaven. Know then that the
world exists for you. For you is the phenomenon perfect. What
we are, that only can we see. . . . Build therefore your own
world. As fast as you conform your life to the pure idea in your
mind, that will unfold its great proportions.'"

To conform one's life to the idea in one's mind, to live, as
Thoreau wrote while he was composing *Walden*, "that you may
the more completely realize and live in the idea which contains
the reason of your life, that you may build yourself up to the
height of your conceptions"—this was to live greatly, to use
one's life wisely. "The whole duty of life," Thoreau said in 1841,
recognizing the problem of vocation, "is contained in the question how to respire and aspire both at once." Already discon-
tented with the tame life he was living as a schoolteacher and
with the fact that he was not marching to his own music, he
proposed that he help himself by "withdrawing . . . [by] deter-
mining to meet myself face to face sooner or later." The solitary
position in which he had pictured himself in his lecture on
"Society" now became the "most positive life that history
notices"—"a constant retiring out of life, a wiping one's hands
of it seeing how mean it is, and have nothing to do with it." And
farming, which he always felt was a noble vocation, first
suggested itself as a solution. But before he could act on it, he
went to the Emersons as handy-man, expecting in the adventure
of friendship that "a great person . . . will constantly give you
great opportunities to serve him."

Friendship was the supreme transcendental relationship, for
without it, Thoreau learned, Nature ceased to be morally significant. He had gone to Emerson with high hopes that in their
relationship the world would learn "what men can build each
other up to be, when both master and pupil work in love." Their
relationship, however, had its undercurrent of antagonism, if
only because of Thoreau's ideal expectancies and Emerson's
benevolent but patronizing attitude toward his superserviceable
Henry. "We do [not] wish friends to feed and clothe our

bodies—neighbors are kind enough for that," Thoreau complained, "but to do the like offices to ourselves. We wish to
spread and publish ourselves, as the sun spreads its rays." Before
long he found that "life in gardens and parlors" was unpalatable
to him, that he was growing "savager and savager every day,"
that his wish, still unfulfilled, was to be "nature looking into
nature," that from this recess he might "put forth sublime
thoughts daily, as the plant puts forth leaves." "When any scorn
your love," he wrote at this time, "let them see plainly that you
serve not them but another. If these bars are up, go your way to
other of God's pastures. . . . When your host shuts his door on
you he incloses you in the dwelling of nature. . . . My foes
restore me to my friends." Even at Emerson's, Nature became
the refuge for his discontent, and before a year had passed, he
wrote: "I want to go soon and live away by the pond, where I
shall hear only the wind whispering among the reeds. It will be
success if I shall have left myself behind. But my friends ask what
I will do when I get there. Will it not be employment enough to
watch the progress of the seasons?" And the next day he added: "I
don't want to feel as if my life were a sojourn any longer. That
philosophy cannot be true which so paints it. It is time now that I
begin to live."

But he lingered because, with Emerson so much away
lecturing, his services were indispensable, and because the
deaths of his brother John and Emerson's son Waldo had united
them in grief. Still the feeling of delay did not abate, but
intensified: "What . . . can I do to hasten that other time . . .
[when] there will be no discords in my life? . . . My life, my life!
why will you linger? . . . How often has long delay quenched my
aspiration! Can God afford that I should forget him? Is he so
indifferent to my career? Can heaven be postponed with no
more ado?" And when he went to Staten Island it was with
reluctance, the stigmata of which were an "unaccountable"
bronchitis and a "skirmishing with drowsiness" that interfered
with his literary projects. The city, moreover, unmanned him,
for though he was always the most perceptive of travelers, he did

28

not have a traveler's temperament; the strange surroundings and the multiplicity of sensations disturbed the tranquillity and stability, the pastoral routine, that he needed. The herds of people—"the pigs in the street" that he wrote of to Emerson—a great tide entering the Narrows and flowing West, all bent on progress, taught him, as he said in "Paradise (To Be) Regained," that "we must first succeed alone, that we may enjoy our success together."

But the most valuable thing his first—and longest—stay in the city taught him was his need for roots; it crystallized his longing and discontent into a hut beside a pond in Concord. When he wrote "The Landlord" for the _Democratic Review_ he not only described a hut in a retired place but made it a symbol of his own sincerity and sociality—here was the open and hospitable hut, the one lofty room in which all the secrets of housekeeping were exposed that he imagined in "House-Warming" in _Walden_; and in "A Winter Walk," which he also wrote at this time, he first canvassed the scenery of his life: Walden Pond, Fair Haven Cliffs and Bay, and the Concord River. Here, too, was a deserted woodman's hut that suggested the rude shelter he later built. And as he sat within it, he enjoyed "the friendship of the seasons" that he described in "Sounds" and "Solitude" in _Walden_, and felt the appeal of the life it would permit him to live. The pond, furthermore, first began to acquire the personal associations that he would explicitly develop in _Walden_, but the lesson it symbolized now was the Oriental wisdom in which the Staten Island interlude had schooled him: "'sitting still at home is the heavenly way; the going out is the way of the world.'"

Staten Island, then, drove him back to Concord and to Nature. "Where nature ceases to be supernatural to a man what will he do then?" he had asked despairingly in this first crisis. "Of what worth is human life if its actions are no longer to have this sublime and unexplored scenery? Who will build a cottage and dwell in it with enthusiasm if not in the Elysian fields?" His determination on Walden, however, even after the delay of a year in the pencil factory, was not easily fulfilled. His friends, understanding his proposal in theory—as one sees in Charles Lane's "Life in the Woods" in *The Dial*—did not approve of the "simple, fibrous life" in practice; and when one considers that Thoreau's experiment was one of the most daring and dramatic of transcendental acts, their sullen silence during his years at the pond, as if he had gone out of the world, showed the strength of their disapproval. In fact, it was partly to get away from the ceaseless transcendental debates in Concord parlors that Thoreau wanted to go to the pond. To live in the woods was not only an economic expedient that would permit him the leisure to write; it would permit him to make his relations on his own terms, free from the expectations of his friends.

Once there, at last face to face with "the great facts of his existence," Thoreau was overwhelmed by a joy that was every-thing he had anticipated. This, he later realized, was the great occasion of his life—an adventure that mounts in excitement from day to day as one follows in the *Journal* his own sudden sense of release from bondage. At last, he said, he walked the fields "with unexpected expansion and long-missed content, as if there were a field worthy of me." The usual boundaries of his life were dispersed, and he learned, as he later dramatized his belief in the uncommitted life in his conversation with John Field, that "your fetters are knocked off; you are really free." "Yes," he told himself, "roam far, grasp life and conquer it, learn much and live. . . . Dismiss prudence, fear, conformity. Remember only what is promised." Free "to adventure on life now, his vacation from humbler toil having commenced" and blest by his "hard and emphatic life" in the Elysian fields, his joy at the pond helped him transform his 1839 excursion on the Concord and Merrimack into the spiritual holiday of the *Week*. This book, in fact, with its confidence in Nature and its daily adventures in ecstasy, was a rhapsody to wakefulness, the record of his "morning work," a form for thought itself. And compared with *Walden*, which was the form for the growth of conscious-ness and the record of his wakening, it was more faithful in spirit to the life he had had at the pond.

There was nothing in this life, moreover, that justified the
fears of his friends that he would lose himself in the solitudes of
his own ecstasy. For, as it had for Whitman, self-realization in
Nature suffused him with love. Neither life nor love could be
shared, he learned, until he had found his own center and the
confidence of self-reliance. Then, indeed, he could brag for
mankind. And then he saw the representative value of his
private reform; he even saw himself as a stock personality, better
able to speak for common working men than Emerson because
he had known and surmounted the conditions of their lives. His
life in the woods had put in perspective the life of village and
city, and counting his gains, he hoped that his example would
begin the social redemption of New England. For unlike the
many social experiments of his day (Alcott had gone to Fruitlands in 1843, and Brook Farm was in its Fourieristic phase
when Thoreau lived at Walden)—unlike the ideal lives that
Alcott had said "none of us were prepared to actualize practi-
cally," Thoreau's experiment had been successful. He had "reduced a fact of the imagination to be a fact to his understanding," as he said in *Walden*, in the hope "that all men will at
length establish their lives on that basis."

He had not planned to live permanently at the pond, however, and the Walden experiment came to an end when
Thoreau, at the bidding of Mrs. Emerson, returned to manage
the household during Emerson's absence in England in 1847–
1848. In many respects, Thoreau took up his life where he had
left it before going to Staten Island, with the advantages now of
being the master of the house and of having the manuscript of a
publishable book in his possession. Walden had healed his
defeat and restored his confidence, and he felt ready now for a
life of successful authorship. He immediately set to work preparing lectures, and the reception of some of them seemed to
promise success. But again he was thwarted by delay, this time
by the refusal of publishers to print the *Week*, his bid for fame.
Advised by Emerson to issue the book at his own expense, he
finally published the *Week* in 1849, but the sale was so poor that
Thoreau did not hazard another book until he had paid his

debts. That delay, however, providing the background of new and more difficult obstacles, was the making of *Walden*.

For faced once more with the problem of economy in the years following Emerson's return, Thoreau had turned again, this time permanently, to the pencil factory—and had added to his chains those of the surveyor. This life, of course, was hardly satisfactory; it robbed him of the time to work for and with his nobler faculties; it was "trivial"; and surveying, which forced him "to live grossly or inattentive to [his] diet," he felt had made his life "prosaic, hard, and coarse." In "Life Without Principle," where the bitterness of these years was distilled, leaving his gladness for *Walden*, he said that "a man had better starve at once than lose his innocence in the process of getting his bread." Indeed, the despair of his later years, those autumnal years of "decay" in which he was literally the "'god in ruins'" Emerson spoke of in *Nature*—the god who was once "'permeated and dissolved by spirit,'" who "'filled nature with his overflowing currents,'" and the laws of whose mind had "'externized themselves into day and night, into the year and the seasons'"—was over his lost innocence. This loss, this impurity, was measured by the loss of communion with Nature, and his world, as Emerson said of the fallen man, now lacked unity and lay "broken and in heaps." There were, of course, other contributory "stains"; the bustling nineteenth century that destroyed his repose, binding him to society with the ligature of his own desire for social justice—Negro slavery and Irish "slavery," the Mexican War, the Anthony Burns affair, and his own night in jail, all teaching him that "life itself being worthless, all things with it, that feed it, are worthless"; the irreparable alienation from his friends; and his strenuous efforts to overcome the first advances of illness by an outdoor life, which, intensified by the strain of the scientific attention he gave to Nature in his attempt to find communion, became a permanent disability. Moreover, from his arduous study of Nature—he had now embarked on the staggering labor of finding in the seasons of Nature the corresponding seasons of man—he learned that his pristine youth or

springtime was passed, that the "second spring" of autumn was
not a time of germination but of ripening, and that to achieve
this seasoned virtue, the sloth and sensuality and impurity of the
hot summer of growth had to be overcome. Summer was no
longer the extended spring it had been in his youth, but the
season of his present manhood, when "Pegasus," he confessed,
"has lost his wings; he has turned a reptile and gone on his
belly." The reptilian imagery of *Walden* (as well as the imagery
of carrion, stagnation, and slumber) were the results of these
years when, living "this slimy, beastly kind of life," Thoreau felt
that he had become "the very sewers, the cloacae of nature."

In his desire for purity, Thoreau transferred the values of
spring to autumn, for autumn, with its cooler days and purer
atmosphere, its returning birds and late flowerings and running
crystal streams, was a rejuvenescence. At the same time, however, he returned in memory to his youth. He longed again for
"those youthful days!" He wished again to be a child. Nothing,
he felt, was "comparable with the experiences of my boyhood."
If the seasons of Nature taught him the inevitability of the
seasons of man and even assured him that harvest was superior
to seedtime, still the "knowledge of ourselves" that came with
manhood spoiled his satisfaction. In spite of (and because of) his
discipline and asceticism, he could not win back the time when
"nature developed as I developed, and grew up with me" and
"my life was ecstasy." He could only remember that before his
"losses" he had been "all alive, and inhabited my body with
irrepressible satisfaction." As he wrote *Walden* in these years, he
knew that his life had been one of obstacles, that once, at the
pond, he had overcome them. The spring he now desired was
the rebirth he hoped to earn by the purity of his manhood, a
rebirth that he believed was possible because of his former
victory and guaranteed by a law of Nature as certain as that of the
seasons—the law of renewal. With this double truth, he found
that he could be true to the course of his life: to the seasons of life
and to his faith in an eternal spring that would transcend the
seasons themselves. In *Walden*, the fruit of his ripening year, he

hoped to keep this faith alive by memorializing the period that had crowned his life. Still undaunted, he believed, as he once told Harrison Blake, that "what can be expressed in words can be expressed in life."

## III

The knowledge of the seasons was the most important addition to Thoreau's thought after 1850. It made possible the metaphors of ripening and completion that give his last work a tone of acceptance and quiet satisfaction; and it also made possible the fable of the renewal of life in *Walden*. When "for convenience" Thoreau put the experience of his two years at the pond into one, when he saw that the narrative action might be related to the seasons, he had the "fable with a moral" with which to express the meaning he now gave to that period of his life. Unlike that of the *Week*, which made the day the unit of time and of inspiration, the fable of the seasons enabled Thoreau to be true to the trials, changes, and growth he had known—to actualize by means of his former life his present aspirations. "Some men's lives are but an aspiration, a yearning toward a higher state," he wrote in 1851, "and they are wholly misapprehended, until they are referred to, or traced through, all their metamorphoses." In the seasons of *Walden* he could trace his metamorphoses: the passage from servitude to liberation, and the self-transcendence of his transformation from impurity to purity—the rebirth of new life out of the old.

The day, of course, had its seasons; it was the epitome of the year: "The night is winter, the morning and evening are the spring and fall, and the noon is summer." The spiritual change from sleep to wakefulness—the prospect of the dawn that closes *Walden*—was proper to it; and the chapters nearest in fact to his ecstatic years employed it—"Where I Lived, and What I Lived For," with its morning philosophy, and "Sounds," with its account of his summer reverie, of a full day in Nature. He had used the day in the *Week* as the very possession of ecstasy, but now that he was earning it, he needed a longer cycle of time in order to participate in the organic processes of rebuilding and renewing his world. There had to be time to clear his land, build his hut, plant his seeds, and harvest his crop: time for that "something even in the lapse of time by which time recovers itself."Change, gradual transformation, now preoccupied him, and sleeping and waking, admirably fitted to the sudden advent of inspiration, were neither as adequate nor as rich in the details of change as the metaphors he now chose: ice-thaw-flux, seed-flower-fruit, grub-chrysalis-butterfly. These natural facts became the metaphors in terms of which he told of his desire to pass from a lower to a higher form of life, from fixity to fluidity (he would share again the "circulations" of Being), from the innocence of youth to the wisdom of maturity, from larval sensuality to aerial purity.

These transformations, moreover, were examples of change in obedience to the organic principle, by means of an inner expansion. In terms of Thoreau's personal life, their possibility was dramatized by his withdrawal from society to Nature, that is to say, from a condition fixed beyond growth (society for Thoreau was always a machine) to a condition permitting him to build his life from the inside out in obedience to his idea. "Our moulting season, like that of the fowls, must be the crisis of our lives," he explained. "The loon retires to solitary ponds to spend it. Thus also the snake casts its slough, and the caterpillar its wormy coat, by an internal industry and expansion." In society, however, he remained his old "scurvy self," and society, as he now used it in *Walden* to enclose his experiment in renewal, was the sum of all the anxieties and constraints and failures he wished to leave behind. Not only because he was preaching self-reform, but because he wanted to show what he had surmounted, he began *Walden* with the long social analysis of "Economy," setting up the emphatic polarities and perspectives that would awaken his readers to see their—and his—condition from a vantage outside of society. As Emerson had done in *Nature*, he began with commodity before turning to spirit. But more fully than Emerson, whose treatise has its

point-by-point parallels in *Walden*, he employed history, anthropology, books (even Scripture), paradox, humor, irony,
ridicule, scorn, philological puns, parables, dramatization,
utopian prospects, and every variety of symbolic statement to
establish the contrasting values of surface and depth (appearance
and reality), transient and permanent, complex and simple,
disease and health, tradition and the uncommitted life, desperation and joy, spiritual emptiness and spiritual fullness. From
externality and circumstance, he turned to the inner dominion
of self-reliance, from collective "humanitarian" reform to self-
discovery, from a world broken and in heaps to the cosmos he
had made. Indeed, in dramatizing these changes from society
and commodity to spirit and self, *Walden* worked inward from
the circumferential to the central life, from the external to the
real self, from extrinsic to intrinsic success.

Thoreau also began with "Economy" because it was the
aspect of his experiment that had aroused the most curiosity.
The life of quiet desperation that he so brilliantly anatomized,
however, had been (or was) his own, and the economic anxieties
merely pointed to deeper anxieties—those of a life gone stale,
without savor or animating purpose. The economy he proposed, therefore, was to the end of getting and spending one's
life, an economy of spirit his readers little expected, one that
denied the Puritan necessity of working with the sweat of the
brow, one that made work itself a joy and a pastime rather than a
duty. The irony of his economy, given to the fraction of a cent,
was that on so little, he had got so much, that he did not carry a
house on his back or possess a corner of the world, but had all the
landscape for his own, and time (which Franklin said was
money) to read, to sit idle all day, to boat and fish, and to saunter
at his ease and enjoy those bounties of Nature that were reserved
for a "Lord of Creation." He had a self that he could hug, one
that was not at society's beck and call or twisted and thwarted by
relations, which, he had found by experiment, were customary
rather than essential. And if the simplicity of his economy
seemed Franklinian, he was not burning incense to the patron

saint of State Street: the end of his economy was enrichment, not denial, and he spent lavishly. "Give me the poverty," he exclaimed when cursing Flint, "that enjoys true wealth." If anything, he was undermining the Franklinian virtues, replacing the *Autobiography* with a model for another kind of success—utilizing the very terminology of business to raise the uncomfortable question of whether possessions actually helped one possess life. This was the purpose of his reductiveness in treating the goods of the world, for the only good he wished to appropriate (and here he added his voice to the swelling clamor of American literature) was experience, the quality or bloom of life. The burden of "Economy," in fact, was that the way to wealth was not the way to health, but to lives of quiet desperation. When he wrote Blake, who was trying to use *Walden* as his guide, he said: "It is surprising how contented one can be with nothing definite,—only a sense of existence. . . . O how I laugh when I think of my vague, indefinite riches. No run on my bank can drain it, for my wealth is not possession but enjoyment."

Standing in the way of this enjoyment, however, was the confusion concerning the means and ends of life which Thoreau had tried to clarify by reducing his life to its simplest terms; and, accordingly, the central issue to those who either rejected or accepted his life was his doctrine of simplicity. He had reduced the means of life, of course, not because he wanted to prove that he could go without them, or to disclaim their value in enriching life, but because they were usually factitious—they robbed one of life itself. And though, like *Walden*, the "shallow meaning" of this economy was "but too clear," the meaning it had for him was not. His economy, like his withdrawal to Nature, was not an ultimate abdication from social life; it was only the means of the self-emancipation, which many, accepting social bondage as the inevitable condition of life, did not find necessary. Economy freed him from society, and Nature provided him the opportunity to share the recreative processes of life; but this life in Nature was also a means, the goal being another, a "higher" and an organic society, shaped by the same principles whose efficacy Thoreau had demonstrated. To this end, rather than the renunciation of society, *Walden* was a social gospel.

He himself had adopted simplicity for many reasons. He believed, for example, that it would bring him nearer to those common influences in which Emerson had taught the poet to delight. And as a social critic, he believed that the only honest or absolute view required the detached prospect of "voluntary poverty." Considering his personal experiment, however, the most important reason was his need to clear away the obstacles that stood between him and the "grand fact" of life. For in order to front the fact and recover reality, he had to reduce the problem of perception to its simplest terms—self and Nature. Simplicity, then, was a discipline and an ascetic as necessary to his purification as the labor in the beanfield or the dietary practices of "Higher Laws," and he often hallowed it with religious associations by calling it "poverty." "By poverty, *i.e.* simplicity of life and fewness of incidents," he wrote in 1857, bringing to the surface the sunken imagery of *Walden*, "I am solidified and crystallized, as a vapor or liquid by cold. It is a singular concentration of strength and energy and flavor. Chastity is perpetual acquaintance with the All [In "Higher Laws" he said that "Chastity is the flowering of man. . . . Man flows at once to God when the channel of purity is open"]. You think that I am impoverishing myself by withdrawing from men, but in my solitude I have woven for myself a silken web or *chrysalis*, and nymph-like, shall ere long burst forth a more perfect creature, fitted for a higher society. By simplicity . . . my life is concentrated and so becomes organized, or a Κόσμος [cosmos], which before was inorganic and lumpish."

When simplicity, finally, was associated with his life in the woods and his hunger for the wild, it raised another issue—that of primitivism *vs.* civilization. In espousing Nature, the transcendentalists, of course, had also glorified the primitive life. But having experienced the wilderness on his trips to the Maine woods in 1846 and 1853, Thoreau knew that his life at the pond and in Concord pastures was far from wild; and though he always maintained that the health of civilization needed the tonic of the wild, his experience had taught him that the pastoral landscape was the best setting for human life. On one level, in fact, he intended *Walden* for a modern epic of farming, and he had purposely begun his life from scratch in order to relive all history and test this model of life against the achievements of civilization.

Had his problem been merely that of doing without society, it would have been easily solved; but his problem—the one that Lane had posed in *The Dial*—was what to do with it: how to join the values of urban and sylvan life. The paradox of civilization that Thoreau exploited (though it was hardly a paradox to one who recognized the enslavement to means) was that it did not civilize but barbarized most men, reducing them to a level of want below that of the savage. His own simple life, however, had been remarkably civil, and much of his satisfaction in it was due to the fact that it had provided the uncluttered and leisurely conditions of truly civilizing himself: savages, after all, did not read Homer or write books in the woods. His stance as a philosopher, moreover, made it clear that his demands on life were not simple or primitive, that only the self-sufficiency and adjustment of the Indians to the natural environment appealed to him—the style of their life rather than the "barren simplicity" of their demands on it. "There are two kinds of simplicity," he had observed in the *Journal*, "one that is akin to foolishness, the other to wisdom. The philosopher's style of living is only outwardly simple, but inwardly complex. The savage's style is both outwardly and inwardly simple." The complex and refined life of society, however, did not necessarily yield a complex inner life. And when he proposed that the civilized man become a more experienced and wiser savage, he hoped that he would retain the physical simplicity of the one in order to achieve the complex goals of the other, that he would "spend as little time as possible in planting, weaving, building, etc." and devote his freedom to cultivating "the highest faculties." This could be

**Thoreau's**
***Walden***

39

done, he believed, as he had done it, not only by simplicity, but by making the organic communion of the sylvan the foundation of a higher life.

In showing the "positive hindrances" of civilization—that its means did not fit the ends of man—Thoreau used examples that also enabled him to develop the theory of organic functionalism so essential to his faith in the renewal of life. Everything— education, reform, clothing, shelter, and furniture—was tested by its fitness to living needs, by whether it answered to the inner necessities of man. Clothing, he found, for example, seldom fit the character of the wearer, in many cases did not even serve its basic function of preserving the "vital heat"; instead it was an outer covering worn in conformity to society. Houses, too, were *"exostrious"* [a pun on *indus*trious], a building from without, a more cumbersome clothing, indeed a "tomb" built by the "coffin-maker," as he called the carpenter, for the next genera- tion. Fine houses, like fashionable clothes, he said, were not the expression or function of the indweller; they had not been built up from the "foundation" of "beautiful housekeeping and beau- tiful living." And furniture was *exuviae,* the cast skins of others, that cluttered the house, the spider's web of tradition that trap- ped the "gay butterfly." Accordingly, having by withdrawal and simplicity divested himself of these impediments, he built his life from the inside out; and he proposed that others build in the same "Orphean fashion," that they "grow" their houses. "Let our houses first be lined with beauty," he said, "where they come in contact with our lives, like the tenement of the shellfish, and not overlaid with it." If he acknowledged that in building his hut he had built too heedlessly to build well, still he recommended that others consider "what foundation a door, a window, a cellar, a garret, have in the nature of man." For he knew that the circumstances that man creates also shape him, that "this frame," as he said of his hut, "was a sort of crystalliza- tion around me, and reacted on the builder."

These principles, as well as the prospectus of his hopes and the initial stages of his experiment, were placed in the intervals of the social analysis of "Economy." The contrast they provided, however, was immediately realized in "Where I Lived, and What I Lived For," for in his determination to adventure on life Thoreau was already reborn. When he went to the pond in March, 1845, he had already felt the influence of "the spring of springs"; he had overcome his "torpidity"; in the woods, as Emerson said in *Nature*, he had "cast off his skin, as a snake his slough" and had again become "a child." Though Thoreau buried this spring in "Economy" and deliberately began his account with summer, with his going to the pond to live on Independence Day, the imagery of the melting pond, the returning birds, and the stray goose were the same as in his second "Spring." This additional season made it possible for Thoreau to recapitulate the entire history of his life from youth to maturity: the first spring, the dewy, pure, auroral season of the Olympian life, was true to his youth, and the subsequent seasons and the second spring were the record of the growth of consciousness and of his conscious endeavor to earn the new world of his springtime again.

Thoreau most patently dramatized this process of organic growth and renewal by building his hut, the container of his vital heat and the symbol of the self, to meet the developing seasons of man and consciousness. The seasons of man, of course, corresponded to the seasons of Nature: summer represented the outdoor life, when man was alive in all his senses and Nature supplied his vital heat; autumn, the gathering of consciousness; and winter, the withdrawal inward to self-reflection. This development, moreover, had its counterpart in the seasons of history, for, as Emerson had noted, "The Greek was the age of observation; the Middle Age, that of fact and thought; ours, that of reflection and ideas." Thus, when Thoreau went to Walden, he found that "both place and time were changed and I dwelt nearer to those parts of the universe and to those eras in history which had most attracted me." Spring was the Golden Age, that morning time of heroic endeavor that he always associated with Greece; and this explained why his first spring was so full of    41 allusions to Greece, why Homer was the proper scripture for his morning discipline, and why the second spring recalled his reading in Ovid's *Metamorphoses* and brought back the Golden Age. His year was the cycle of human history, and by renewing it he was trying to prove his proposition that the joys of life were not exhausted, that the counsel of despair of his elders, who believed that the whole ground of human life had already been gone over, was untrue.

The frame and foundation of Thoreau's hut came from Nature, the boards or outer covering from a shanty Thoreau purchased from James Collins, an Irish laborer whose life, like his "dank, clammy, and aquish" dwelling, was the very sum of quiet desperation. Dismantling this hut, Thoreau bleached and warped the boards in the sun; he purified the materials of his life, as he did again the second-hand bricks he used for his chimney; and with the stuff of the old, for he knew that men must borrow from civilization, he built the new after an Orphean fashion. When he first occupied his house in the summer, it was "merely a defence against the rain, without plastering or chimney," with "wide chinks" between the boards, open, as he had been in the summer, to the influence of Nature. "I did not need to go out doors to take the air," he observed, "for the atmosphere within had lost none of its freshness." This was the time of his rich communion with Nature, when there were no barriers to the rapture he celebrated in "Sounds," when his solitude (which he defined in terms of his nearness to God) was a satisfaction his friends never suspected. As long as possible, therefore, he preferred to remain outdoors, warmed by these genial influences; but, anticipating the bleaker seasons, toward the end of summer he began to build his chimney and fireplace—"the most vital part of the house." The foundation had already been laid in the spring, and now in the cooler days of autumn, he carefully and slowly built his chimney a layer of bricks at a time. The chimney, of course, was his very self or "soul"—an "independent structure, standing on the ground and rising through the house to the heavens"—and he built it deliberately because it "was

calculated to endure for a long time." Finally, when the north wind came and the pond began to cool and he needed a fire to warm him, he first "inhabited" his house;
he plastered and shingled, completely closing himself off from the elements—he internalized his life. "I withdrew yet farther into my shell," he wrote, "and endeavored to keep a bright fire both within my house and within my breast." In this season, as he told of it in "House-Warming," his chief employment was gathering wood for his fire: he was trying to keep alive, to maintain "a kind of summer in the midst of winter." For he found, during this "barren" season when he had only his heart to gnaw, that he began to grow torpid, that what he had gained in maturity by his self-confinement—by the change from outer to inner, from unconsciousness to consciousness—had brought with it an estrangement from Nature, the sense of "otherness" that bespoke his greatest loss.

If this development was true to Thoreau's life, so were the occupations or disciplines by which he hoped to burst the shell of his cocoon. His summer and morning work, for example, was cultivating beans, a discipline that was hardly consonant with the "fertile idleness" he had appropriately described in "Sounds" and "Solitude." During the Walden period he had, of course, hoed beans, but solely for the purpose of paying his way; from the vantage of his later years, however, this labor became the discipline by means of which he participated in the natural process and renewed his intimacy with Nature. "They attached me to the earth," he said of his beans, "and so I got strength like Antæus." The value of farming, or of any unspecialized vocation in Nature, he also found, was that it helped one catch Nature unaware, that it restored unconsciousness and permitted one to see out of the side of the eye. He advised the American scholar to live by this manual labor, moreover, not only because it was honest and because it rooted one in the native soil, but because it taught one how to reason from the hands to the head: here was the very creative process that would instruct him in the symbolic use of things, that would make the concrete object yield its truth and that, accordingly, would remove the "palaver" from his style. In his own case, he had been "a plastic artist in the dewy and crumbling sand" in order that his work might bear the "instant and immeasurable crop" of "tropes and expression." And the expression it yielded was the parable of the chapter itself: how to plant the seeds of "sincerity, truth, simplicity, faith, innocence, and the like," how by constant vigilance to make the "germ of virtue" bear, how by redeeming the "lean and effete" soil of Massachusetts—the "dust of my ancestors"—the seed of one man might bear the harvest of "a new generation of men." Here was a parable of both individual and social reform, of the kind of moral reform that went to the root of things and that could not fail because, as Thoreau pointed out in the case of the word "seed," its root was "spica," "spe," and "gerendo"—hope-bearing.

The most important result of this discipline was that it helped him "clothe that fabulous landscape of my infant dreams." At the beginning of "The Bean-Field" he told how he had first been brought to the pond in his childhood, and in "The Ponds" he told how the woodchoppers had since laid waste its shores. These alterations in the shore, he now realized, were the evidence of his own coarsened, actual self. For the pond itself, he discovered, was "the same water which my youthful eyes fell on," that "all the change," as he confessed, "is in me." The pond, then, was his own pristine, eternal self, and by cultivating beans, by discipline, he was changing the aspect of its shore, making it more agreeable to his imagination. If in his "decay" he lamented that the poet could not sing because his groves were cut down, he was heartened now because, he said, "one of the results of my presence and influence is seen in these bean leaves, corn blades, and potato vines."

That the pond was his real or essential self and the shore his actual self was made clear in "The Ponds." "It is no dream of mine," he said of Walden. "I cannot come nearer to God and Heaven/Than I live to Walden even. /I am its stony shore." In a variant of this verse, he wrote: "It is a part of me which I have not profaned/I live by the shore of me detained." And he even punned on its name—"*Walled-in* Pond." In "The Ponds," however, he did not linger over his shores, but lovingly related all the details of the "crystal well" that he had once been made. There he described the remarkable purity, depth, and transparency of the pond, its coolness and constancy, the cerulean color that made it a "Sky water," the "earth's eye," the very window of the soul. It was the "distiller of celestial dews" whose seasonal tides and daily evaporations kept it pure; it was alive with the motion imparted by the "spirit" of the air, and its surface was "a perfect forest mirror," reflecting all phenomena perfectly as an untarnished mind should. Even its bottom was "pure sand," with only the sediment of fallen leaves (Thoreau's autumnal decay); "a bright green weed," the token of life, could be found growing there in winter; and its fish—its "ascetic fish"—were "cleaner, handsomer, and firmer." Having in his *Journal* thanked God for making "this pond deep and pure for a symbol," Thoreau accounted for its creation with a "myth" of the "settler," the same old settler he had used to explain why he was not lonely in "Solitude" and was to refer to again in "Former Inhabitants; and Winter Visitors" to explain his notion of society. "That ancient settler [God] . . . came here with his divining-rod [pun]," he wrote, "saw a thin vapor rising from the sward, and the hazel pointed steadily downward, and he concluded to dig a well here." Walden was " 'God's Drop.' " He also gave it Edenic associations, describing its immemorial breaking up in the imagery of his first and second springs, making the rebirth this signified Adamic. Finally, having told of the ecstasy of his youth upon its waters, he likened it to himself; for it was "the work of a brave man," it lived "reserved and austere, like a hermit in the woods," and like his life, which he had "deepened and clarified," it was "too pure to have a market value." And yet he "bequeathed it to Concord," hoping that it would serve society as an example of "greater steadfastness," that "this vision of serenity and purity" would "wash out State-street and the engine's soot."

"The Ponds" was a summer chapter, the record of the time when he floated on the bosom of Nature and even in the darkest night communicated with her by fishing her mysterious depths. Now, fishing, he explained in "Higher Laws," was the proper vocation of the Golden Age; with hunting, it was "the young man's introduction to the forest, and the most original part of himself." Following the inevitable cycle of the seasons, however, this youthful pursuit was soon over: "He goes thither at first as a hunter and fisher, until at last, if he has the seeds of a better life in him, he distinguishes his proper objects, as a poet or naturalist it may be." When unconscious communion was gone, showing him what his proper objects were, the fisher angled instead (in "The Pond in Winter") for the pond itself, seeking the bottom or foundation "that will hold an anchor, that it may not drag."

But before this conscious exploration became necessary, Thoreau went afishing in the summer days. In "Baker Farm," he extolled the easy self-sufficiency of this uncommitted life in the wild and contrasted it with John Field's grubbing. Coming home with his string of fish, however, he turned to "Higher Laws," as if suddenly aware of the fact that in respect to diet he was as much in the larval condition as Field. Aware now that only discipline would help him continue his culture after manhood, that the instinct for the wild had been challenged by an instinct toward a higher or spiritual life, he repudiated his former mode of life and adopted the Oriental rituals of purification—bathing and diet and the conscious discipline of earnest labor. This resolution on purity, like the invocation to Hebe in "Solitude" and the martial vigilance of "The Bean-Field," betrayed an autumnal mood which Thoreau tried to dispel by the humorous dialogue that began "Brute Neighbors." There, his going fishing was a breach of discipline that destroyed his "budding ecstasy"; but, having covered his loss by self-protective humor, he nevertheless seriously explained the higher uses of Nature for which he was purifying himself. Nature, as Emerson had said and as Thoreau first introduced

46

this theme in "Sounds," is language. Thoreau's proper objects now were the correspondences of Nature; his brute neighbors were "beasts of burden . . . made to carry some portion of our thoughts." The partridge, for example, suggested "not merely the purity of infancy, but a wisdom clarified by experience." And the loon, whose return marked the advent of autumn, carried the heavy burden of his personal lapse. Enacting the play of inspiration by chasing this deep-diving bird, Thoreau told the story of his decay: consciously trying to pursue it—"While he was thinking one thing in his brain, I was endeavoring to divine his thought in mine"—he was balked; and even his passivity would no longer help him. Always the loon, he said, raised its "demoniac" laugh "in derision of my efforts." Finally, he wrote, the east wind came and "filled the whole air with misty rain, and I was impressed as if it were the prayer of the loon answered, and his god was angry with me." Like the "tumultuous surface" of the pond, here were signs that the serene communion of summer was over.

The chapters that followed—"House-Warming," "Former Inhabitants; and Winter Visitors," "Winter Animals," "The Pond in Winter"—recapitulated the themes of the summer chapters, taking up solitude, the resources of the natural scene, sounds, and the pond. With the change to the season of inwardness, however, the mood changed: now was the time of Thoreau's greatest solitude, a sleepy time when life was reduced to routine and staying alive was a problem, a time when he retreated to memory and held communion with the former inhabitants whose lives suggested the possibility of failure. Every image, from the pond whooping as it turned in its sleep to the fox "seeking expression" and "struggling for light," conveyed a sense of impoverishment and spiritual restlessness and the need for bravery under duress. Now he longed for the "Visitor" who never came and turned to the spiritual necessity of friendship, recalling those days when the faithful Alcott had come and their discourse had summoned the "old settler" and "expanded and racked my little house." And even though he knew that "moral reform was the effort to throw off sleep" and "to be awake is to be alive," he found that, like the pond, he could not escape his dormant season. "Every winter," he observed, "the liquid and trembling surface of the pond, which was so sensitive to every breath, and reflected every light and shadow, becomes solid to the depth of a foot or a foot and a half. . . . It closes its eyelids and becomes dormant for three months or more. . . . After a cold and snowy night it needed a divining rod to find it."

In the midst of his winter of discontent, however, Thoreau began his intellectual search for faith. In "The Pond in Winter," he told of the question that he had tried to answer in his sleep, the question of "what—how—when—where?" which only dawning Nature, by her living presence, had answered for him. This awakening *to* life was the preparation for rebirth, the beginning of the long process of conscious penetration to the law of the "spring of springs." This finally brought the rewards of "Spring," warranted his injunctions on self-exploration, and provided the testimony of his "Conclusion"—"Only that day dawns to which we are awake." Now his morning work was the "scientific" exploration of the bottom of the pond; for he "was desirous," he said, "to recover the long-lost bottom of Walden Pond," that "infinite" which its reputed bottomlessness suggested. In this survey he found that the fabulous pickerel (fish and fishing, as early as the *Week*, were symbols of thought and contemplation) still lived beneath the surface of the ice and that the "bright sanded floor" of the pond was "the same as in summer." And what was even more important for the foundation of his faith, he discovered and verified by accurate measurement the spiritual law of correspondences. The general regularity of the bottom—of the unseen—conformed to the shores: the correspondence was so perfect that "a distant promontory betrayed itself in the soundings quite across the pond, and its direction could be determined by observing the opposite shore." This universal law, which he applied to his own character, was also supported by the fact that "the line of greatest length intersected the line of greatest breadth *exactly* at the point of

48

greatest depth." By these soundings he renewed his faith in the transcendental method; and reading his own life correspondentially, he found that the disciplines of his outer life indicated the purity of his inner life. Though winter was the barren season, it brought the compensation of "concentration"; in the purity of the Walden ice he could see the symbol of his steadfastness. He could meet the priest of Brahma at his well— and the pure Walden water could mingle with the sacred water of the Ganges—because he had observed the purificatory disciplines, had bathed his "intellect in the stupendous and cosmogonal philosophy of the Bhagvat Geeta."

At the bottom of the pond he also found the "bright green weed" that symbolized the everlasting life of organic Nature, the law of life to which even the frozen pond undulated in its sleep, to which it thundered "obedience . . . as surely as the buds expand in the spring." Its booming, accordingly, was the sign of its awakening, a morning phenomenon, when, responding to the sun, it "stretched itself and yawned like a waking man." It sounded the signal of spring, prefigured that irresistible thaw when "all things give way to the impulse of expression." Indeed, with the warmer weather, the snow and ice began to melt, the "circulations" began, and the blood of winter was purged. Once more Nature supplied her "vital heat" and, in the thawing clay of the railroad cut, gave way to the impulse of expression—to the impulse of life.

The most brilliant passage in "Spring," Thoreau's description of the thaw, was a myth of creation as expression. This elaborate metaphor of the organic process that proceeds from the inside out, that creates and shapes by means of the Idea—the process of Nature, art, moral reform, and social reform—was also for Thoreau the metaphor of his purification and rebirth. Not only did the "bursting out" of the "insides of the earth" and the unfolding of "the piled-up history" of geology prove that there was nothing inorganic and that life provided fresh materials for the fictile arts of man, it showed that "Nature has some bowels, and . . . is mother of humanity." The frost coming out of the ground was Spring, a newly delivered child; and the flowing clay was an analogy of the development of the human body. The shapes and forms it took in its passage reminded him of "brains or lungs or bowels, and excrements of all kinds," but, as he explained this process in terms of "sand-foliage," the leaf-like character not only appeared in liver and lungs, but in feathers and wings. This evolution from excrementitious to aerial forms was a process of purification: "You pass from the lumpish grub in the earth," he wrote, "to the airy and fluttering butterfly. The very globe continually transcends and translates itself, and becomes winged in its orbit."

If the thawing made him feel that he was "nearer to the vitals of the globe," its leaf-like forms also reminded him that he was in the presence of "the Artist who made the world." The Creator was still in his laboratory, "still at work, sporting on this bank, and with excess of energy strewing his fresh designs about." In this analogy to the creative process, the earth was laboring with "the idea inwardly" and expressing itself "outwardly in leaves." For, as he had learned from Goethe, the leaf was the unit-form of all creation, the simplest form of which the most complex, even the world, was composed. "This one hill side illustrated the principle of all the operations of Nature," he explained. "The Maker of this earth but patented a leaf." This process, of course, not only applied to art, but to all re-forming and shaping. It illustrated Emerson's belief that "Nature is not fixed but fluid. Spirit alters, moulds, makes it"—that not only poems and individual lives, but institutions were "plastic like clay in the hands of the potter." Hoeing beans, Thoreau had himself been a plastic artist making the earth—that granary of seeds—express itself in leaves; and of all the former inhabitants he had identified himself with Wyman the potter, whose fictile art pleased him. Moreover, unknown to his neighbors, he had practiced that fictile art himself—for himself and society. He was not, however, the reformer who broke things, but one whose method, like that of the thaw with its "gentle persuasion," melted things. By recasting his life he hoped that Nature again would try with him "for a first settler." He was a "Champollion," deciphering the hieroglyphics of Nature, that "we may turn over a new leaf at last."

As a symbol of ecstasy, however, the thaw, even with its remarkable suddenness, was spoiled by the intellectual purposes Thoreau made it serve. Whatever ecstasy the passage conveyed was intellectual rather than spontaneous or unconscious; it followed from his long observation of Nature, and it showed that he had with his intellect riven into the "secret of things." The faith he had earned by this conscious endeavor, however, was rewarded, at least in the pages of *Walden*, by his long-awaited ecstasy. This "memorable crisis"—"seemingly instantaneous at last"—came with the melting of the pond, when he saw its "bare face . . . full of glee and youth, as if it spoke the joy of the fishes within it, and of the sands on its shore." For in the sparkling water, he realized the contrast between winter and spring: "Walden was dead," he said, "and is alive again." The change he had awaited—"the change from storm and winter to serene and mild weather, from dark and sluggish hours to bright and elastic ones"—was at hand. "Suddenly," he wrote, "an influx of light filled my house, though the evening was at hand, and the clouds of winter still overhung it, and the eaves were dripping with sleety rain. I looked out of my window, and lo! where yesterday was cold gray ice there lay the transparent pond already calm and full of hope as in a summer evening, reflecting a summer sky in its bosom, though none was visible overhead, as if it had intelligence with some remote horizon. I heard a robin in the distance, the first I had heard for many a thousand years . . . the same sweet and powerful song as of yore. . . . The pitch-pines and shrub-oaks about my house, which had so long drooped, suddenly resumed their several characters, looked brighter, greener, and more erect and alive, as if effectually cleansed and restored by the rain. . . . As it grew darker, I was startled by the *honking* of geese. . . . Standing at my door, I could hear the rush of their wings . . . they suddenly spied my light, and with hushed clamor wheeled and settled in the pond. So I came in, and shut the door, and passed my first spring night in the woods."

With the coming of spring, with renewal and rebirth, had

come "the creation of Cosmos out of Chaos and the realization of the Golden Age." Like Ovid, Thoreau was ready to tell of bodies changed by the gods into new forms, even glad, in the presence of this alchemy, to accept the life in Nature—served though it was by death—as the grand fact. Once again he lived in the eternal present, reborn to innocence, with an overwhelming sense of freedom, release, hope, and pardon. But even though he had regained the Golden Age before the fall of man, his metamorphosis took the form of the hawk rather than that of the butterfly; for having won his renewal by lonely heroism, he saw his transcendence in the soaring, solitary hawk, the bird he associated with nobleness and knightly courage. The hawk, he wrote in his *Journal*, soared so loftily and circled so steadily and without effort because it had "earned this power by faithfully creeping on the ground as a reptile in a former state of existence." It symbolized his ultimate liberation, the emancipation from the senses. At last, as he copied from *The Harivansa*, he was "free in this world, as birds in the air, disengaged from every kind of chain."

As the logic of his metaphors demanded, however, Thoreau closed his book with the fable of the beautiful bug that had come out of the dry leaf of an old apple-wood table. This fable recapitulated his themes: "Who knows what beautiful and winged life, whose egg has been buried for ages under many concentric layers of woodenness in the dead dry life of society, deposited at first in the alburnum of the green and living tree, which has been gradually converted into the semblance of its well-seasoned tomb . . . may unexpectedly come forth from amidst society's most trivial and handselled furniture, to enjoy its perfect summer life at last!" This was the fable of organic renewal. But the fable of the creative enterprise that made it possible—the transparent parable of his own life and vocation—was that of the artist of the city of Kouroo. This artist, Thoreau wrote, "was disposed to strive after perfection." Determined to make a staff, he went to the woods to select the proper materials, rejecting stick after stick until "his friends gradually

deserted him." In his striving, however, he lived in the eternal
now of inspiration which made the passing of dynasties, even eras, an illusion. Finally, in fashioning his staff, merely by minding his destiny and his art, he discovered that he had "made a new system . . . a world with full and fair proportions." And because "the material was pure, and his art was pure," the result, Thoreau knew, could not be "other than wonderful." *Walden* was that staff, that fuller and fairer and supremely organic world, because it was, by Thoreau's own test of sincerity, the form and expression of the life he had lived in the desire to live. But it was also—for in it he had enacted the process of creating scripture—the kind of heroic book that was worthy of morning discipline, a book so true "to our condition" that reading it might date a new era in our lives.

My interest in Thoreau was concurrent with my interest in
Emerson and developed with it, though Thoreau may have been first in my thought. A sacramental act of our coming East had been to visit Walden Pond, to wet ourselves (the three of us then) in its waters and to walk its shores. Could we have managed it, in that time of housing shortages and of impecuniosity and carlessness, we would have chosen to live in Concord. We did, somewhat later, live nearby for a year: at Fort Devens, where Harvard had converted some hospital barracks into apartments and had created an independent community of graduate students—the most rewarding arrangement for living I have yet experienced. Fort Devens, near Ayer, was admirably situated, and I remember most, or most favorably, not the early rising and huddled, cold, silent hour's drive to Cambridge, but the hilly countryside, much of which we bicycled over—Harvard, where the view of the Nashua valley is so fine and Alcott had tried communal living at Fruitlands; Shirley Center, the perfect village (the colonial background in Lewis Mumford's early film on the city), where Benton MacKaye, whose work on regional planning and geotechnics I read

later and with whom I would correspond, still lives. Though
we never walked to Wachusett, we lived in the landscape
Thoreau explored and became familiar with it.

I first read Thoreau in graduate school and published my
first paper on him at that time. With lectures I later worked up
for a course on Transcendentalism, this paper was the seed of
*The Shores of America: Thoreau's Inward Exploration* (1958),
the writing of which preceded and prepared for the introduction to *Walden* reprinted here. Rereading both now and recalling the circumstances of their composition, I wonder, even as I
wonder at a day's delay in undertaking any writing, whether
(and how) they would have been different if they had been
written in Cambridge. In one respect the circumstances at
Urbana were the same as those at Cambridge—in fact a con-
tinuation of them—and the reason I found myself writing
about Thoreau in a study under the eaves of the University of
Illinois library and not in a carrel in Widener, and surrounded
not by woods and water and hills but by flat, endless prairie.
(The change in libraries was not significant, for the library at
Illinois, where I spent so much of my lifetime, was almost as
"great" as Widener and as "good." And the landscape, as I
learned by attending to it and from the remarkable photographs
of Art Sinsabaugh, was not without beauty.) What continued
the same at Urbana—and would have at other universities—
was the necessity to advance.

To advance by writing about Thoreau! Institutionally, that
paradox is easily explained: publish (almost anything) or perish;
be productive. Harvard had wound me up; scholarship was a
strenuous life—I can feel now, in my muscles and stomach,
the tight, determined character of my daily existence. According to some of the "homeguarders," I had the Harvard tic, but
they did nothing to help me or other "cosmopolitans" cure it
and, to survive in the university-world of the late fifties and
early sixties, even tried to acquire it. Scholarship and teaching
are so essential to each other, so little divisible, that one is
troubled to find them existing together uncomfortably, each
54    pursued, because of limited time, at the expense of the other,

and both pursued at the expense of health and the larger life of family, friends, and community. My memory of the five years I spent completing this book is one of three classes to teach (then a fairly light "load") and of time snatched, sometimes even the hour between classes, in order to get on with it. I was two years writing it.

But writing itself opens a space truly one's own, and when one enters it, he is no longer moved by pressures of survival or ambition, but by the wholly different, imperious pressures of intellect and art. Personally, there was nothing paradoxical about my writing about Thoreau: it allowed me, as the classroom did, to live in my vocation, and gave me a way of being-in-the-world and the well-being without which the academic situation would have been less tolerable. In what mattered to me, I wasn't denied, only placed, because of what I felt was indifference to the claims of teaching-and-scholarship, under needless pressure. Could it be that *Life* and *our lives*, the words that enclose the introduction to *Walden*, were fortuit-ous?

I now find pervasive in my writing on Thoreau a desire for openness, for natural goods—the goods of life. These works seem to have, perhaps because the metaphor of exploration is prominent (is this metaphor a hidden connecter with my studies of Williams and Olson?), a visionary quality, an idealis-tic complement of a search for right relations of all kinds. The period during which I pondered and completed them was dis-mal: the time of the hydrogen bomb and the Korean War, of Joseph McCarthy and Eisenhower's presidency, of the Hunga-rian revolt and Sputnik. Undoubtedly, they speak, through Thoreau, for my own "opposing self," for my dissatisfaction with the world and the withdrawal—the title of my book suggests this inwardness—that accompanied it.

The writing itself, I think, is better than that of my book on Emerson, and the way in which ideas are treated developmen-tally in relation to the texture of an entire life and art and, accordingly, become act and expression is an improvement. But the concord of tone pleases me most: mine is not discordant with Thoreau's, and only consonance with him—my exploration, too, had been inward—assured it. The resonances I hear tell me that in writing about Thoreau I was living more agreeably in my imagination and was thereby enabled to write as I did of the joy and contemplativeness of the uncommitted and unbounded life. And I know better now that this was not wholly self-expressive. *America*, which figures in the titles or subtitles of my early books, declares the particularity of my concern, both devotion to and desire to change my country. Like Thoreau, I was impatient with its actuality and dedicated to its promise, responsive still, as others were at this time—Kerouac, for example, in *Dharma Bums*, Snyder in *Myths & Texts*—to an old dream.

With all this in mind, I regret most using *anarchical* in its popular sense. Now I would use it and its cognates, as Paul Goodman does, to designate not only the standing out of the way that permits the operations of nature, but responsiveness to need, or function, and the desire to be responsible for all that its satisfaction entails—in Thoreau's phrase, living one's life.

# THE IDENTITIES OF
# JOHN JAY CHAPMAN

*I*

IN 1928 John Jay Chapman published a translation of *Philoctetes*. Like his other translations from the *Iliad* and *The Divine
Comedy* and of *Antigone* and *Medea*, its freshness and fidelity
won the reluctant approval of scholars; for like all of his inva-
sions into literature, whether into Plato, Shakespeare, Balzac,
Goethe, or Emerson, it was issued under the banner of an
"amateur" who used every occasion to assault "the camp-
followers and sumpter mules of learning." He only claimed that
the translation was the pastime of an elderly gentleman with
time on his hands.

But Chapman had more than time on his hands. He was not
simply refurbishing his Greek, not even, as one always suspects,
finding another way, however polite or remote, of relieving
himself in attack. Nor was his profound concern for revitalizing
the humanities at the bottom of this work. He had no literary
preoccupations. "Belles Lettres is the devil after all," he had
once remarked of Lowell. "It spoils a man." He might reverse his
political views, but not his literary ones. He was not a gentleman
of letters like Lowell, a "literary fop." Everything he wrote was
struck from the rock of his life. With him the essay became again
what it had been for Emerson and Thoreau and would become      57

for Randolph Bourne, the robust and challenging expression of Man Thinking. Even his lesser work, his traditional poems and plays, especially his plays for children, reveal the man for whom time had created insupportable burdens.

By 1928 the aging reformer and "agitator" had earned the right to let Philoctetes speak for him. Nearly three decades before, he had broken under the strain of unsuccessful political reform activity and the sudden death of his first wife, Minna Timmins. When he began to write again several years later, the fairy-tale trappings of his plays for children disguised his self-analysis. "To tell thy guilt dissolves it," one character says; he wrote to confess and to assuage himself, to ask forgiveness. *The Hermits*, for example, reenacts the jealous rage that led to his assault on Percival Lowell and the expiatory act of self-mutilation. He now asks pardon and accepts solitude as repentance. In *King Ithuriel, Christmas in Leipsic,* and *A Maid's Forgiveness* he recalls the loss of his son who drowned in 1903, a "sacrifice" which restored the disabled father much in the same way as did the loss of another son in the war. *The Lost Prince* treats of "mother love" and the restoration of right. He is haunted by remorse for the "betrayal" of his first wife in *A Maid's Forgiveness*—its setting is the kingdom of "Minneberg." The kings in *King Ithuriel* and *A Maid's Forgiveness* are old, brain-sick, put upon, unkinged; one is willing to renounce a crown that isn't rightly his, the other to be delivered from the need to be a king. Old age, ebb of life, loss, solitude are the themes of *Christmas in Leipsic*; here the aging husband will be a child to his wife, as the invalid Chapman undoubtedly was to Elizabeth Chanler, his second wife.

Obviously, these plays were not meant for children. But the children's play was congenial to Chapman's imagination. Pitting good against evil, it permitted him to express his sense of evil and his conspiratorial mentality. His evil characters work by means of *Realpolitik*, his good characters by means of love. His moralism is strong because his view of morality is weak. His world is composed of simples, of "two hierarchies of power." He sees it as a child sees it.

The sense of conspiracy still oppresses Chapman in *Philoc-* *tetes*. He identifies himself with Philoctetes because he, too, believed that he had been abandoned by others because of his illness; he, too, had a "nameless, blasting wound" and had become (especially in the 1920s) "a maniac in hate." He can understand the pain that makes Philoctetes desire to cut off his foot, for in his youth he had himself been driven to destroy an offending hand. But he feels his kinship most when Philoctetes tells Neoptolemus, who in Chapman's case might represent the younger generation,

> O infamy of outrage! Not content
> With casting me out, they kill my fame
> By keeping silence: not a word of me
> Lives in the land of Hellas! O my son,
> Hast thou perchance heard tell of Philoctetes.

Fortunately, recognition came. In 1929 Edmund Wilson broke the silence with a long review in the literary supplement of the *New Republic*. He assessed Chapman's career in order to show that he had "much to say to the younger generation," that here was a genuine humanist who loved literature and wrote poetry, not a schoolmaster like Babbitt or More. He praised Chapman's early companion volumes, *Causes and Conse-quences* and *Practical Agitation*, connecting them to his generation by noting their influence on Croly's *The Promise of American Life*. Acknowledging Chapman's crankiness, he emphasized the sage and prophet rather than the agitator, and placed him in the intellectual tradition of Emerson. The intensity of his spirit, the brilliance of his literary gift, the continuity of thought embodied in Chapman's work—these, he concluded, made him "an American Classic."

When the *Times Literary Supplement* devoted its lead article to the "American Moralist" in 1930, Chapman felt that at last he was "afloat." More than this, however, was needed to keep alive a reputation that had never been secure. Thirty years earlier he had won the praise of Henry James, had been acclaimed as *the* American critic, and he knew that people now had the right to ask, "But where are the works of this man?" His answer—"The

works of this man perished in the Eruption of Vesuvius"—was
true enough. The fires that kindled him had also destroyed him.
He had created in his fiery engagement with his times the lava of
his own oblivion. His most substantial claim to fame was in his
letters, published posthumously in 1937. They showed how
brilliant and destructive the fires had been, and how much his
reputation, in his time and ours, depended on sympathy for and
fascination with his temperament and predicament.

Based on Chapman's letters, Edmund Wilson's later essay in
*The Triple Thinkers* was the most important critical study of
Chapman and is probably the source of whatever general enthusiasm for him there has been ever since. Now his reputation
rests with the graduate students, whose scholarship Chapman
would have deplored ("the earthworms of scholarship are destined to go on forever fertilizing the soil by going up and down
in it"), but who nonetheless have treated him carefully and well.
They have uncovered almost all that can be found in the ruins of
his Pompeii. His thought has been explored and systematized in
the theses of David M. Stocking and Melvin H. Bernstein. The
study of his life, which his friend M. A. DeWolfe Howe did not
sufficiently make in *John Jay Chapman and His Letters*,
Richard B. Hovey undertook in a thesis covering the early years.
Hovey published the first book on Chapman, *John J. Chapman:
An American Mind*, in 1959; Bernstein's *John Jay Chapman*
appeared in 1964.

One soon learns in reading about Chapman that nothing tells
as much as his own words. Chapman's words are bolts of
character. What he said of Emerson can be said of him: "Open
his works at hazard. You hear a man talking." His voice is still
one of the most engaging in American letters. Essayists are out
of fashion and memorialists are rare; Chapman's literary
achievement is in the essay and memoir. This must be acknowledged. But this is not so much in question as his stature.

Ferris Greenslet once told Chapman that the history of his
"education (*à la* Henry Adams) would be a record of the American people during the epoch and one of the greatest books ever

written." Whether Chapman refused to make good this suggestion because, as he claimed, the past bored him, or because he
had mixed feelings about Adams' *Education,* or because to
rethink the past and explicitly note where he had failed would
have unsettled his precarious serenity, one will never know. The
book was never written, only the briefest of "recollections." But
critics who glean the passing references, such as F. O. Matthiessen's coupling of Adams and Chapman as "two of our most
symptomatic minds," are often led to make untenable claims.
For the fame Chapman gains by association, he loses by comparison; and none of Chapman's critics has taken the risk of
comparing him. Is he, as one gathers from the testimony of
Jacques Barzun and from Hovey's subtitle, an American mind,
a critic whose reputation can no longer be deferred because we
stand in need of his qualities? Does he belong in another order,
that suggested by Austin Warren when he said that Chapman
was "a saint writing about saints, himself not the least of them"?
Or is he after all, as Bernstein believes, only a minor representative figure? And one wonders most just what it is (since it is not
his skill as an essayist) that we have overlooked, and what arouses
the sympathy of his recent champions.

## II

Whenever one attempts to measure Chapman's achievement he
should remember that his contemporaries included such nota-
bles as Thorstein Veblen, Louis Sullivan, Paul Elmer More,
Irving Babbitt, George Santayana, Owen Wister, Theodore
Roosevelt, and Alfred Stieglitz. He belonged to the generation
that was born about the time of the Civil War, whose entry into
manhood might be marked by the enactment of the Sherman
Antitrust Act in 1890, and whose energies and intellects were
absorbed by a revolution in economic, political, and social life.
For Chapman, molded by the legacies of Jay stewardship and
Chapman abolitionism and trained at St. Paul's, Harvard College, and Harvard Law School to carry on the traditions of his
class, most disturbing was the fact that the changes he witnessed

constituted a "status-revolution." Edmund Wilson speaks of that "difficult" time in a memoir of his father, who belonged to Chapman's generation. The young men, he explains, had been educated to serve as their fathers had, and they had become casualties because of their "fundamental lack of adjustment to the American life of the period." Wilson tells us that "of his father's close friends at college, but a single one was left by the time he was in his thirties: all the rest were dead—some had committed suicide." And Chapman, explaining his brother Henry's death in 1913, attributes it to the fact that "it's a pretty killing age . . . the society of it was at its worst just in our time." Other casualties, like those of Chapman and Wilson's father, were of a subtler neurotic sort, so that just "to have got through with honor that period from 1880 to 1920!" was, Wilson feels, a kind of victory.

By birthright and nurture Chapman had a special burden to carry into the new America—an urgent conscience. In everything else a cosmopolitan New Yorker, in his conscience he was a New Englander. He had the "excess of the individual spirit manifested in the exaltation of conscience" that William C. Brownell ascribed to Puritanism. Religious training at St. Paul's School had only exacerbated it, and the boy was shattered. "Early holiness in boys," he later remarked, "goes with pneumonia." Nevertheless, this training fixed the religious disposition that provided the hidden link of a life broken over the problem of how to make conscience a direct agent in human affairs. It strengthened the Hebraic, the ethical passion with which Chapman struck in word and deed. At the end of his life he could identify himself with Lucian because he had "a non-Hellenic, ethical passion, which has the heat of religion, yet does not appeal to authority or use the symbols of religion." Like Lucian's, his theme was conduct, his appeal to courage; he employed his talent to a similar end, "to break down every screen of theory that lies between the private mind and practical life." It was easy for Chapman to welcome Lucian in his attack on the "disease" of the Greek mind because earlier he had embraced Emerson and Garrison, the "purgers" of what Chapman believed to be the chronic American disease of moral cowardice, a disease bred alike in the slavery of Emerson's time and the "commercialism" of his own.

Emerson and Garrison were Chapman's heroes of conscience. During much of his life he pitted them against each other as he wavered between the efficacy of saying and the efficacy of doing. Courageous men both, they needed each other; they were the "head" and the "heart" Chapman hoped but failed to unite in himself. Emerson was the seer, an artist of ideas, for whom utterance was enough; he wanted to reform society without visible means. Garrison, however, knew what Chapman had learned as an agitator, that "reform consists in taking a bone from a dog. Philosophy will not do it." Where Emerson, with the "better element" in New England, responded to slavery only when Webster defected, Garrison, twenty-five years before, had made the "agonized protest" and had brought the heat and passion and action needed to stir a cold and conciliatory age. He was not a moralist who read lectures; he enacted lessons; and he broke the conspiracy of silence that followed the Missouri Compromise. Garrison had the prophet's emotion in the face of innocent suffering; he laid hands on visible, particular evil. Had he been a "no-organization" man capable of standing alone, the Chapman who wrote his own farewell to reform movements in *William Lloyd Garrison* would have found him the perfect practical agitator.

Chapman's criticism of Emerson was severe not simply because the seer lost power by not acting, but because Emerson had become profoundly a part of himself. No one ever gave himself over so entirely to Emerson as Chapman did. Speaking of his "rag-dolls" (Emerson and Goethe), Chapman recalls that he found his Emerson "in an old family trunk" and that long ago he began "to show signs of wear and tear." He was always grateful to Emerson for standing him on his feet; the college boy had been "intoxicated with Emerson." "He let loose something within me which made me in my own eyes as good as anyone

63

else." On completing "Social Results of Commercialism" he told Elizabeth Chanler: "It's all Emerson. I should have had neither the ideas reduced so clearly nor the public to understand them if it hadn't been for Emerson. I can't imagine what I should have been if it hadn't been for Emerson." Though he later repudiated the "Emerson madness"—the fanaticism and self-will Emerson had released—he never repudiated the individual moral heroism that had made it acceptable.

No, Emerson failed Chapman where he was most vulnerable—in the heart. When he wrote his brilliant essay on Emerson in 1897, Chapman qualified the praise with reservations he had earned: "Regarded as a sole guide to life for a young person of strong conscience and undeveloped affections, his works might conceivably be even harmful because of their unexampled power of purely intellectual stimulation." Not only had Emerson made a dogma of the moral law, but he had "lied" about human nature when he preached the self-sufficiency and invincibility of individual spiritual power. He had the "anaemic incompleteness" of the Puritan; he needed "incaloration." He never understood life "in its throb and passion," and his asceticism was simply the old cross on which New England had always crucified the natural instincts. After his own devastating experience of conscience inflamed by love and hate, Chapman was ready to learn from Browning that "it was right to love, hate, and be angry" and that "we had some inheritance in the joys and passions of mankind."

But Chapman personally tested Emerson in another way: he animated him with the Garrisonian passion. He became a full-blooded "American Scholar." Garrison, he felt, best fulfilled "Emerson's ideal picture of the influential individual"; he was "self-reliant, self-assertive, self-sufficient." And Chapman began his career as a Garrisonian. When he entered the political reform movement in New York City in 1888, he believed that he was making good just where Emerson had failed. Chapman's activity—cart-tailing, organizing the Goo-Goos, writing the *Political Nursery*—turned out to be the "excursions into pragmatic romance" that Veblen said typified "the contingent of well-to-do irregulars." He had achieved nothing; the bosses remained. But Chapman learned the lesson of compromise, though he put his own interpretation on it: "In all the politics I have ever known compromise means change of faith." He was unwilling to sacrifice conscience to the pragmatism of politics, as he believed that Theodore Roosevelt had—and for which Roosevelt had called him a traitor. He preferred to work alone and to limit the reformer's activity to the educative function of raising moral issues. By this time, the action he had undertaken to restore his psychic health had partly broken his spirit; "I feel like Atlas, lifting the entire universe." Family disaster completed the breakdown in 1901. And by the time he wrote the *Garrison*, it was too late to apply the lesson his life had taught him, that if the end of agitation is education, then by writing he might have truly influenced his generation—might have provided, as William James said, "a gospel for our rising generation."

Now Chapman could turn again to Emerson and accord him the lasting victory. Acts, Chapman believed, are more expressive than words, but the "great artist is the most educative influence upon the globe." Garrison had been luckier than Chapman: when he blew the "brazen trumpet" the walls of Jericho fell. But Garrison's power died with him. "The small, inner, silver trumpet of Emerson," Chapman now realized, "caught and sounded the same note, and it continues to sound the note, shaking down the walls of inner Jerichoes of men of later and even later generations." The victory of the artist had been one of passivity; he had dissolved his will in God and had become a channel for the spirit, the ultimate "influence." Thus, having abdicated the self-will of his early Emerson, Chapman accepted the mysticism of the Emerson who had always drawn his power and solace from the Over-Soul. Outbursts, such as those occasioned by his fears of Germany, of the Jew, and of the Catholic, marred Chapman's later life. But whatever serenity he had was the result of a lifetime's struggle with the will. "At first we desire to help vigorously," he explained, "and we do all in our power to assist mankind. As time goes on, we perceive more and more clearly that the advancement of the world does not depend on us, but that we, rather, are bound up in it, and can command no foothold of our own. At last we see that our very ambitions, desires and hopes in the matter are a part of the Supernal Machinery moving through all things, and that our souls can be satisfied and our power exerted only in so far as we are taken up into that original motion, and merged in that primal power." Chapman not only wished to return to the "Mansion of Religion" which enclosed the "Houses" of philanthropy, art, social caste, and grief in which he had lived, he wished to yield up to God that American conscience which no one had been strong enough to bear.

### III

None of Chapman's critics sympathizes with his escape into a personal transcendental religion. They prefer the early Chapman of the Emersonian will. One gathers from the moral touchstones they cite that they are attracted to the Chapman who went alone to Coatesville to do penance for a lynching that had occurred there. His strenuousness, his courage and nonconformity, his willingness to be the conscience of his age and to serve only the authority of the moral sense, attract them. His individualism and moral intransigence make him a type we do not like to see become obsolescent; we would like to believe that a man of his qualities could still be a power in American life. From Emerson's day to ours, the intellectual has hungered for individual influence and has felt guilty because of his ineffectualness in liberating the "beneficent energy" and making the "good" turn the wheels of society. Nostalgia for the time when the individual could earnestly accept the calling of the American Scholar with the duty to bring about "the conversion of the world," perhaps self-pity because of the difficulty of becoming an intellectual force in our time—these may account for the respectful attention Chapman has received. What the cowboy is to the lowbrow, the hero of conscience emboldened by the "nerve of failure" may be to the highbrow.

Chapman's attractiveness, as Edmund Wilson's special relationship to him makes it easier to see, is due not only to the fact that Chapman is a fascinating case of what he called "the nemesis of temperament," but to the fact that he was patrician. He is an example of the democrat with an aristocratic sensibility. A cultivated amateur, a critic in the world of affairs rather than in the academy, he was more genuinely humane in his concern for the classics and the humanities than were the scholars themselves, and he reproved them for opening the universities to the commercial interests of the time. His humanism was acceptable because it united an awareness of the social values of continuity, standards, and tradition with the need for romantic impulse. Unlike Babbitt, he knew that art was the language of the emotions, that it ministered to emotional health, and that America needed not so much the will to refrain as nourishment at its emotional roots. In his youth he had discovered that Europe was his "natural habitat" and that America was a "desert," and yet this man of culture wrote one of the first and best indictments of expatriation. Though he enjoyed the social arts and was at home in club and country house, he was seriously interested in the problem of art and society. The study of how commercialism corrupts society and frustrates art in *Causes and Consequences* and *Practical Agitation* is still worth reading and places Chapman in the line of critics who, like Wilson and Trilling, devote themselves primarily to matters of cultural health.

In these books, in *Emerson and Other Essays,* and the *Political Nursery,* Chapman had much to say to a younger generation as deeply concerned with the politics of culture as he was. His attacks on the genteel tradition, on the reputations of Stevenson and Kipling, and on the "iron grey commercial civilization" which fostered in "half-educated people" a taste for "second-rate things," should have become their starting point. His views on art were romantic; he stressed its unconscious sources and ex-

67

pressive ends. And the polar terms of his cultural analysis—
"selfishness" and "unselfishness"—were simply the moral
equivalents of "acquisitiveness" and "creativity" which were later
used by Van Wyck Brooks. If only Brooks had found the Emerson of his *America's Coming-of-Age* in Chapman instead of in
Vernon Lee! If only the few years between the generations had
not opened such an unbridgeable gap!

But Chapman was already out of things when the younger
generation came of age. In 1910, in *The Treason and Death of
Benedict Arnold*, a play which was Chapman's most poignant
statement of his position in American life, Arnold puts on his
old American uniform, exhibits the sword-knots Washington
had given him, and says, "I must go back / To where I lost the
way." In 1915, Chapman wrote that "we are becoming the
oldest generation." By 1918, he confessed that the new age
presented "strange symbols that I could not understand."
*Memories and Milestones*, published in 1915, seemed to be a
valedictory volume; and the critic who never got beyond Shaw
and Ibsen, and who had said of Whitman, the saint of the
younger generation, that he had the "soul of the tramp," was
easily put aside with the Babbitts and Mores. Followers of John
Dewey, the younger generation disliked the moral rhetoric of
the elders; they were suspicious of a "belated abolitionist" who,
as Wister said of Chapman, was a "soldier of God against
Mammon." They did not see the World War religiously, as
an occasion for self-sacrifice. Believers in a "trans-national
America," they resented the hysteria of an Anglo-Saxon
crusader, hardened in caste, who occupied himself with the
affairs of private schools and Harvard College and who fulmi-
nated against immigration and found support for his prejudices
in an alliance with the Ku Klux Klan.

An abolitionist who writes poety for the Klan! This is but one
paradox in Chapman's career. But this and the other paradoxes
that one finds in Chapman are the detritus of social change.
They are common enough in "stranded" intellectuals who after
a lifetime's devotion to American culture may feel, as Edmund

Wilson did that "I don't want any more to be bothered with the kind of contemporary conflicts that I used to go out to explore. . . . When, for example, I look through *Life* magazine, I feel that I do not belong to the country depicted there, that I do not even live in that country." The choruses in *Benedict Arnold* chant: "For an old [man], only death remains. He hath no strength for new things." And when Arnold dies, they chant Chapman's epitaph: "Surely the past must be allowed to all men. . . . What good there was in us cannot be lost. God forgets not the virtue of those who have failed; and why should men seek to judge them? Verily all courage is immortal."

Perhaps the unsettled and unsettling year we spent in Vienna began the turning of which this essay is representative. I had chosen to teach in Vienna because I associated it with the achievements of Freud and of the logical positivists—Feigl and Bergmann had been at Iowa, and Bergmann had been one of my teachers—and because I wanted, in preparation for a book on Transcendentalism, to study Goethe and German Romanticism closely, nearer the font. Neither was offered in 1957–1958, and since study was not facilitated and I was attracted more by the city itself, I read other things, among them Lewis Mumford's *The Culture of Cities*. I already knew some of Mumford's work—*The Golden Day, The Brown Decades*, and *Herman Melville*—but this book, because of my situation, was decisive, and I followed it with *Roots of Contemporary American Architecture*, an anthology that I, having an interest in the "organic," found especially stimulating and full of discoveries. By the time we returned to Urbana, I had postponed the book on Transcendentalism for studies in what I called the Emersonian or "organic" trandition. I began corresponding with Mumford, and in August, 1959, we visited the Mumfords at Amenia. That autumn I taught "American Criticism and Culture," a course growing out of these studies, progressing with and consolidating them.

This turning involved a leap to the generation of critics that had most conspicuously expressed the Emersonian inspiration—the generation of Randolph Bourne and Van Wyck Brooks. But since I also wanted to chart the continuity from Emerson, I wrote at this time not only about Whitman, who was the central figure for Bourne and Brooks, but began to search for someone who belonged to the intermediate generation. What I had read of John Jay Chapman, especially his famous essay on Emerson, led me to think that he might serve. But after doing my "homework" (as Austin Warren calls diligent scholarship), my disposition was, in a double sense, to dispose of him. He disappointed me. With him, Emersonianism ended in a trial of character; it did not open, as I happily found that it had with Louis Sullivan, into the main currents of modern thought.

And yet, as rereading this essay informs me, Chapman served by pointing up the moral predicament of the intellectual. He knew the excruciating problems of action vs. contemplation, of finding an effective purchase for social change. What seems notable now is the moral imperative that moved him and that, in 1960, prefigured the imperative of another generation—a generation the presentiment of which, even then, may have moved me to write of generation gaps and the politics of culture.

# PAUL ROSENFELD

THE CLASS of 1912 at Yale wasn't unusual. Of its 298 graduating members, 57 expected to go into law, 54 into business, 20 into medicine, 10 into banking and brokerage. There was a conquering confidence: "Symington will enter Wall Street." According to a poll, the most valuable courses had been "Social Conditions" and "Elementary Economics," with "Tennyson and Browning" not far behind. Kipling was the favorite prose writer, Tennyson the favorite poet, and "Crossing the Bar" the favorite poem; *Ivanhoe* was the favorite novel. A majority of the class favored William H. Taft as the presidential candidate in the coming election.

One of its members who was still undecided about his vocation and whose tastes, one suspects, were not entirely represented by the class polls was Paul Leopold Rosenfeld. He does not appear in the lists of "most to be admired," "best athlete," "best natured," "most brilliant," "most original," "most optimistic"—not even "best dressed," for Yale had succeeded in getting others into Brooks Brothers suits. At the bottom of the list of "most scholarly," his name appears, his scholarly bent having been recognized by seven of his classmates if not by those who award Phi Beta Kappa honors. The face in the photograph in the *History of the Class of* 1912 is a bit Prussianly severe; perhaps the moustache and high collar account for it. But there is no familiar nickname in the personal history printed beneath; and we learn that he had always roomed alone and that he had been an editor of *The Lit.*, the least popular college publication according to the polls, its six votes undoubtedly cast by the six members of its board.

Military school had prepared him for Yale, but it had not prepared him to be a conqueror in what he later called—taking the phrase from Henry Adams—a "coal-power civilization." His father, Julius Rosenfeld, had been a small manufacturer; his mother, Sara Liebmann (Clara in the class history), was an accomplished pianist. Until her death in 1900, when Paul was ten, the family lived the well-to-do brownstone existence of upper West Side Manhattan that also characterized the cultivated middle-class German-Jewish families that produced Alfred Stieglitz and Waldo Frank. The father had literary, the mother musical taste; and the manner of their life, to judge from Rosenfeld's story, "The Dark Brown Room," and his novel, *The Boy in the Sun*, would have put him at ease in the drawing rooms of bourgeois Vienna or Berlin. They summered on the New Jersey coast, typical of those families that later disturbed Henry James and that led John Jay Chapman to cry out: "Judea—Israel—the Lost Tribes—lost no more! found—very much found, increased—multiplied—as the sands of the sea—upon the sands of the sea—in the city of the sea—Atlantic City." The mother's death destroyed the family. The children were cared for by their maternal grandmother. The father, whom the son spoke of in the class history as "retired" but who died before Paul entered Yale (according to his friend Jerome Mellquist), disintegrated under his sorrow.

Riverview Military Academy at Poughkeepsie, where Rosenfeld was sent in 1903 presumably to improve his posture but actually because "choicer institutions," as he admitted, would not accept him, did not make a soldier of him. His memories of the place are empty of military occasions. "On its parade-ground," he relates, "I discovered the advantage of piano lessons. Correctly to execute the maneuvers when the command was 'Squads right!' or 'Squads left!' I found I had merely to imagine myself at the keyboard. Promptly I knew which of my hands was left, which right. It made me a trifle slow, but never fatally so. Finally I attained a sergeant's rank." He always remembered the low highlands and the Hudson, for he later took Sunday excursions there; and he remembered a Mr. Charles H. Hickok who ran a music store and who, pretty much at his own expense as it turned out, twice brought the Boston Symphony Orchestra to Poughkeepsie. At the Academy he took piano lessons; first from a "lady teaching by the noiseless method," the "pathetic, bosomy" Miss Virginia Gorse who began the first lesson with, "I'm glad to see you have rounded finger-nails. People with flat finger-nails, you know, are always deceitful"; later from a pale young man named Arthur Moore Williamson. If Mr. Hickok remained in his memory as an exemplar of the selfless devotion that makes culture possible, Arthur Williamson figured there as an exemplar of the talent that cultural wastes like Poughkeepsie (all the world's Poughkeepsie, he said) failed to nourish. No humor is intended when Rosenfeld describes this spectacled, infinitely sensitive, suffering young music master, who at five was rapturous over a Mason and Hamlin piano, who developed heart disease at fifteen and suffered from gastric disturbances, and who fainted when calling on a young lady to whom he intended to propose. For in his unpretentious way, Williamson opened the door to the world of music which by 1920 Rosenfeld had made his own. Cadets may contrive strategems in order to go home, but certainly not, as Rosenfeld did, to escape to New York for a concert. His debt to Williamson is recorded in the dedication of his first book, *Musical Portraits* (1920).

Rosenfeld left few recollections, musical or otherwise, of his years at Yale. In his sophomore year he read George Moore and Arthur Symons, and Moore, he later acknowledged, influenced his feeling (already partially developed by his reading in George Meredith, Morris, Pater, and the early Yeats) for a "high," sensuous style. He heard Horatio Parker, professor of music, play the organ in Woolsey Hall, but Parker's *Mona*, an opera which Rosenfeld heard in 1912 and ever afterward defended as the best American opera, was never associated with his college years. He has nothing to say about his work on *The Lit.* or about his initiation into journalism on a New Haven newspaper. Journalism, however, seems to have been the career he had in mind, for he entered the Columbia University School of Journalism in the fall of 1912, and following his graduation in 1913 began to report for the New York newspapers. Six months of journalism were apparently enough and probably brought about the "revelation" we are told occurred on 42nd Street, where Rosenfeld decided that, having a private income of five thousand dollars a year,[1] he could follow his own calling. The calling was still uncertain, but it led immediately to Europe; and there, in London, in May 1914, he discovered in Bechstein Hall what Randolph Bourne was also discovering in Europe—his own generation and its "modern desire" to reach beyond the material to more spiritual satisfactions.

The experience of music was Rosenfeld's passport to this new world. He heard his way into things, and music undoubtedly kept his sensibility fluid and responsive. Such courses as "Social Conditions" and "Elementary Economics" did not enable him to see the social manifestations that Bourne saw so well and reported so carefully. Concert halls filled his horizon, not the rallies of socialists and suffragettes, the lecture rooms of Oxford and the Sorbonne, or the new architecture and planned communities to be seen on the Continent. He would grow in social awareness, but this awareness always sprang from his knowledge of the travail of artists whose heroic mission, he believed, was to explore and to shape contemporary experience. The signposts of his awareness of the experience of his generation are the concerts he heard; the Armory Show of 1913 did not jolt his eye in the way that the music of Stravinsky and Schönberg (which he

1 Lewis Mumford believes his annual income was nearer ten thousand dollars.

later described in cubist terms) jolted his ear. He came to painting and literature by way of music, and his account of his own discovery of modernism in "Grand Transformation Scene—1907–1915" is a story of concerts.

The first concert goes back to the Riverview days when he had slipped away to New York and had heard the *Pathétique* symphony. As in almost everything he wrote, such backward steps prepare for the leap into modernism; it dates an epoch, and Rosenfeld's truthfulness about his response, that "awareness passed into ecstasy," dates a sensibility that would learn increasingly to pass from ecstasy into awareness. The second concert in London shocked the young listener because, although he had already left Tschaikowsky behind, he still felt that music with the power to exalt and satisfy had ended with César Franck and that recitals of new music promised him nothing. Perhaps his account of his tastes benefited in the retelling by his mature criticism, for he had already worn out his enthusiasms for Wagner, Debussy, Mahler, and Loeffler. As for American music, it was idealistic, a "pale wash," represented by the "gentlemen of Boston," the Chadwicks and Converses. What one got in the concert hall was "Victor Herbert emerging from the wings with an invisible shillalah to conduct his Rhapsody of favorite Irish airs." Such music left him among the "flat buildings on upper Broadway" with their electric signs and automobile displays feeling that he was in a world "without bloom, without mystery; dusty, smart and empty." Even the music of the Europeans, of Strauss, Reger, and Mahler, disclosed "the banality of a world posthumous to the wet, singing one"; and until that night in Bechstein Hall, with the cheap seats crowded with intent young people ("it was my generation—and alert, and out in life as gardens were"), with Scriabin, hitherto unknown to Rosenfeld, at the piano, there had been no one to tell him that "not lyric impulse but the rhetoric of romanticism, the passion for passions—and New York, were dead."

The nineteen-year-old boy in the black velvet jacket and slippers who played his "atonal ectoplasmic compositions" one winter afternoon in 1915 in the playhouse on 57th Street completed the transformation. After this concert by Leo Ornstein ("It was all new, this music."), there was for Rosenfeld a "singular bloom on 57th St. . . . So strong, so promissory, New York had never lain." This music registered what Rosenfeld had believed to be lost: "The direct sounds of souls in contact with present existence: infinitely delicate and serious representations of the complex and nervous patterns of experience rising out of the relationship between the organism and the modern environment; encouragements to the accurate expression of every living sensation, perception, emotion." One imagines Stieglitz's photograph of the single slender tree rising from the wet city pavement when Rosenfeld expresses his sudden sense of "the perennial fecundity and youthfulness of life" and his realization that the new world he had discovered in this music would be "less dream-laden, more realistic with material than the romantic had been" and more "democratically affirmative of the natural variety of attitudes and impulses."

The years from 1914 to 1916 when the new music seemed to Rosenfeld to be saying, "YOUR TURN, AMERICA!" were devoted to literary apprenticeship. He worked at a novel, and though he never succeeded as a novelist, he remained a *writer* who approached critical writing, as few have done, as a creative art.[2] In retrospect and in the dedication of *Port of New York* he gave the credit for his awakening to Leo Ornstein, but his critical work and the program it served must be credited to the mediation of the ebullient Waldo Frank. Frank had been sent to Yale rather than to Heidelberg because his father wanted him to be an "American"; he had taken his degree, even an M.A., had gone into journalism, and shortly afterward had packed his bag for Paris. There he found that he was not "needed"; he returned home where he "belonged," led an itinerant existence in what

2  It is characteristic of his generation of men of letters that his style more often than his judgments was criticized. Criticism was a personal art, and though Rosenfeld valued impersonality he never relinquished the testimony of his personal contact with the object.

he later called "the American jungle," and began his career as
novelist and critic, fully aware that in matters of expression "the
present generation of Americans [were] more profoundly
pioneers . . . more original adventurers than Columbus."
Rosenfeld probably met Frank at one of Claire Raphael's musical evenings when Frank played the cello in an amateur trio; and
it was through Frank that he came to know Alfred Stieglitz, Van
Wyck Brooks, and Randolph Bourne, each in his way a center of
artistic or creative enterprise, and all devoted to the cultural
possibilities of American life.

Frank was one of the initiators of *The Seven Arts*, a shortlived
but seminal little magazine which rallied the adherents of contemporary art with its declaration of policy, "AN EXPRESSION OF
ARTISTS FOR THE COMMUNITY." Its editorial proclamation expressed the common faith of a group of critics who, unlike the
lost generation that shared the twenties with them, never quite
forsook the generous hopes for America that had stirred them in
their youth. "It is our faith . . . that we are living in the first days
of a renascent period," the proclamation began, "a time which
means for America the coming of that national self-
consciousness which is the beginning of greatness. In all such
epochs the arts cease to be private matters; they become not only
the expression of the national life but a means to its enhancement." *The Seven Arts* was to be the channel for the flow of these
new tendencies, especially of the conviction that the aesthetic is
inextricably a part of the social; and the very existence of the
magazine was to create a community of artists—a school such as
Henry Adams wished to found. Even though it died within a
year, the spirit that animated it and the artists it had united
found outlet in magazines like *The Dial, The Freeman,* and *The
New Republic*; in *The American Caravan,* an annual volume of
new writing; and in *Twice A Year,* a book-length magazine
devoted to the arts and to civil liberties which began in 1938 and
offered a place to those still living and memorials to those who
had died.

Rosenfeld began to write on music and literature for *The New*   77

*Republic* in 1916, but it was Frank, the associate editor of *The
Seven Arts*, who brought him into the community of artists
whom Rosenfeld was soon to champion. He made it possible for
Rosenfeld to appear in the first number, that of November,
1916, with articles on the American composer and on "291."
"291 Fifth Avenue" was the first gallery and workroom of Alfred
Stieglitz, who might fairly be said to have provided the example
and tended the soil from which such literary ventures as *The
Seven Arts* grew. For years he had singlehandedly fought for
both European and American modern art. In 1903 he had
founded *Camera Work*, a sumptuous quarterly, indeed a folio-
sized gallery, in which he presented the history of photographic
art, the work of contemporary photographers such as Paul
Strand and Edward Steichen, and reproductions of the draw-
ings, paintings, and sculpture of Rodin, Cézanne, Picasso,
Picabia, Matisse, Brancusi, Marin—artists whom he had already exhibited for the first time in America at "291." Patron,
teacher, crusader, Stieglitz sponsored Alfred Maurer, John Marin, and Marsden Hartley in 1909, Arthur Dove in 1910, and
Georgia O'Keeffe in 1916; later on when he opened The Intimate Gallery in 1925, he added Charles Demuth to the group of
painters for whom he had established the gallery; and annually,
first in The Intimate Gallery, then in An American Place, he
showed their work.

As an art critic Rosenfeld was almost exclusively the interpreter of the painters in Stieglitz's group. He was fiercely loyal to
Stieglitz, filially bound to him. He emulated him by becoming
a discoverer, patron, and receptive critic of new talents; and the
courage and faith with which he espoused the cause of art were
comparable to Stieglitz's, drawn from the belief in the value of
art that both profoundly shared: "the bridge to consciousness of
self, to life, and through that, to new life and creation again."
He took his aesthetics from Stieglitz, the work of Brooks, Frank,
and especially Bourne, providing the cultural framework for the
findings of his sensibility. More than anyone else, he was the
78   liaison between *The Seven Arts* and "291."

The war broke the momentum of the movement. Indirectly it led to the closing of "291," and it closed out *The Seven Arts* when its backer and some of its editors could not agree with Bourne that the intellectual must choose between "the war—or American promise." It took Rosenfeld to Camp Humphreys, Virginia, and it hastened the death of Bourne, who died in Rosenfeld's apartment in 1918. It chastened many a democratic faith; it brought in its wake those illiberal, reactionary undercurrents that Bourne had fought and that made a mockery of normalcy. For some, like Rosenfeld who remained loyal to Bourne's vision of America, it toughened the faith by revealing the strength of the opposition. If it seemed to be free and hospitable, the age of normalcy was nevertheless a cold war within America for those intellectuals who had taken to heart the lesson of Bourne's death. Critics thought of "Daisy," but did not marry her; and even the "Daisy" Edmund Wilson temporarily possessed was a *jeune fille* of his own sentimental boyhood.

Bourne, Brooks, and Frank were more influential in the early years of the movement than was Rosenfeld. Or perhaps one should say that they had a public stature that the self-effacing Rosenfeld never acquired. They were primarily culture critics; he was a literary, art, and, above all, music critic interested in culture. They did not know or master the arts as he did or leave behind so large and solid a body of criticism. Brooks was the acknowledged leader, having clarified the cultural scene in *America's Coming-of-Age* (1915) and in *Letters and Leadership* (1918). Bourne, as Rosenfeld said, was "the great bearer of moral authority while America was at war," a more political, forward-looking, and resolute "bannerman of values" than Brooks; had he lived, Bourne probably would have been the sovereign intellectual spokesman of his generation, and Brooks and Frank would not have fought, as they did, a subtle battle for leadership. Not only was Frank recognized as a significant experimental novelist; *Our America*, a study of American culture compounded of Brooks's leading ideas and his own mysticism, was acclaimed in 1919, and his collected critical essays,

*Salvos* (1924), and his *New Yorker* portraits of famous contemporaries gathered together in *Time-Exposures* (1926) made him a prominent critical figure in the twenties. His militancy and the avant-garde nature of his fiction were probably more acceptable to the younger writers (an issue of *S4N* and a book were devoted to him) than Brooks's querulousness and indifference to contemporary art. Bourne had been doubtful of the way in which Brooks intended to treat Twain, and none of Brooks's friends, having deferred judgment during his years on *The Freeman*, felt that he had redeemed himself with *The Pilgrimage of Henry James* (1925). That book, as Brooks himself admitted, broke his career and his mental health.

The twenties brought Rosenfeld forward. In that decade he published a novel and seven volumes of criticism. *Musical Portraits, Musical Chronicle, Modern Tendencies in Music*, and *An Hour With American Music* were concerned entirely with music; *Men Seen* treated modern European and American literature, *By Way of Art* the arts at large, and *Port of New York* those Americans who in spirit or in fact were related to "291" or *The Seven Arts* and whose work dispelled the Brooksian gloom about creative America. These books, his private solicitude for innumerable artists, and the editorial labor of gathering and publishing the work of new writers in *The American Caravan* (which he began with Lewis Mumford and Alfred Kreymborg in 1927), represent the largest single effort on behalf of contemporary art of any American critic. Edmund Wilson, always a shrewd observer of his colleagues in criticism, recalls that Rosenfeld "at that time enjoyed a prestige of the same kind as Mencken's and Brooks's, though it was not so widely felt as the former's." Not so widely felt, but deeply felt: if *Paul Rosenfeld: Voyager in the Arts*, the testimonial volume which followed his death, is any indication, then, with the possible exception of Stieglitz, Rosenfeld was the most warmly regarded critic of his generation.

Not only his work but his personality, with which the work is so alive, explains this gratitude. Gentleness perhaps describes his total quality, a genial (in the Emersonian sense) responsiveness which permitted him, without grasping, to reach out to people in the same large way that he reached out to art objects and to the environment. Lewis Mumford speaks of his "lyrical wisdom," that profound wisdom of experience emotionally mastered. This wisdom took him to the creative springs of art and taught him that "good equals the communication of life" and that "the personality with a living object [never] goes into itself." Sin, he believed, was the withholding of love; the most intense emotion was tenderness.

By temperament Rosenfeld was a romantic. His values, however, must be placed between the evils of romantic yearning for the past and Flaubert's horror at man's everlasting filth and ferocity. He is a romantic in his belief in the primacy of the heart; for, though he is classic in his desire to see the external world clearly, he knew that the intellect could not fully capture the rhythms of life. Neither a Transcendentalist nor a naturalist, he was the kind of humanist who takes life for his scripture. In his own experience he had had the doubt of all things earthly and the intuitions of some things heavenly of which Melville had spoken, and from his own suffering and awareness of the reality of death he had won a tragic sense of life and liberated his joy in living.[3] "To live," he said, "is to touch others with the antithesis at the heart of the world, with sorrow as well as joy."

His response to art and life was therefore something more than aesthetic. He judged both art and life by the possibility of "life completely used, exercised to the fulness of its capacity for tragedy and for delight, and deprived by death of nothing of worth." Though he appreciated the pioneer aesthetic achievements of Joyce and Eliot, he rejected the "comédie intellectuelle" of the one and the "fantasy of The Waste Land" of the other; and it was not that he overlooked the actual wastelands, but rather that he believed them to be relative conditions. Even now—he found in the case of D. H. Lawrence—"someone is always finding his age propitious to his form of artistry [,] the world and someone's idea are always managing to harmonize."

3 See "The Hospital," *Men Seen.*

To Lawrence, Rosenfeld accorded the highest praise. For Lawrence had not succumbed to the "parasite" of mind; he had had "new, increased and more complex capacities for feeling," and had therefore beaten out the rhythm of his age and helped men live more truly. Rosenfeld's measure of art was individual and social health: "We cannot be sincere and not crave fullest living."

Such attitudes were not prescriptive, yet had a seriousness that artists at least responded to. They were embodied in his person and exuberantly expressed in his own rich art of living. What he wrote in admiration of Guillaume Apollinaire applied to him: "Possessed of a voracious appetite for many kinds of experience, a swift sensibility and an inextinguishable intellectual curiosity, he communicated his joys and games and sensations not less through the forms of ordinary existence than those of literature." The Apollinaire of "metro'd electric Paris" was everything that the cosmopolitan and cultivated Rosenfeld wished to be in New York—a "vivid and distinguished person," a "cavalier of life." No autointoxicated D'Annunzio searching for some grandiose situation, posture, or movement to fill his emotional emptiness or using art to compensate for "inward incapacity," Apollinaire "had the gift of procuring for himself aristocratic pleasures among the ordinary house-walls and in the ordinary paths of urban life."[4] He was one of those people, as Henry James might have said, on whom nothing is lost. He nourished his art with every motion of the boulevards, with convivial talk, and with the pleasures of good food which he often prepared himself—as did Rosenfeld. And beneath his bonhomie was a strongly developed communal feeling and a combativeness in behalf of ideas that made him the champion of the cubists much in the same way that similar traits made Rosenfeld the champion of the artists of his time. The portrait that Rosenfeld drew can stand for his own, for its surest lines are those that delineate his "sensuous alertness," that show his

---

4 Edmund Wilson noted Rosenfeld's "capacity for presenting even the most abortive incidents in the life of human intelligence as events in a significant, exciting and highly picturesque adventure."

awareness of the fact that he was "deliberately used by those interested in the advancement of their own affairs," and that his willingness to serve the general cause had cost him his own complete self-expression.

Everyone acknowledged Rosenfeld's cultivation, and no one more than Sherwood Anderson. Anderson, whom *The Seven Arts* and *The Dial* had lifted to fame, had come to believe, as he said in a letter, that he was the product of the "same thing Brooks talks so much about in his *Mark Twain.*" Having been raised in a "different atmosphere than most of you fellows," he felt that he never really deserved the praise of a "truly fine aristocrat" like Rosenfeld who had done him the honor of leading him through Europe. Alyse Gregory, managing editor of *The Dial*, noted Rosenfeld's fine manners and remarked that he "followed the Latin rather than the Anglo-Saxon tradition and made of human intercourse an art." And Edmund Wilson, perhaps with a tinge of envy, said that more than any other American writer Rosenfeld had "the real freedom of the Continent," the gift of living "in touch with the great artistic life of the world." In the curious way in which his father's generation had marked the Jew (Justice Holmes, for example, called Harold Laski "the Jew"), Wilson attributed Rosenfeld's gift to the concurrence within him of American, European, and Jewish backgrounds. But whatever the reasons, and Wilson's have their share of truth, Rosenfeld did absorb European culture in an unself-conscious way and more wholly than did early apostles of culture like Lowell and Norton and later apostles like Eliot and Pound. This may account in part for the fact that he did not feel the need to adopt in criticism the magisterial tone. It accounts, certainly, for the reverence with which Wilson treated Rosenfeld in his brilliant imaginary dialogue between the older critic, who represented the living and human values of tradition, and Matthew Josephson, expatriate editor of *Secession*, who represented the explosive cultural nihilism of the younger generation.

Looking back in the forties over his career, Rosenfeld observed that the present state of culture in America at best "possesses a

memory with a span of possibly ten years." It is a telling observation about the large work and small expectation of the intellectual in our society—a society still Jeffersonian in its belief in the
sovereignty of the present generation—and it was true enough
in Rosenfeld's case. Rosenfeld lost his place, but not as Edmund
Wilson wanted to believe as early as 1925 when, perhaps with
the possibilities of his own *Axel's Castle* in view, he wrote that
Rosenfeld had broken down our provincial prejudices and in-
hibitions against artistic expression and had permanently
bridged the gulf between Europe and America, and that therefore the need for his services was over. Rather, he lost his place,
as Wilson recognized when Rosenfeld was dead and possibly
from his own later experience, because the climate of each
succeeding decade was different. Rosenfeld knew that it was "an
era of sudden developments"; generations were "littered every
four or five years." And therefore Rosenfeld knew that work such
as his was never done. Goethe expressed his acceptance of the
thankless and unremitting job of criticism: "We acquire little
thanks from people when we try to elevate their inner necessities, to give them a great conception of themselves, to bring to
consciousness in them the magnificence of a true, gracious way
of being. I say this not to humiliate my friends. I merely say that
thus they are, and that we ought not to be astonished that
everything remains as it does."

Many things but mainly the discontinuity of the cultural
conditions of the thirties and forties brought about Rosenfeld's
decline. The public indifference and the burning-out—so Wilson generalized on the depressing story of the American
intellectual—seemed to go together, and many of Rosenfeld's
friends noted his loss of confidence. But the only book he
published after the twenties, *Discoveries of a Music Critic*, was
his ripest work. It should have made clear to those who had
doubted (was the dedication to Wilson ironic?) the depth of his
awareness of social, historical, and intellectual forces and his
skill in relating them to art. He had already rejected, in the case
of D'Annunzio, an art subservient to preconceptions and political formulas, and once more took his stand in "The Authors and

Politics." He had no mercy for the exhorter in art, not even for a friend like James Oppenheim, poet and editor of *The Seven Arts*; and where the artist was an "advertiser" like Gershwin or a propagandist like Shostakovich, he had abdicated for Rosenfeld the essential individual integrity of aesthetic vision. In an essay on "The Nazis and *Die Meistersinger*," he defined the uses and abuses of nationalistic art and reaffirmed his belief that "art is one of the great potential agents among a democratic people." But these views did not endear him to the majority of artists and editors who in the thirties had moved politically to either the left or the right and had accepted the security of doctrine.

Other changes, such as T. S. Eliot's ascendancy in elite critical circles and the commercialization of what had been an independent press, reduced the outlets for his highly personal, emotionally evocative prose. Even *The New Yorker* refused to print the articles it had asked him to write and Knopf turned down his proposed book on *The Seven Arts* group. And these rejections were doubly severe because the crash of 1929 had destroyed his financial security and forced him to play the game of supply and demand for which he was not equipped.

Personal difficulties—the crucial years after forty which he said were "devilish"—compounded the difficulties of survival. Fully aware that irresolution gets down to the "nucleus of sex," he tried unsuccessfully to resolve in an autobiographical novel, *Concert in Rome*, what he could not resolve in life. But this failure was not due, as some suspected because of his political stand, to his unwillingness to forsake bourgeois comforts, though it may have been due to his unwillingness, in reduced circumstances, to ask another to forsake them. He refused not so much to embrace life as to offer his life without all of its former resources. Diabetes, the war, the book on literary genres that he began after rigorously reeducating himself—all these things taxed the limited strength with which he maintained his quiet cheerfulness and dignity. Judged, however, by his desire to live boldly and dangerously "in the fashion of the artist" and by the critical necessity of remaining at the "battle-line," he was not the kind of failure he believed Brooks to be. Often lowered to menial

and perfunctory reviewing, he was still able to speak out for the
courageous publishing of *New Directions* and for new talents
like Henry Miller.

The photograph of Rosenfeld taken in these years by Stieglitz
catches the limpid sorrowful eyes and the full heavy inclined
head; the severity, if ever it were that, of the college photograph
is gone. No conqueror of an age, only its sensitive recorder
whose "activity of spirit [was] an infallible sign of health,"
Rosenfeld died in circumstances of "indecent unceremonious-
ness" (a phrase from *Port of New York*, written two decades
before) that only make more ghastly the terrible anonymity of
American life. Stieglitz died on July 13, 1946; eight days later,
having already sent a memorial article on his beloved mentor to
*The Commonweal*, Rosenfeld had a fatal heart attack while
attending the neighborhood Loew's Sheridan motion picture
theatre at Seventh Avenue and Twelfth Street. The cold and
careless obituary in the New York *Herald-Tribune* reported that
the movies were *The Green Years* and *Night Editor*. Toward the
end, it mentioned that Edmund Wilson had said of Rosenfeld
that "he gave himself away to the artists of his period." Essentially that was just what Rosenfeld had written of the lonely
Stieglitz.

## II

Appreciative, aesthetic, impressionistic, romantic—these are
some of the terms that have been used to define the criticism of
Paul Rosenfeld. From the standpoint of current critical "authority" they are all invidious terms. We establish our own rigor by
means of them and with them we cauterize portions of our
sensibility and exclude values we do not wish to accommodate.
Our criticism is but another mirror of our response to life:
intellectual, discriminating, precise, it is curiously impersonal,
dry, beggarly. Turning in on itself, it manifests the dehumaniza-
tion of the other arts. Although it is concerned with defending
the ways in which art uniquely realizes the fullness and com-
86    plexity of experience, in practice it anatomizes the work and

only infrequently summons a personal sense of those values it cherishes most. Criticism has become a discipline and, like the discipline of science, its individual practice (or art) has been constrained by the common program it serves. For at least three decades we have been afraid to show our passion in criticism or to push on to the moral of our aesthetic experience. For many in our time it is perhaps enough that art is thus made safe and the values it enshrines secure. We have come closer to Dr. Johnson's desire for a criticism with the certainty and stability of science; we have quoted but neither fully understood nor practiced what Henry James said of criticism, that "to criticize is to appreciate, to appropriate, to take intellectual possession, to establish in fine a relation with the thing criticized and make it one's own."

Rosenfeld used criticism in the large Jamesian way. James judged both critic and novelist by the same standard; for criticism, he said, "springs from the liveliest experience" and offers an opportunity, like fiction, for the active mind and the free play of intelligence. Everywhere in James the bedrock is sensibility—vital intelligence. The critic therefore is judged by his "indefatigable suppleness," by his capacity to remain open to impressions, by the quality of his feeling for life. He is "to lend himself, to project himself and steep himself, to feel and feel till he understands, and to understand so well that he can say." Where the novelist gives us the "sense of life," the critic gives us the "sense of art." But if, as in Rosenfeld's case, the critic is a novelist (with Jamesian proclivity), then perhaps his criticism gives in a less realized form than that of fiction a sense of life as well. For the impulse of all his writing, Rosenfeld wrote, was in response to "the latency pressing, directly upon me and my time."

This is not to say that Rosenfeld is the paragon of critics, but only that such qualities as he brought to criticism give his work a permanent value. To place him, as many still do, with James Gibbons Huneker helps to distinguish his virtues rather than to maximize his faults. Both of course had gusto and an unremitting devotion to the life of art; "bohemian" describes both of them only if we remember that it also describes the Rudolphs of *La Bohème* and the Thoreaus of this world. Both approached art temperamentally and emotionally and both wrote lush and lapidary prose in order to convey their vivid impressions and to excite response. They were impressionists then, for isn't bejeweled prose a hallmark? And friend and foe alike found fault with Rosenfeld's prose.

Some tripped over the infelicities of his Frenchified and Germanicized English. Many felt the prose unnecessarily rich. Malcolm Cowley even says that Rosenfeld's "obstinacy" in clinging to this "style" after the literary fashions had changed accounts for his decline. The style, however, was never a manner or fashion; it changed with the critical occasion. There are times at the beginning, middle, and end of his career when Rosenfeld writes as lucidly as Edmund Wilson. The style was in fact a means of exact emotional notation. Joseph Warren Beach perceptively observed that it was "complicated, intensified, knotted up, tangled up, speeded up"; that the lapses which brought Huneker to mind were not characteristic; that it registered the world of the skyscraper—a fit prose, certainly, for one who shared the new world of Ornstein and Marin. The prose also tended to be richest when Rosenfeld was most wholly engaged. Its ebb and flow is one measure of his vitality. It is incomparably full and fine in *Port of New York,* probably because this book is most profoundly and generously *his* book, warmly alive with his men and his ideas and the hope of the future. Most important, the prose did not exist for itself; there is none of Huneker's exhibitionism in it. It serves the object and the experience of the object, always to the end of translating the experience of new, inaccessible media—Stravinsky's music, O'Keeffe's painting, Anderson's prose—into the more familiar verbal one. If this is paraphrase, then it is paraphrase by way of sensibility and not, as it is so often in others, by way of intellect alone. The simplest test of this method, which might be called objective impressionism, is to look at pictures or listen to music

with Rosenfeld in hand. "I have never seen a picture of Marsden
Hartley," Beach wrote, "but I shall recognize without a label the
first one I come upon." The critic who can help us to such
recognitions (more than identification is involved) has himself
taken possession. He understands so well that he can say.

With such criticism of Rosenfeld as that by B. H. Haggin and
Thomas Craven we need do nothing but note it. In a radio
address, Haggin said: "Mr. Rosenfeld has been engaged all these
years in over-estimating the second- and third-rate pioneers of
our own time, and this, I think, in order to raise himself in the
estimation of others. Ordinarily one does not speak of motives;
and I am not questioning the honesty of his intentions when I
speak of a pose, in the sense of a determination to appear
comprehending and sensitive to everything new, which is evident in the very manner, the mannered manner, of his writing,
and in the pretense of discerning in a piece of music what is not
there." Thomas Craven said as much indirectly when he wrote
that he could only see clouds in Stieglitz's cloud studies.

The most serious criticism of Rosenfeld is that of Edmund
Wilson. With the freedom that characterized the fraternity of
men of letters in the twenties, he addressed the author as well as
the book. The heart of Wilson's criticism is that Rosenfeld "gives
us loosely imaged rhapsodies when what we are demanding is
ideas." The "orchestral style" does not perform the "closer and
severer function of analysis and exposition." Rosenfeld, therefore, is not a critic of the "philosophic sort." When Wilson is
generous, Rosenfeld is a "romantic commentator on [the arts]
who is also a commentator on life"; "he is sensitive, intelligent,
well-educated and incorruptibly serious." When he is niggard-
ly, Rosenfeld is said to be "unreflectively appreciative"; "receiv-
ing in his soul the seed of a work by some such writer as
Sherwood Anderson, himself one of the tenderer plants, he will
cause it to shoot up and exfloreate into an enormous and rather
rank 'Mystic Cabbage-Rose.' " Wilson is embarrassed most,
apparently, by the evidence of Rosenfeld's emotion. The virtue
he wants in Rosenfeld is his own: the ability to follow "intellec-

tual tides," to fully appreciate the social, political, philosophical, and scientific currents of the day.

Some of this criticism was well taken at the time, but most of
it is curiously off-center and ambivalent. Though Wilson represents Rosenfeld in "The Poet's Return" as one who understands
the value of tradition and standards of excellence, he says
elsewhere that Rosenfeld has no political, moral, and aesthetic
ideals; and because he covets Rosenfeld's cultivation, he enjoys
having Matthew Josephson say, "I tell you that culture as you
understand it is no longer of any value . . . the subway and the
shower themselves are more magnificent poems than anything
by Schubert or Goethe."[5] In matters of art and life Rosenfeld, of
course, had aristocratic tastes; every fine sensibility is aristocratic. This does not, as some would have us believe, gainsay the
democratic faith. Democracy is more than a "popular" manifestation and, as the democratic Rosenfeld knew, was not irreconcilable with every human excellence. The best was its proper
goal. But the tenor of Josephson's speeches is that Rosenfeld is
not in touch with popular culture; he doesn't consider jazz, for
example, or the writer of advertising copy who forges our literature. Yet Rosenfeld wrote on jazz and scored its sentimental
evasions with an edge as sharp as F. R. Leavis' in his attack on
the "literature" of advertising. Rosenfeld was not unsettled by
the dichotomy between highbrow and lowbrow, a dichotomy
presumably of taste but actually of class, which established the
need of proving one's democratic allegiance by a show of lowbrow preferences. One has only to read *I Thought of Daisy* to
realize that Wilson, though writing extensively about popular
culture, personally never really liked it.

Except for a fine memorial article, all of Wilson's criticism of
Rosenfeld was written in 1924–1926. The books under review
were *Musical Chronicle* (1923) and *Men Seen* (1925), both

5  1924. In 1956, Wilson wrote: "For myself . . . I have not the least doubt that I
have derived a good deal more benefit of the civilizing as well as of the
inspirational kind from the admirable American bathroom than I have from
the cathedrals of Europe."

admittedly miscellaneous collections. *Port of New York* (1924) was not explicitly mentioned in the review of *Men Seen* or in the memorial article. Even more curious is the fact that Wilson's essential judgments never altered; for his friend John Peale Bishop had shown in his brilliant review of *Men Seen*, and Rosenfeld's later books and essays demonstrated, that Rosenfeld had political, moral, and aesthetic ideals. Every critic of course has such ideals and it is the business of a critic of critics, as Bishop knew, to locate them. Wilson was perhaps objecting that in Rosenfeld's work these ideals were not sufficiently intellectualized. Or it may be that they amounted to profoundly emotional commitments which he did not share. His misgivings over Rosenfeld's reluctance to ally himself with the Communists in the thirties seem to be a clue to Wilson's earlier response. (In his own uncertainties, as his *Imaginary Dialogues* and *I Thought of Daisy* show, he has felt the need to formulate not his ideals so much as his positions.) Rosenfeld's ideals are clear enough and conviction certifies them. Broadly humanistic, they cohere in his concern for the artist who must be free in his art so that he may bring men to fuller consciousness and a more abundant life.

**Paul Rosenfeld**

The artist is Rosenfeld's representative man or stock personality, and the adventure of art the most rewarding way of life. "Artist" of course must be liberally construed. The nineteenth-century's special interest in art and culture is freighted in the word. Educators like Margaret Naumburg and "intellectuals" like Brooks and Bourne are artists. Anyone qualifies who has thrown off the traces of the bourgeois—even the "new" professor Bourne described—if he takes the adventure of art seriously. For the adventure of art, like Thoreau's uncommitted life and Whitman's life on the open road, is in fact what Bourne meant by the experimental life; it discovers new worlds because it leaves behind the preconceptions that make the world old. It is a serious matter and not a game because the stake is life. Leisure class parasites of culture and literary dandies are its greatest betrayers. "Peacocks" like D'Annunzio and Ezra Pound play the rôle of artist; they use art for costume and gesture. They share the faults of those self-pitying artists who follow art without genuine conviction and who are overborne by the modern malady of fear. Eliot and Wallace Stevens are their representatives, for they made of Laforgue's Pierrot "the spiritual type of all correct young men in mourning." The artist for Rosenfeld is a composite of Emerson's American Scholar and Whitman's poet. He is especially defined by his lack of nostalgia for the past and by his willingness to "relinquish his old modes of apprehension, be born in harmony with the new order, affirm it, venture forth with it on its voyage into the unknown, cleave to it for good or ill." He is committed to the living present, the node of past and future. The inevitable sorrows and defeats of his adventure overcome neither his love nor his hope. All of his duty is comprised in the need to beat out "the rhythms of his age." He stands for what man might be when he casts out fear and works in freedom. And if we find him grandiose it is because we now mean something less by "autonomous" than Rosenfeld did.

The social dislocations of the industrial revolution forced the displaced intellectual to consider the artist a redeemer. Brooks' diagnosis of the split in American society between the highbrow and the lowbrow and his faith in the leadership of the artist are special instances of the general cultural problem of the nineteenth century. "It is the poet alone," Rosenfeld wrote in presenting Brooks's views, "who can make society take the shape which can satisfy the human soul. It is the poet alone who can end the schism in American men; can turn American life toward personal ends, and develop out of an anarchical competitive horde a community of men who give and enrich themselves in giving." With or without the poet this version of the good society (recently called a fantasy of cultural brotherhood) has behind it a century of American progressive thought; it is the core of the progressive vision. But such views often compelled the artist, whose art alone had not brought immediate social change, to seek political power. The artist was not only the putative shaper of society, he was its product, and before he **Paul** could shape truly, the society from which he sprang had itself to **Rosenfeld** be changed. Here was an old dilemma: Herder's organic thought, which stands behind Brooks's, at once empowered and victimized the artist. Emerson, Whitman, John Jay Chapman—every intellectual—had faced it; for it was the old burden of the American Scholar who must perforce do as well as say, cultivate the soil as well as his art.

Rosenfeld recognized the dilemma, but he did not follow Brooks who fashioned it into a rationale for failure. Rosenfeld was closer to Bourne than to Brooks. More political than Brooks, Bourne nevertheless expected less in the way of "leadership" from the artist. He expected the artist—and all those in socially useful occupations like architecture, education, medicine, and letters—to revolutionize by individual example, by the commitment and life-style of his work. The fundamental problem of the experimental life was psychological; Rosenfeld did not project, as Brooks did, the psychological onto the social and read into a "hostile" environment the cause of the artist's failure. The artist failed because of personal weakness. Rosenfeld, for example, said that Mahler failed not because he was a Jew in Vienna but because "he was a weak man." "He permitted his environment to ruin him." Strauss was spoiled by inner weakness, Liszt by cynicism. An age was never hostile, though it might be "exhausted." That was why the Gilded Age was not "prolific of expressive individuals"; its "determined musicians, men like Paine and Lowell Mason," he said, "were forceless; weak personalities." Of course every society connived with weakness, but even in the most meager, third-rate civilization stalwart artists like Sherwood Anderson (and even the less stalwart like Twain) had been able to achieve greatness.

Personal weakness, moreover, was often seen in the artist who betrayed his gifts and the ultimate social usefulness of art by turning irresponsibly to politics. Rosenfeld remembered the folly of the intellectuals in World War I, and when he wrote "The Authors and Politics" in the thirties, he spoke out with the 93 old conviction of Bourne. The authors accepted the "prophetic rôle,"they turned to politics; but they had allowed themselves to be swept "underneath a partisan flag and into the arms of a dogma." Rosenfeld did not eschew politics. He feared preconceptions—whether they were the neoclassicism of contemporary aesthetics, a Puritan morality of sex and success, or a political line. And in politics he feared most the authors' "readiness for corporative political action," for this readiness soon dissipated the "responsibility toward, or consciousness of, the particular interests entrusted to the artist's care and advocacy."

The fervor of a minority of one sounds in Rosenfeld's defense of these interests:

> It has never been . . . the function of the artist to espouse the cause of "the world" and to defend its special interests. These special interests have everlastingly been those of power and of booty. . . . His concern is not with possessions, but with the uses of things, indeed with a particular use of them . . . how material is had and held, and in what spirit. What he naturally champions is something the world is not interested in: the use and administration of material possessions in sympathy with "vision."
>
> Vision of what? Vision of "life" itself, the mysterious forces which lie in and about and beneath and behind things, the "something" forever beautifully expressing itself in them; the "divine" known to man in his moments of spontaneity, and felt by him through free contact with other individuals and objects. For the artist is himself formed by things to receive his greatest gratifications not through having, or holding, but through feeling life . . . the basic forces of the universe. They themselves, these forces, are perpetually declaring themselves to him through people and their lives, and through inanimate material itself: inspiring him with awe, or wonder; and inspiring him with the desire to represent them. For, wonderful or ghastly, godlike or cruel, they *are*; above all, vision of them brings the visionary into touch not only with the immediate instruments of his revelation, but with other men, and the whole world. . . . And if the artist seeks, through manipulation of material to bring to light that which he has felt in his moment of vision, it is largely for the sake of fully understanding that which has been revealed to himself and making all men see and recognize the truth: but most of all, to

move people toward him in the spirit in which he himself has been moved toward them.

For the most part, the artist's struggle aims at, and ends with, the representation and the social acceptance of the thing which he has "seen." But, as we have said above, he will actively champion from time to time the general administration of material possessions in sympathy with and in the interests of vision itself. That is, he will become the impassioned advocate of things produced out of feeling: things having the quality of life and awakening feeling and bringing men into touch with its divine source and object.

Those who deplored Rosenfeld's refusal to join the Communist ranks overlooked the most telling point in his confession of faith. He saw (as Chapman had seen in the early days of socialism) that the ideal of "rich corporate existence and spiritual growth" had not in fact been furthered by the change in political allegiance. This ideal of social wealth had always been dear to intellectuals caught up in the American game of salvation by individual acquisition; and yet, following closely the political activity of the thirties, Rosenfeld noted the lack of any "quarrel with the whole blindly wasteful tendency of American life." At the rallies he did not hear of the desire for "the right to the good and the sincere job" or of "the social necessity of a living use of materials." Instead, behind the revolutionary talk he heard the old demand for bourgeois comforts. The "revolution" was simply distributive; its end was not a change in the quality of life but "cars, silk stockings and radio sets for all."

History may force us to grant the justice of Rosenfeld's observations, but somehow, in our own preoccupation with things, we find quixotic the partisan of a better life. Rosenfeld might have taken comfort from Thoreau, not only because the thirties taught him a bitter lesson in simplicity but because his stand was never popular. He now feared that the artist's cause had been lost from the beginning and that a society seeking spiritual ends was "incapable of realization in the world." America, he wrote, was not "the first land to believe that, made economically secure and comfortable, life will automatically grow blessed." He did not spare himself hard truths. Perhaps it was the world's misfortune to be destined to belong to "the stupid." But if it were, it was still the "artist's business to tell it so." It was the artist's business to fight for life against death. The wasteland and martyrdom were not the only alternatives.

Rosenfeld placed the artist in the world but beyond the politics of possessions. For the artist was fundamentally an anarchist. His intuitions revealed the ever-changing order in things. To this order he was faithful when he shaped material "in accordance with its own nature and the idea to which it conforms." For in this way his work was "expressive," carrying us, as Rosenfeld said of great music, "out of ourselves and beyond ourselves, into impersonal regions, into the stream of things; permitting us to feel the conditions under which objects exist, the forces playing upon human life." The nature of vision committed the artist to an open world, and in this sense the environment proved "hostile" only when the artist himself refused to embrace it. "What we call a favorable environment, and what we call creative ability," he explained, "are actually two aspects of a single force, basically or at one with itself, and productive in its two-part play. Of these parts, one is the 'not-I,' the other the 'I'; but essentially they are lovers."

This aesthetic might be considered transcendental. It proposes that art mediate the inner and outer worlds. To that extent its symbolic embodiments are "correspondences"; Stieglitz's "Equivalents" are the supreme example. But unlike the Emersonian aesthetic, it has no Over-Soul in which to moor the symbol. In repudiating Zola's naturalism, the generation of artists from whom Rosenfeld took his aesthetic did not return to the Emersonian notion that the "inner" was the "above." They no longer believed that the world was an emanation of the ego. The truth of things is revealed in fidelity to both inner and outer worlds. They believed, however, in the centrality of the self and in the discoveries of feeling; if faithfully responded to, the external world would reveal the inner truth of life. Thus the artist was to seek the "expressivity of the objective world" and therewith fashion the "subjective form." Art, Rosenfeld insisted, **Paul** must get us somewhere new and true, and that somewhere was a **Rosenfeld** new world of feeling. And he listened intently for these new and true "rhythms" because he believed that they disclosed the bases of new social relationships and order.

Only by spontaneously and openly responding to the world can the artist capture the rhythms of his time. Without preconceptions he must woo the "not-I." His love affair with the world is an exploration of reality to the end of adjusting men to the world and to other men. "Ready-made elysiums" therefore do not comfort him. The "pink world of received ideas and sentiments" that Rosenfeld found in the work of Gershwin and other popular artists weakened the "lure of the actual." Such work removed men from contact with reality. It offered easy security, not freedom for living; it was not mature. But judged by this aesthetic, even the work of serious American artists was faulty.

The cultural critics of Rosenfeld's generation investigated the causes of this creative immaturity. Rosenfeld himself did not undertake this work; he took his cultural bearings from Brooks's *America's Coming-of-Age*, Frank's *Our America*, William Carlos Williams' *In the American Grain*, and D. H. Lawrence's *Studies in Classic American Literature*. We now know the inadequacy of these studies, especially those of Brooks and Frank which are neither good history nor good literary criticism. These critics did not read enough or well. They were in fact psychologists rather than historians, and their account of America is more rewarding as psychology than it is as history. They offered their generation the kind of relevant cultural description that we now find useful in the work of sociologists like David Riesman. They used the past, though they were led by Brooks to believe it insufficiently "usable" for a vital American tradition—Brooks acknowledged that "once you have a point of view all history will back you up." The work of Brooks and Frank, therefore, fits the aesthetic or individual problem better than the political or institutional ones. But considered as 97

cultural "myth," it reaches deeply into the American ex-
perience. We are moved by its embodiment in Hart Crane's *The
Bridge* and Fitzgerald's *The Great Gatsby*, and in Rosenfeld's
*Port of New York*.

Rosenfeld most brilliantly applied the "myth" in his criticism
of contemporary art, and because he assimilated its various
elements he provides perhaps the best introduction to it. The
first strand of the "myth" might be called the utopian dream of
America. Columbus had gone to sea to discover the good place,
the "divine land." But America had "interposed"; it was not the
"Earthly Paradise." Mankind, however, did not renounce the
"dream," and the voyage of yearning—"the divine delusion"
—continued on the American continent. This dream left its
mark on the national character: the American was restless and
maladjusted, enamored of the distant and the future; the present
world, the present moment had no wonder for him. In the
pejorative word of the time, the American was a "pioneer."

To call the American a pioneer is to bring forward another
element of the "myth." We might, with Richard Hofstadter who
analyzed its relation to populist thought, call it "soft agrar-
ianism," or with Lawrence who had more in mind than a
*mystique* of farming, the "spirit of place." The common point,
however, is the need for roots and the love of the soil.
"Pioneersmen," Rosenfeld explained, "are not earth-builders,
not people who take root and love the earth that nourishes them,
and have a sense of responsibility to the men who are to come
after them." The pioneer scratches the earth and moves on; he is
an unrelated and solitary despoiler. Even worse when one
recalls Rosenfeld's aesthetics, he withholds love: "something
that is in the human power to give had never come and opened
[his] pores to the light and the green and the wind." He does not
feel as the people of older countries do, that the earth is an
organism like himself and that it has to be "cared for." He has
not learned from the Indian (whose corn dance Rosenfeld saw in
Sante Fé in 1926) that "if he put himself in harmony with
nature, nature would put herself in harmony with him." Ameri-

cans, then, did not have "the land love, ground love" Anderson appreciated in Dove's paintings; they were not like Thoreau, "deeply earth-submissive."

The dream and the restlessness left the "testimony of disinherited things" of which Brooks spoke so eloquently: things "old without majesty, old without mellowness, old without pathos, just shabby and bloodless and worn out." America was an impoverished civilization. "The trip from the old to the new world upon which we are all in spite of ourselves embarked," Rosenfeld said, "has gotten most of us not to a city spreading 'its dark life upon the earth of a new world, rooted there, sensitive to its richest beauty.'" The green breast of the new world had succored something else; we had come "no further than a low smoky shore looking rather like the Bayonne littoral from the Staten Island ferryboat on a sunless winter's day: a slatey weed garden of wharves, gas-tuns, church spires, chimneys, habitations set against ghostly blueless hills." There was nothing in this landscape to warrant Whitman's confidence that the life disembarked here would be a good one. "We have been standing at the rail," Rosenfeld said of his generation, "uncertain whether the shore before us is indeed solid earth upon which one can walk and nourish oneself."

Disenchantment with an America without a conception of the nonacquisitive, creative life is at the bottom of the historical explanation that followed from this sunless view. (One need only read the letters of Bourne, Hart Crane, or Anderson to sympathize with it.) From the beginning the American had been self-seeking; that might explain why in the closing paragraphs of *The Great Gatsby* Fitzgerald had written that America "pandered in whispers." Protestantism had emphasized individual salvation; it had not been conducive to communal life; and its fear of "earthiness" had made men "avert their love from the soil and the things that nourished their bodily life." The devil in the garden was in fact not so much the historical Puritan as it was the contemporary puritanism with which he was confused. But the historical Puritan (if Tawney was right) had done enough harm: his secularized faith was capitalism, his gospel "success," his modern avatars the lowbrow business man of practical grasp and the highbrow professor of genteel spirituality. Pioneer, Puritan, Professor still lorded it over America.

While Brooks told his generation what this triumvirate had done and what they were doing or not doing for American expression, Rosenfeld undertook in terms of their formative influence to explain the shortcomings of contemporary artists. He pointed out, for example, the "sexual fear" disclosed by the undeveloped foregrounds of Ryder's paintings. "Ryder," he wrote, "could not bring his whole man into entire contact with the object. The upper, spiritual regions of the body were singing flesh to him. The lower he could not fit into his scheme of beauty." Hartley, too, had "not been able to lose himself in his 'object'"; though he employs sexual forms, the mournfulness of his canvases suggests withholding, an unfortunate result of the Yankee alienation from the soil. [6] In the case of Kenneth Hayes Miller, an excellent painter of the nude, Rosenfeld perceived "the not entirely successful struggle with the blood." Why Miller should paint his feeling for flesh "more swimmingly through the smooth and stubby protuberances of the landscape than through the body itself," that, Rosenfeld remarked, "is known to God alone, who alone can sound the mysteries of the Yankee soul." In any event, this struggle with the "blood" could not be overcome in a generation.

Alienation—lack of relationship to thing, flesh, soil—this is the deepest source of incapacity, of truncated life and incomplete expression. "From a lack of touch," Williams wrote, "lack of belief." The relationship of the artist to his object, Rosenfeld found, was "typical of the American in his general contacts." Behind the weaknesses of Ryder, Hartley, and Miller was "the attitude taken by the whole of society to the soil that nourishes it." We are reminded also by Rosenfeld's "struggle with the blood" of Lawrence's blood-emotion—the emotional con-

6  Rosenfeld forecast in 1924 that the wandering Hartley would have to return to Maine, the place of his deepest feelings. Hartley returned in the 1930s.

sciousness or consciousness unmediated by concept and abstraction that makes for flowing, immediate contact. This emotion embraces equally the flesh and the soil; indeed the relationship to the soil for which Rosenfeld speaks is something sexual, something compounded of passionate desire, yielding, and tender care. The romantic feeling for nature, he later wrote in an essay on "Mozart the Romantic," is feminine; in "The Land Awaits," America is "She," still very much Pocahontas awaiting the husbandman—the artist—who will touch her stirring body lovingly.

Finally, the nationalism fostered by these cosmopolitan critics was only another way of calling attention to the need for such vital relationships—relationships other than those of the cash-nexus. Patriotism was absent in this nationalism. And this nationalism, which Bourne called trans-national, was not limited to those of certified Anglo-Saxon stock. America, Rosenfeld claimed, is "the native soil of anyone who *feels* it to be his." That is why these particular critics and artists were able, when even the hundred percenters failed, to rediscover America.

Signs of vital relationship or organic connection became the evidence of the creative readiness of American life. Sandburg, whose sentimentalism disturbed Rosenfeld, was valuable because he helps us "feel roots beneath us in the soil . . . feel the tie ineluctably come to be between us and this new world earth." The poet feels "the woman power in the soil," and knows Pocahontas' body, "lovely as a poplar, sweet as a red haw." He at least does not have to return to Europe "to feel his rootfastness"; he has approached and helps us approach a forbidding environment; he has whetted our desire for New York and Chicago, not for Paris. Dove's work, a "sort of 'Leaves of Grass' through pigment," communicates a "direct sensuous feeling of the earth." Marin, too, is fruit-bearing because he is rooted in America, and perhaps with Thoreau's essay on wild apples in mind, Rosenfeld says of him: "Marin is fast in American life like a tough and fibrous apple tree lodged and rooted in good ground."

With this acceptance of the soil (an acceptance large enough to include the possibilities of the industrial machine on its surface and all the past plowed into its depths) there was new response to the body. If Hartley had not gone far enough in referring the universe to the body, others had, among them Anderson, O'Keeffe, Dove, Williams, and Stieglitz. Anderson, who never really appreciated the title "phallic Chekov," reminded "an age that it is in the nucleus of sex that all the lights and confusions have their center, and that to the nucleus of sex they all return." He plumbed the American loneliness and the truth of human relationships. Georgia O'Keeffe was *woman* painting, Dove *man*. And Williams, able to relate the "white thighs of the sky" and "the round and perfect thighs / of the Police Sergeant's wife / perfect still after many babies," was, with Stieglitz, himself unrivaled in catching the vitality and spirit of sex, a surety that life might grow hopefully beyond the Bayonne littoral.

This "myth" of "the soil, the unconscious, the community" answers a very real problem. It arises from the need in our culture for intimacy, communion, and fulfillment. The stranger in Anderson's story, "Tandy," speaks its very essence: "I am a lover and have not found my thing to love." This "myth" may look backward, as so much thought since the industrial revolution has, to a more golden day; but it also looks forward to a "new generous way of life." One may cavil with its simplicities, with the melodramatic shape it takes, and with its reading of the malady of an entire civilization in terms of the artist and his difficulties of expression. And yet, after all, it is only another version of the constant vision of realized personality and being that one finds in Emerson, Thoreau, and Whitman; in Chapman and others who felt that commercialism had destroyed significant social life. If the artist has become the stock-personality, it is because he represents for us the highest measure of consciousness and the most life-furthering activity. "The land has no need intenser than the need of men who see justly," Rosenfeld believed, "men who go the artist's personal, passionate, disinterested way." For only when men willingly turn the self outward to the object is art and civilization possible: "Giving alone builds cultures and cities for men."

## III

*Port of New York* is Paul Rosenfeld's best book. *Men Seen* has a wider range—twenty-four poets, novelists, and critics from eight literatures; *An Hour with American Music* perhaps because of brevity hews the exposition to a sharper line; *Discoveries of a Music Critic* is more mature. But composed in the fullest confidence of his powers, *Port of New York* is a *book*, almost perfectly organized, thematically developed and controlled to the last word. It is not a collection of essays, a miscellany like *Men Seen*. Where *Men Seen* expressed Rosenfeld's "happy realization that the world is filled with individual, separate destinies" and that this pluralism was equally right for the imagination and for democracy, *Port of New York* expressed his sense of the desirableness of communal ends. It was, he said, a "picture of a number of individualities moving through several gateways toward a common point." The common point, as we have seen, was the discovery in expression of the "new" America. This mighty theme Rosenfeld was capable of handling notably. He had the gifts of understanding various media and of sympathizing with personalities as different as Sandburg and Hartley; he was a portraitist in the Jamesian tradition and a critic who unfolded his criteria within the book with the mastery of an artist. The substantial achievement of *Port of New York* was itself an assurance of the creative vitality it affirmed.

The personae of this drama of cultural awakening (these critics were fond of metaphors of dawn and day) are all treated with large sympathy. In *Port of New York*, moreover, the sympathy never softens the critical judgment as it does in *Men Seen*, where minor talents and friends (like Jean Toomer, to whom he dedicated *An Hour With American Music*) are placed among the host of great modern writers. There may be a lapse in the case of Roger Sessions, the only composer in the book, who at the time had demonstrated his gifts in a single composition; and he may have been included, as the chronicle-writing of this essay suggests, because he recalled the kind of excitement Rosenfeld had once felt in listening to Ornstein. Ornstein of course had figured in *Musical Portraits*, but by 1924 he was on his way to obscurity, remembered in the dedication by the sadly aware but ever-generous Rosenfeld. Of the writers connected with *The Seven Arts* and "291," those he could not fully or heartily endorse were relegated to the less exacting *Men Seen:* Kreymborg, Oppenheim, Frank. Frank, the most serious omission when one considers his stature at the time, was probably neglected because Brooks provided the essential cultural themes—and without Frank's special pleading to the Jew; but we know that in 1921 Rosenfeld had justifiably but severely criticized Frank's novels and that this had ruptured their friendship. Margaret Naumburg, Frank's wife, was included, in her own right and not by way of reparation. Others, like Lewis Mumford and Hart Crane, whom we would now place in such a book, had not yet arrived.

Where Wagner had served to summon the nineteenth century as the background for *Musical Portraits*, Albert Pinkham Ryder, a painter inspired in several canvases by Wagnerian themes, served to summon the dark American past as the background for *Port of New York*. He did not express with Wagner the material triumph of the age; he expressed its terrible homesickness. In his haunted moonlit pictures we are still at sea, Flying Dutchmen or Christopher Columbuses without compass and chart, driven on by the "romantic inhuman lure" so characteristic of American idealism. We see beauty only at night in these Poe-like paintings; we cannot accept the sunlit world; the moon betrays us and life emptily glides by. We are restless and without will, victims of what Brooks, not yet Freudian enough to call sublimation, called the malady of the ideal: "the sickness of those who are captive to some shadowy unsubstantial ideal order and, while possessing little faith in the ideal which holds them, are

nevertheless prevented by it from slaking their thirst for experience in the real substance of the world." Ryder, the most
original and deeply expressive American artist of the nineteenth
century, records and thereby ends our wandering; he brings us to
the shore of "the inhabited solid earth." Rootless and solitary,
fearful of sudden experience and sexuality, unskilled in his
medium and only partially expressive, he provides in the negative those themes whose positive aspects Rosenfeld will use to
strike up for a new world.

Brooks follows because he supplies the compass and the
chart, and also, one suspects, because his significant work is
done. Rosenfeld devoted the longest essay to Brooks. He
thought him the most important critic since Whitman, a
much-needed model of the cosmopolitan man of letters committed to America. But he felt that Brooks was personally in-
completely integrated, that his personal irresolution had
loosened his grasp of American reality, and that (as *The Pilgrimage of Henry James* soon proved) he would have to clarify his
own life before he could see America clearly. Rosenfeld gratefully acknowledged the debt his generation owed Brooks: "With
him came the philosophical and intellectual basis of the movement, the analytical scheme of the past." His criticism itself had
relieved the cultural situation. And yet, tried by his own belief in
the leadership of the man of letters, he was beginning to show
signs of failure. After *Letters and Leadership* his prose began to
decline; Rosenfeld noted that personally he had less vigor and
vivacity. *The Ordeal of Mark Twain* revealed a "strabismic
vision," and its "perverse thesis" accused Brooks of "shooting
with loaded dice." Intent on finding victimization everywhere,
Brooks had lost faith in the heroism of the artist; by preaching
and by indulging passivity, he had himself become a hostile
environment. Rosenfeld's greatest fear was that in "playing safe
with life" Brooks had renounced the bold and dangerous life-
style of the artist, for this would have been the earnest of his
commitment. As it was, he had retreated from the "critical
battle-line" and had turned away from the contemporary writers   105

who needed him most. The young man who had once adventured on life now sat unmindfully behind a closed door. Unsparing criticism, but so prophetic! And Rosenfeld had the right to judge because he followed the credo of the early Brooks more closely than did Brooks himself. By implication Rosenfeld thus defined his own positive critical stance and work. The remainder of *Port of New York* made it good.

In turning West to Sandburg, Rosenfeld hailed a half-formed poet who at least took chances with life. Here he struck earth. Some of the fog enshrouding the Flying Dutchman is dispelled: "We drift aimlessly in the currents of air that circle the globe; strain away to some otherwhere. But for Sandburg the magnetic pole of life has situated itself in mid-America." We are no longer homeless. Hartley, with his New England delicacy and refinement, complements the raw Westerner. Both, however, are only partially successful: Sandburg is sentimental and Hartley uses his brilliant technique to shield himself from the bitter emotional assaults of life. Rosenfeld develops the theme of "soil" with Sandburg; with Hartley he advances his aesthetics; and in William Carlos Williams, who follows and concludes the first movement of the book, he portrays a successful artist. Williams gives himself completely to the American environment and the medium of his art. Superior to Eliot in his "mature capacity for insight," Williams is able to face the evils of life and the harshness of America. Because of his work, Rosenfeld feels at last that the land is "habitable." The journey from the old to the new world "has led us somewhere."

The second movement of the book deals with teachers who devote themselves to the necessary education in realities. Margaret Naumburg, director of the Walden School, represents the kind of social vocation Bourne had called for; she is the artist-as-educator, the Bronson Alcott of the group, who works in the living medium of the child. Her experimental school is comparable to Stieglitz's gallery: it opens into life and is dedicated to the development by expression of the full personality. "The human being is poisonous," Rosenfeld says, "in proportion to the

amount of his unfulfilment." The "organic" education of the **Paul**
Walden School, which mediated the extremes of old-fashioned **Rosenfeld**
authoritarianism and Dewey progressivism, proposed to reduce
the poisons by liberating the child. Opposed to the routines,
repressions, and values of the bourgeois world, trans-national in
character, this school is a new society: the possible American
society in which the artist-man would fulfill his inner needs for
expression (individuality) and for fellowship (communal life).

Another teacher with a realistic spirit is Kenneth Hayes Miller
of the Art Students' League. A minor but honest painter, he is
important because he does not indulge in the "illicit revery" and
pre-Raphaelite evasions of prominent artists like Arthur B.
Davies. His work rids us of "the burden of fraudulent idealism
which lies heavy on each American back." Finally, Sessions, a
New Englander of ancient Puritan stock, typifies the young man
whose promise the new education might release. Trained by
Horatio Parker at Yale and commissioned by Smith College to
compose the score of the "daring" commencement play, An-
dreyev's *The Black Maskers*, Sessions represents in his preparation and the occasion of his work, a native creative insurgence
within the enclosure of the American college.

Major figures and eminent creators comprise the final
movement. Themes are recapitulated in terms of strength and
success. John Marin, for example, is an ancient mariner wholly
unlike Ryder. Rooted in Maine and New York, American in
every fibre, courageously and completely true to himself and his
medium, he is for Rosenfeld the prototypal artist. With Stieglitz, who climaxes the movement, he stands on the peak of
assured achievement, one of the greatest painters and discoverers of our time. Dove, Anderson, O'Keeffe—all indebted to
Stieglitz—express in their realized art the favorable results of
root-taking and sexual liberation. In addition, Anderson's
career, his struggle to become a writer in an acquisitive society,
makes him the heroic artist whose victory over the environment
refutes Brooks's thesis. Bourne, too, is an exemplary individual,
the "artist-fighter," who formulated as no one else did "the

creative will of American men." He is placed here, next to
Stieglitz, because both are spiritual guides to a trans-national
democracy. Bourne of course countervails Brooks. He dedicates
us anew to the unfinished task of American culture.

Had *Port of New York* been a historical narrative, the portrait
of Stieglitz would have begun rather than ended it. Stieglitz
ends it perhaps for the very reason Anderson wrote:

> Old man—perpetually young—we salute you.
> Young man—who will not grow old—we salute you.

He ends it, where Ryder began it, because in his art he transformed the moonlit landscape of the soul into the daylight
modern world. He was the master of light. He created a new
traditionless art. He conclusively demonstrated the aesthetic
use of the camera, making a "machine" serve the spirit. With
the camera he "cast the artist's net wider into the material
world than any man before him." He captured the inner meaning of every manifestation of life—soil, grass, water, tree, sky,
cloud, animal, woman, house, skyscraper, airplane, city. His
brave individual life was steadily affirmative. And the history of
his work at "291" summarized the entire movement only to
elicit once more the desire for the creative group and to stir again
for similar ends a combativeness for ideas. For Stieglitz was the
outstanding example of the initiator: he showed how groups
answering to the living needs of men begin in the interstices of
institutions.

Rosenfeld's world is the world of Stieglitz's pictures. In the
"Epilogue," we stand with the immigrants of Stieglitz's "The
Steerage"; we watch the shuttle of ferryboats and trans-Atlantic
liners. We come to port at last. Europe no longer pulls us back.
There is an almost unaccountably subtle change in the spirit of
place. "Through words, lights, colors, the new world has been
reached at last." The good sun shines on America;[7] in its light
the "smug safe bourgeois values" are gone. The mature life of
work, growth, and love is possible now. The root has found
welcome soil. In the dazzling brilliance of this picture, in

7 Emerson: "The sun shines to-day also" (*Nature*, 1836).

Rosenfeld's overwhelming lyrical affirmation, we may
momentarily forget that every generation, even those thankful
for this tilth, must put to sea. Should we remember, we may take
courage from the adventure of one generation willing to hazard
for the gift of life.

This essay, which I finished in April, 1960, is important to me
because it crystallized the extensive studies I had undertaken. It
was written at a time when I was enjoying one of the great
excitements of scholarship, that of entering and charting a new
field and of trying to occupy it all at once. How avid one's
reading and search! I follow the chronology of publication here
because there is no better way to order the continuum of
thought. While reading Rosenfeld, I was writing about Chapman, and while writing about Rosenfeld, I was reading
Bourne's correspondence and Sullivan's manuscripts. By the
time this essay appeared, I had published a little on Sullivan in
book reviews.

Though I never intended to write a prospectus, this essay
includes amost all of the writers I have treated at length in the
past decade or so, even Hart Crane, to whom I thought I had
come by other routes. My intention in writing it was introductory: to reintroduce a group of writers and critics who had been
neglected, even dropped, as a result of selective tradition-
making, from the textbooks. Alfred Kazin, in *On Native
Grounds* (1942) was perhaps the last to espouse them; not until
Richard Chase's *The Democratic Vista* ( 1958), a challenging
book that received too little attention, did they figure again in a
dialogue of culture. By writing about Rosenfeld, I wanted to
add the chapter that rightly belongs to his book, and I wanted to
make this book available because it was the best introduction to
the resurgent spirit that I hoped it would help to revive.

My partisanship is evident. This essay was a sally against the
New Criticism. In it, I declare myself. Though I did not endorse Rosenfeld's strictures on Eliot, Stevens, and Joyce (in my

advocacy this is not made clear), I endorsed him, and not
merely by commending his way of criticism but, in my own,
by going beyond declaration to demonstration: speaking forthrightly to present vital issues and relying more than hitherto on
my own voice. That I had been able to enter the body of my
own criticism was for me momentous. Nothing so severe as the
breakdown Seymour Krim reports in *Views of a Nearsighted
Cannoneer* had prepared for it, and the result was hardly so
dramatic. Yet in kind it was similar.

I remember vividly the way the first sentences filled my
mind as I was leaving my study, how I turned back to write
them down, knowing, as I did this, not only that in catching
the right cadence and tone the essay was secure, but what I had
done. I had seldom used contractions before, certainly not in
an opening sentence; nor had I committed myself so fully to
the task of evocation. And evocation—the reconstruction of a
milieu in fidelity to its thought and feeling—was part of the
demonstration. I did not ignore the literary work; it was still, as
it must be, a central object of attention. But now, more consciously than before, I placed it in relation to biography and
history. And I tried my hand at portraiture—could I so soon
have learned from Edmund Wilson how to use photographs
and significant details?—and gave the essay a tripartite structure which did not confine so much as focus my concern with
self, world, and work.

# LOUIS SULLIVAN AND ORGANIC ARCHITECTURE

*Architect of American Thought*

*LOUIS SULLIVAN AS HE LIVED: The Shaping of American Architecture.* By Willard Connelly. Horizon Press.

Louis Sullivan was not only a great architect, one of the triumvirate that includes H. H. Richardson and Frank Lloyd Wright, he was also a penman for modern building and an architect of American thought. For him architecture was "not an art, but a religion, and that religion but a part of democracy." In his writing he did not speak primarily to architects, but, as he said, to the "laity." And all of his writing—*Kindergarten Chats,* "Natural Thinking," *Democracy: A Man Search, The Autobiography of An Idea* and A *System of Architectural Ornament According with a Philosophy of Man's Powers*—fills the claim he first made for *Kindergarten Chats:* it tests architecture by human nature and democracy.

In *Genius and the Mobocracy,* that Sullivanesque book on Sullivan (and Frank Lloyd Wright), Wright said of architects: Expect [of them] a system of philosophy and ethics." More than any other American architect, Sullivan worked on such a system and cogently developed it; for the very forces in American life that led to his solution of the tall office building prompted him to become a social critic and educator. In his hands his famous architectural maxim—Form Follows Function—became a tool of social analysis; and if he placed too much blame for the betrayal of an indigenous architecture on the World's Columbian Exposition, we can now see that it was because he saw in the imperial façade social forces it could neither glorify nor hide. The most eminent architect of the nineteenth-century Chicago School, he was also a critic who deserves a place in the galaxy of Debs, Darrow, Jane Addams, Dewey, H. D. Lloyd and Veblen. Inspired by Whitman and a student of history, psychology and sociology, Sullivan brought forward the "organic" tradition. No one in our literature more thoroughly assimilated the "organic" idea—the "supremacy of interior order," as Wright put it—to democracy. No one, not even Whitman, was a more determined enemy of "Feudalism."

When Sullivan wrote Claude Bragdon that "what my heart yearns for now is justice, and a sympathetic interpretation of that which I have loved, and for which I have lived," he had in mind what we must now consider his total achievement. Sullivan scholarship is slim, and the most notable work, that of Hugh Morrison, is almost entirely devoted to his architecture. The clue to further study, however, was provided by Ray Ginger in Altgeld's America, where Sullivan was first properly placed as a social thinker. One expected, accordingly, that Mr. Connely's book on how Sullivan lived would probe more deeply the heady intellectual milieu of the Chicago Renaissance. The materials are abundant, and even Sullivan, who often overlooked his intellectual debts in his writings, left ample evidence of his development.

Unfortunately, Mr. Connely's book is popular biography. It does not do justice to the architecture, the writings, or the man. It is valuable for new disclosures, but their significance is often missed. It is ill-proportioned and theatrical; bravura effects add a questionable color to Sullivan's life. One's total impression of a book so close to vulgarization and superficiality is one of distrust.

And yet everything Mr. Connely tells us is true—if not quite right. We are grateful to him, for example, for revising the Sullivan chronology. He has established the length of Sullivan's stay in Paris, a brief term at the Beaux Arts. But he has not seen its meaning for the *Autobiography*, where Sullivan extended his stay and lengthened the narrative of his brilliant achievement, probably to match or surpass Mrs. van Rensselaer's glowing account of Richardson's apprenticeship there. Nor has he used this new material, in connection with the healthy masculine camaraderie at Lotus Place on the Calumet River, to discredit Wright's repeated slur concerning the bad habits "Lieber Meister" acquired in Paris. In fact, he prefers to follow Wright's lead. His account of Sullivan's unhappy marriage is insensitive; he merely alludes to a relationship with the wife of a professor at the University of Chicago; and, in describing the years of decline, he overworks Wright's reference to the little henna-haired milliner who offered companionship, if not color, to the sick and lonely man in the shabby Warner Hotel.

Mr. Connely's most welcome discovery is the notebook Sullivan kept from the time he entered M.I.T. in 1872, until 1881, when he became the partner of Dankmar Adler. This notebook is valuable not so much for the athletic records of the young men at Lotus Place, which Mr. Connely exploits, as it is for the record of Sullivan's reading and intellectual apprenticeship to the architect, John Edelmann. Sullivan paid tribute to Edelmann in the *Autobiography*, but he was irritatingly vague about the people whose influence had been formative. We now learn that the ebullient Edelmann set out courses of reading, answered questions on ornament and native art, and first employed Sullivan as the decorator of the Moody Tabernacle and the Sinai Temple. And this relationship, repeated with Sullivan as the teacher when young Frank Lloyd Wright began to work for him, was probably the inspiration for the educational situation Sullivan used so effectively in *Kindergarten Chats*. Here, moreover, was the seed which Wright, perhaps with a backward glance at Richardson's *atelier*, developed into an institution at Taliesin.

**Louis Sullivan and Organic Architecture**

113

Mr. Connely has not been as fortunate in finding materials for other portions of Sullivan's life. He overdoes Sullivan's artistic debt to his mother (did he have in mind a parallel with Wright?), missing the fact that Sullivan impugned the notion of heredity. He carries beyond fruitfulness the broken relationship of Sullivan and his brother Albert, who might have been more interesting as a typical railroad executive of the time than as an athlete. When he lacks information he relies on the *Autobiography*; when he has information (much of it, in Northrop Frye's phrase, the "history of rumor") he repudiates Sullivan's record and what might be read between the lines.

Heedless of Sullivan's dictum that every problem provides its own solution, Mr. Connely misconstrues the problem and fails the solution. For the problem was not one of retelling Sullivan's life with such slender means, but of re-creating Sullivan in the arduous task of re-creating his age. Then the Sullivan who related in the *Autobiography* that "Daniel Burnham [his rival] was obsessed by the feudal idea of power [and] Louis Sullivan was equally obsessed with the beneficent idea of Democratic power" would stand forth in his largest significance. And we would know something more of how he lived from the line Sullivan added: "Daniel chose the easier way, Louis the harder."

## Architect of Society

DEMOCRACY: A *Man-Search*. By Louis H. Sullivan. Introduction by Elaine Hedges. Wayne State University Press.

"To discuss American architecture and its possibilities, while ignoring the repressive force of feudalism and the expansive force of democracy, is sheer lunacy." This was Louis Sullivan's response to his colleagues who were still peddling styles without reference to the social crises of their time. He had always related art and society. Early in his career he had been concerned with the more strictly architectural aspects of the relationship, with achieving a personal utterance for the aspirations of society. The financial crises of 1893 and 1907, however, broadened his emphasis. The first crisis began the decline of his fortunes, the second completed it. Sitting in his office atop the tower of the Auditorium Building (which he was forced to abandon in 1909), he had little to design, but much to read and think about—and much to write.

The betrayal of American architecture at the World's Fair turned him to education. He challenged the American Institute of Architects by leading the draftsmen who in 1899 formed the Architectural League of America. For them he wrote *Kindergarten Chats*. But it was impossible for one who lived in Chicago to overlook a greater betrayal. Chicago, Henry Adams wrote, "asked in 1893 for the first time the question whether the American people knew where they were driving." If they did not know that they were on their way to feudalism, there were philosophers, psychologists and social critics in Chicago who could tell them. Sullivan was one of them.

He read widely and he learned from Dewey, Veblen, Oscar Triggs, and Henry D. Lloyd. He found that what he called "natural thinking" was confirmed by functional psychology, that his notion of beneficent power was comparable to Veblen's instinct of workmanship, and that the Whitmanian gospel of experience in the "open" which he espoused had been given scientific support. The new thought, he believed, was as significant for the history of man as the Copernican revolution had been. With its "publicity," he hoped to clear away the "survivals" of feudalism.

Feudal thought was "inverted"—untenable dualistic thinking that had externalized the powers of man and alienated him from himself and the universe. Its psychological origin was fear, and whatever had been created in the image of this thought contributed to the culture of fear and to the "dance of death" which for him symbolized past and present civilizations. To remove the "mind-forg'd manacles," to show man to himself that he might realize his powers—such was the aim of the Nietzschean transvaluation of Sullivan's man-search. In his battle for democracy the real issue was not simply man's "natural rights" but the liberation of his actual, naturally creative powers.

Sullivan was a man of good hope, one of many progressive prophets who upheld the claims of honesty and justice and announced the advent of a genuinely social democracy. It is easy to deny such men, to mock them as Veblen did, until one realizes that every subsequent generation has been kindled, if at all, by their faith. Those who are accustomed to the blander sociological vocabulary of our time may be put off by Sullivan's rhetoric; those who are cynical about democracy and unwilling, even as historians, to understand what it meant to another generation (a fault, I think, of Burchard and Bush-Brown's recent *The Architecture of America*), may not wish to return to books that challenge their little faith. But perhaps that is the value of Sullivan's book, which only now has found a courageous publisher and a perceptive editor.

*Democracy: A Man-Search* was written more than fifty years ago. To fully appreciate its singular achievement one must go back to a time when sociology was the new master science. It had then an aura it later lost. Sullivan said in *Kindergarten Chats* that it was the unitary science, the explorer and evangel of democracy. It fulfilled "the main and the immediate business of democratic philosophy"—"to simplify, to clarify and to know itself." For him it defined a new mode of thought (the "face to face" experience of *Democracy*), a new area of study (that of the forms and functions of man in society throughout history) and an immediate end in reform (the social salvation of man in democracy). This feeling for the redemptive possibilities of the new thought explains Sullivan's prophetic posture, the manner of his writing, and his personal fear lest society let its dreamers perish. And it helps us understand those deep and continuing currents of thought and emotion which carried democratic idealism from the transcendentalism of the early nineteenth century to the pragmatism of our own era.

What makes *Democracy* so singular is the fact that it is not a social tract. It is a work of art, and now that Sullivan's buildings are being demolished, it may remain, with his other books, as a testimony of his creative impulse and of his tremendous imaginative vitality. His ends were always social and his means were always artistic. (He knew, as Raymond Williams reminds us in *The Long Revolution,* that art is a social activity and that the communication of creative impulse is a necessity of democratic society.) It was not enough for him to tell men about the new thought; he would make them *see* it—and its consequences. He would dramatize on the stage of history the story of "man's self-eclipse," he would show them how they themselves had created the culture of fear, and he would force them to accept the burden of choice and responsibility for the thought that was the spring of history. As his examiner in history at the Beaux Arts had prophesied, he would turn the teachings of history upside down. And he would do in his way what recent studies like the Goodmans' *Communitas* and Mumford's *The City in History* have done: liberate choice by showing alternatives.

*Democracy* is not a perfect work. Repetition, especially toward the end, produces the effect of shrillness. Nevertheless, it is boldly conceived and written with restraint. Its theme—man's search for himself—is grand; its method—the socio-psychological—is profound; its intent—the passionate desire to redeem man—is Messianic. In theme as well as technique (for example, the conscious use of archetypes and the complex fusion of past and present) it anticipates much in modern literature. The result is a landmark in democratic thought. Sullivan's book belongs with those great affirmations of the human spirit which for want of another name might be called the permanent sociology of man.

### For Love of Chicago

CULTURE AND DEMOCRACY: *The Struggle for Form in Society and Architecture in Chicago and the Middle West during the Life and Times of Louis H. Sullivan.* By Hugh Dalziel Duncan. The Bedminster Press.

THE CHICAGO SCHOOL OF ARCHITECTURE: *Early Followers of Sullivan and Wright.* By Mark L. Peisch. Random House.

Mr. Duncan is a sociologist; Mr. Peisch is an art historian. Mr. Duncan has a cause to plead—his book is dedicated "to all Chicagoans who struggle to keep alive the soul of a city guarded by the spirit of Louis Henri Sullivan"; Mr. Peisch has a story to tell, which quietly contributes to that struggle. Both, and especially Mr. Duncan, have the intense devotion, and sometimes partisanship, that characterize students of the Chicago School. "New York is not the country. It is in this land physically to be sure, but spiritually it is on the outskirts"—this comment of Sullivan's informs Mr. Duncan's book. But having granted the fact that no other architectural achievement in America has been so great and portends so much for American democratic culture, one still wonders whether Frank Lloyd Wright's remark, "But, well, I like Chicago," isn't after all the most solid reason for its defense? Mr. Duncan insists, however, that "we must either deny Chicago's greatness or develop a new cultural history," and he has written a very large book to prove that he is not being merely rhetorical.

As a sociologist of art, Mr. Duncan does not develop a social theory of art so much as exemplify or re-enact its emergence in the cultural history of the Middle West, in the architecture and social arts of Chicago, the capital city of the democratic heartland, and in the thought of such Chicagoans as Dewey, Veblen, Mead and Sullivan. He understands the spiritualization of money, as a student of Kenneth Burke should, and ably presents the cultural process by which it so swiftly took place in an agrarian, religious community—a transformation from church to department store that took hardly a generation—and he recognizes in Veblen's writing especially, but also in the work of other writers and artists, the countervailing force for its desanctification.

Burke contributes to Mr. Duncan's dramatistic awareness of culture, as do Mead, Dewey, Veblen and Cooley: social process as well as social cohesion depends primarily on language—on communication by symbols that are forms and thus stages for the drama of life. Transform the symbols and life is transformed:

Marshall Field and Potter Palmer create the stage of the department store and feminize shopping (spending); George Pullman
builds a model town that dramatizes paternalism, what Ghent
called "benevolent feudalism"; the stockyards, whose assembly
line impressed Henry Ford, stage the efficient mechanization of
death. The social process is essentially the work of art—and
sometimes a work of art. It is a matter of creating forms (social)
for functions (social); art is action, creation creates. In the
central and best chapters of Mr. Duncan's book, art is treated as
a "form of sociation." Here we learn that the most characteristic
form of sociation is conversation (Dewey said that "democracy
begins in conversation," or, as we now say, having rediscovered
this simple necessary social idea, in "dialogue") and, remembering the quintessential function of speech in early American
agrarian community life, we begin to understand better not only
Sullivan's desire to create buildings that are presences but buildings that speak. For Sullivan, as for Emerson and Whitman,
nothing matched eloquence.

This book may be read as a history of Chicago, but it is also Mr.
Duncan's attempt to possess the tradition of its best architects
and social philosophers. He properly makes Sullivan the focal
figure of this cultural history because he was the *artist* who best
understood and explained this social theory and related it to the
creation of democratic culture. In doing this, Mr. Duncan also
more firmly establishes Sullivan's importance as a thinker, a
role sometimes questioned by those whose notions of "thinking"
are needlessly strict. Sullivan's *Kindergarten Chats* is, as Mr.
Duncan claims, "the most profound book yet written on American architecture"—the most important statement of the pragmatic, organic aesthetic until Dewey's *Art as Experience*, which
appeared more than thirty years later. It is salutary to remember
this as the razing of buildings destroys the visible signs of Sullivan's genius.

But Sullivan is also the focal center because Mr. Duncan is
rehearsing a struggle in which he himself is still engaged, and
because the "tragic" life of the artist is wonderfully dramatic. His

book is written in a "Western" style—loose, affirmative, uncritical, abundant, aggressive. He is more the gatherer than the interpreter, is loosely analogical rather than tightly developmental; for him repetition is an aspect of style. Omnium-gatherum prevails in paragraph, page and chapter (chapter 30, for example, does not, as announced, treat "Sullivan's Principle of Mobile Equilibrium"). Paraphrase, even unpunctuated quotation, mixes with direct quotation; entire chapters, such as those on Root and Adler, are simply restatements of the subject's own words—a procedure not so damning as unendurable—and a good portion of Sullivan's *writing* is used. Coherence and proportion are lacking. Yet the form fits the function *pleading*: the chapters are short, followed by footnotes in which Mr. Duncan carries on vigorous polemics with contemporary sociology, and though the chronology is disturbed, the book ends with Sullivan's account, in *The Autobiography of an Idea*, of his own childhood and early manhood. The symbolic action proclaims victory out of defeat, and the verbal action works up a lively sense of the genuine importance of this period of democratic resurgence.

For a book devoted to the democratic value of communication (sharing), it is curiously reticent about the contributions of fellow workers whom Mr. Duncan surely knows: John Szarkowski (a photographer), Maurice English (an editor), Ray Ginger (a historian), Paul Goodman (a generalist),[1] Vincent Scully, Jr., (an art historian), Albert Bush-Brown (an art historian). This lack of generosity is perhaps attributable to a provincialism that makes too much of the new and the local. Not everything of value for democratic urban culture arose in Chicago. Sullivan, in his most formative years, was an Easterner, and he carried West with him, as well as found there, the fertile seeds of a still earlier democratic thought, that of Emerson and Whitman, which the pragmatic social thinkers of the Chicago School also knew well.

1 In *Little Prayers and Finite Experience* (1972), Goodman distinguishes between generalist and man of letters and establishes his claim to the latter.

There is little that is new about Chicago architecture in Mr. Duncan's book, much that is new in Mr. Peisch's monograph. The Chicago School, set back by the World's Fair of 1893, did not disintegrate but rallied under the leadership of Sullivan and the Architectural League of America, for which Sullivan wrote *Kindergarten Chats*. (Neither Mr. Duncan nor Mr. Peisch seems to be acquainted with the League, which for a brief time rivaled the American Institute of Architects, and toward the formation of which the Chicago Architectural Club had been instrumental.) In the years after the fair and up to the First World War, the Chicago School quietly flourished, adding a second chapter to its brilliant history.

Mr. Peisch tells this story—tells of the work of Richard Schmidt and Hugh Garden in designing hospitals, Dwight Perkins in designing schools, George Maher, William Purcell and George Elmslie in designing banks and other public buildings; the landscape architectural work of Jens Jensen (the subject of Leonard K. Eaton's recent study, *Landscape Artist in America*) and Walter Burley Griffin, for whom Olmsted's work at the fair had been a positive influence; the domestic architecture, in particular, of Wright, Maher, Garden and Griffin; the city planning of Griffin and Daniel Burnham, which again, according to Mr. Peisch, testifies to the positive influence of the fair; and the church architecture of Barry Byrne.

These architects, and others whose work is briefly mentioned, serve as background for the one complete architect of the group, Walter Burley Griffin. Purcell and Elmslie are credited with continuing the work of Sullivan, now in eclipse; Daniel Burnham is accorded eminence; and Frank Lloyd Wright, even when Mr. Peisch restrains him and puts him down, manages to assert his claim to attention. Yet Griffin (1876–1937) dominates this book, not so much for the artistic merits of his accomplishments as for the fact that he focuses the various architectural trends of the Chicago School. "He was," Mr. Peisch explains, "a student of Ricker, an Oak Park assistant, a social planner, an architect in the new idiom, and a city planner." To follow Griffin's career is therefore to learn about the significance of the school of architecture that Nathan Ricker established at the University of Illinois, the architectural lofts in the Steinway Building which housed some of the younger members of the Chicago School, the Oak Park Fellowship, Frank Lloyd Wright's first *atelier* (where Griffin met his wife and collaborator, Marion Mahoney, and where others, Barry Byrne, for example, were trained), the early attempts at neighborhood planning in Evanston, Winnetka and Mason City and, finally, the successful competition for the planning of Canberra. With Griffin, as with Wright, Chicago architecture became world wide.

## Interior Order

FRANK LLOYD WRIGHT: A Study in Architectural Content. By Norris Kelly Smith. Prentice-Hall.

One needn't accept the assumptions or conclusions of this study to appreciate the kind of inquiry Mr. Smith has undertaken. He is interested in the "architectural content" of Frank Lloyd Wright's work—in its metaphorical expression or meaning; with how it stands in relation to his awareness of the world, the philosophy and ethics he believed to be the ultimate gift of the architect. Others have contributed to such an understanding of his thought (for example, Lewis Mumford, Vincent Scully, Jr., Paul and Percival Goodman, Morton and Lucia White—none of whose work, incidentally, is acknowledged by Mr. Smith); but no one has gone so far in treating Wright's work as a history of ideas.

Smith's concern with the history of ideas, however, is of less importance to him than the polemical ends to which he puts it. He is a partisan—rarer, it seems, in architecture than in literature—of the religious and socially conservative ideas so fashionable today. To present Wright as an advocate of such ideas, he has had to deny the importance of Wright's relation to the modern movement, and to reject the notion that the art of an age is its reflex, its expression a unity. The distinction he wishes to make between the efficient functionalism of contemporary building (and science) and the expressive vital organic functionalism of the Romantic tradition is a valuable one that could have been made without fixing religion to the latter, or pushing beyond the facts of Wright's case. He does so, I think, when with the help of a single book, Thorlief Boman's *Hebrew Thought Compared with Greek*, he presents Romanticism in terms of Hebraism—to no other purpose than to give Wright's work religious significance. "It will be one of my purposes," he says, "to demonstrate that though the Bible has played an incalculably important role in shaping western thought for some two thousand years, it was only with Wright that Biblical thought found expression in the art of architecture, which has been dominated almost exclusively by the Greco-Roman tradition."

No one will deny that Wright "disliked the Hellenic way and its principles" (I quote Scully), or that he considered himself an artist-seer, one of those great personalities that Van Wyck Brooks, for example, valued so highly for their social force in the nineteenth century. Like his master, Louis Sullivan, he lived in "the cause of architecture," and "total architecture" was his religion. But he would not have found agreeable the association of his work with Hebraism, for Hebraism (as Matthew Arnold, if not Boman, defined it) was for Wright connected with all that was rigid and retributive, and was repugnant to him. "The boy," he says of himself in *An Autobiography*, "grew to distrust Isaiah"—that "Mosaic Isaiah" to whom he preferred the gentle, beauty-loving Celtic prophet Taliesin, and against whom he sought refuge in his work.

As for the place Smith seeks for him in "the cause conservative," no one will deny that Wright, who needed so much the security of his ancestral valley, was conservative in some respects. Yes, conservative in impulse but radical in idea, as Richard Chase has characterized the best American minds, including those who influenced Wright, like Emerson and Whitman. Wright was too much opposed to the institutions of our society to be conservative in the special sense that Smith has in mind: that architecture is the art of the Establishment, of constituted social relationships (not necessarily new ones). Wright, at least, thought himself radical and described the essence of his being in the anecdote of deviation from the straight way with which he begins *An Autobiography*. He was, if any American architect was, a *reformer*, with an "imperturbable readiness," Mumford says, "to break old molds and improvise new ones"; and he also had the radical's utopian expectation that his work would create the conditions of new life—and that others should conform to it.

The claims of growth were for Wright superior to any other; growth is the idea he dramatizes throughout his essentially open, unending autobiography. *An Autobiography*, modeled on Sullivan's, parts of which he heard the master read aloud, is an *autobiography of an idea*—of the growth and nurture of genius in the cause of architecture and in behalf of the idea of "the supremacy of interior order." The event in his life that probably disturbed him most, and that the story of his achievement was intended to justify, was the first domestic crisis, his desertion of his family in 1909. He reads it back to instances of flight in his boyhood and youth, and forward to his many *Wanderjahre*; and he gathers about it his resentment of his mother's gentility and of the sentimentality and stuffy domesticity of the time.

The reader may, with Smith, consider Wright's early houses (the Winslow house is his example) "sacramental homes"; Wright was a great domestic architect, who understood the many uses of home and was always profoundly moved by the eternal feminine. But he was also, in keeping with the realistic spirit of the age, a simplifier of relationships in the interest of truth; and his own flight, anticipated in the Coonley house, the prototype of Taliesin, was part of the contemporary sexual revolution against the hypocrisy of middle-class family life. At the end of the first version of *An Autobiography*, Wright tries to explain its lesson: "The sufferings of growth, the agony of sentimentality that tries to hold life by 'institution' and establishment and extend the fleeting hour until the simple inevitable becomes high tragedy—are they not all punishment for violation of the first simple law of Freedom: the law of organic change."

As a proponent of organic change Wright was fully aware of the need for roots—for the ground and shelter of genius—a necessity wonderfully expressed in respect to his own life in Taliesin. With him, security is not so much a conservative idea as an aspect of the bipolar unity of his thought, and one might even say that Wright was never more radical than when advancing it. The tensions of such thought are seldom resolved, as Smith shows, in the most valuable part of his book, by analyzing its architectural expression in several representative designs: the Winslow and Coonley houses, Taliesin, the Barnsdall house, Fallingwater, the Johnson Wax Company Building and Broadacre City.

Smith follows Wright in considering the work an integral part of his life and using it for biographical purposes. His interpretations differ from those of *An Autobiography*, a book he cites but insufficiently studies as autobiography, that is, as the foundation for a much needed biography. For Wright the Barnsdall house was, in the language of Sullivan he frequently uses, a "romanza"; for Smith it is an expression of his need in unsettled years for security and shelter. This is perceptive, as are many of his insights—that Taliesin, for example, was his Camelot, and that the tree, his organic model, represented for him a free solution to the social problem of the relation of part to whole.

When one feels especially critical of Smith's study it is because of the encumbering polemical tone, the loose construction and the lack of rounded presentation and balance. He does not adequately characterize Wright's mind (in some ways a Populist mind) in terms of its time and place. And he lets his religious argument mislead him when, in a major instance, he treats Broadacre City as Wright's supreme statement—as a secular version of the City of God. Taliesin, it seems to me, would have been a better example of Wright's "vision"; a vision of the natural house become a principality, where the abundant life is possible ("the exuberance of life in all these rural riches"), and all the things Wright valued—Family, Fellowship, Work,

Freedom: the headings of *An Autobiography*—were brought
together under one roof. Much about Taliesin is "feudal" and
"agrarian," but not necessarily the joyous spirit with which
Wright hoped to invest it. His genuinely conservative ideas are
conserving and relate to human well-being in an urban culture.
When they fail in this it is usually due to inadequate thought, for
his thought was not always equal to the scope and spirit of his
designs, and to the authoritarianism he sometimes permitted his
genius.

## No Loitering!

*STREETS FOR PEOPLE: A Primer for Americans.* By Bernard
Rudofsky. Doubleday & Co.

Mr. Rudofsky is an excellent photographer and book designer;
his book is an art book, large, sleek, well illustrated. It may be
used to good purpose as a picture book, for it will, as he modestly
hopes, whet our appetites for "the world of foreign streets"—for
the porticoes of Bologna, the Galleria of Milan, the ramparts
(promenade) of Lucca, the suq at Marrakesh, the mazes of the
white towns of Apulia—and may send us in search of fountains,
stairs, street markets, street drama and spectacle. In search of:
for these primary amenities (hence primer) are not, and never
have been, ours. We need, as Mr. Rudofsky cites *The New
Yorker* lamenting, "something to lift and brighten our fancy,
and if we cannot have bridges and vistas and colonnades and
canals and window boxes filled with flowers and a humane and
smiling architecture, we should have a little street music."

Though no one would deny the substantial truth of this, the
argument is as old as the condescension that accompanies it.
One remembers Henry James's long list of things of high civilization absent in American life but also his awareness that "the
American knows that a good deal remains; what it is that
remains—that is his secret, his joke." Mr. Rudofsky is not in on
the joke and doesn't really wish to be. He prefers, like a romantic

in search of the picturesque, to take his camera to Europe, to write charming sketches of such colorful things as the Italian story-singer (already disappearing from the streets) and to rummage, not delve, in the social history of the distant past.

The only American city he considers is New York, which is not the only city in the United States; and then it is not present-day New York City that interests him so much as New Amsterdam, where pigs used to scavenge in the streets. His book cannot be placed seriously in the category of social history—it is too thin, too impressionistic, a book of savory gleanings, each chapter heavily illustrated and perfectly suited to the women's clubs, to the very passionate pilgrims he despises. Everything about the book—its design, price, style and tone—belongs to familiar low-grade (but expensive) popularization, and perhaps most of all its subject, which is not pursued with the intent to remedy by implementation a dire civic situation, but rather to gratify us with the sick pleasures of nostalgia and cultural masochism.

A book that begins, "This book is about the great outdoors . . ." and asserts that Americans don't "give a hoot for streets" is immediately suspect. This is not the language of serious discourse or of discourse to be taken seriously. Style of this order is a public nuisance as lamentable as our streets, and writers who adopt it are likely to clutter their books with spurious notions (Americans like ugliness, Rudofsky believes, because they feel beauty undermines their toughness) and downright nonsense ("It is a melancholy comment on what we perversely call American civilization that in order to recapture the taste of human dignity, if only for a few precious days, one has to cross an ocean"). Rudofsky knows very little about American civilization past or present. He thinks that, because pigs once ran in the streets, we are eternally damned and can never attain a requisite sense of amenity; we are, he feels, all of us, from the beginning to the end, greedy and without civic sense. The fault of our streets lies in our national character, which is irreparable. But if

this is so, why advertise one's book as a primer? Why omit such
important basic studies as that on piazzas by Camillo Sitte? Isn't
it rather a travel book?

I think so. Rudofsky should have been advised to concentrate
on Italy, the great good place with which he always contrasts
America, and to put aside the attempt at comparative study. As a
book on Italy his work has merit; that he yokes what he loves to
what he hates is unfortunate. Or Rudofsky should have been
advised to "study out the land," as Whitman said, to see if our
streets have been as empty of people as he thinks and, if so, to
find out where they have gone. Is there nothing in the design
and life of college campuses (not unlike small Italian cities), in
people's parks, in other forms of living and associating alfresco
(picnics, camping, rock festivals, etc.) to give him hope? Why,
even here in Iowa City one can still walk. The nine blocks I walk
to work, some shaded by trees (the elms were once our portico),
include a small park where people of all ages eat, converse,
contemplate, study and play (chautauqua was once held here,
now there are rallies), a small creek which a few people with
civic feeling tried to clean, a downtown business district made
lively and interesting more than anything else by the variety of
people, and the campus animated by people day and night. And
this week, at *Oktoberfest* in nearby Amana, the people will
certainly be in the streets.

I welcome reviewing most when it is an opportune occasion of
work in progress and, as with these reviews, helps to precipitate
thought. These reviews represent *Louis Sullivan: An Architect
in American Thought* (1962), but I also reprint them to mark
what I considered a public stage in my work. They were my
first publications in a national magazine of opinion—in anything besides scholarly journals and little magazines (these
boundaries are no longer so sharply drawn)—and it is significant that I was asked to write them not because of literary
credentials but simply because I was interested in architecture

and city planning.

My interest in them was not entirely the scholarly one of
following the course of organic thought in one of its most
important contemporary expressions. The source was deeper:
in the need to fulfill the demand for active thought with which
Emerson tasked the American Scholar. In graduate school this
need had prompted me to seek an internship with the TVA
(my letter was never answered), and it accounted for the strong
appeal I felt in the teaching of F. O. Matthiessen. In the
preface to *American Renaissance*, he had joined Emerson and
Sullivan in his own avowal of critical purpose and democratic
faith, and his scholarship bore, as Sullivan said scholarship
should, "a genuine relation to the vital, aspiring thought of our
day and generation." In my book on Sullivan, I use, as epigraph to the chapter on "The American Scholar," the passage
Matthiessen cited: "his work [it begins] must so reflect his
scholarship as to prove that it has drawn him toward his
people, not away from them." It had been in my mind long
enough for me to forget my debt—so long that it struck me
forcibly when I found it again. I owe to Matthiessen, whose
lectures I attended, my introduction to Sullivan and also, I
realize now, a reinforcement of the Emersonian spirit in which
I wrote about him. The example of his criticism, which was so
much wider and richer than the New Humanism and New
Criticism he had assimilated, provided a warrant for including
architecture in my own.

My book on Sullivan is dedicated to the Mumfords to com-
memorate the visit to Amenia and a subsequent meeting in
Philadelphia and to acknowledge Lewis Mumford's immediate
influence. His work had turned me to architecture, and I
began to read about it in order to prepare to write about him.
The book on Sullivan was a by-product—but no less central to
me on that account. It got written, and what I had planned to
do and worked at for a few years did not: a composite biography
of Mumford after the fashion of my friend Edward Nehl's biography of D. H. Lawrence and a critical study, which was to
provide one of four overlapping perspectives—studies of Van
Wyck Brooks, Randolph Bourne, and Edmund Wilson were to

provide the others—on the critical (cultural) situations during
the period from World War I to the present. At Mumford's
request I abandoned the former, and I didn't complete the
latter, only some of the preliminary work it entailed. *Edmund
Wilson: A Study of Literary Vocation in Our Time* (1965) is
one of its fragments; the essays on Brooks and Bourne reprinted
here are others.

*Louis Sullivan* is primarily a work of intellectual history. Its
style is straightforward and descriptive, and its structure is minimal. This may be due to considerations of function and form,
but nevertheless I find it curious—not alien to me so much as
unexpected—and wonder if it is also due to the serious illness
that preceded its composition and allowed me time to put my
notes in ready order. What pleases me most, reading it now, is
the way the movement of thought returns to Emerson and
Whitman and, as it moves forward, deepens and clarifies their
ideas. I possess them more fully, it seems, by meeting their
issue in modern thought. Sullivan, who was so much their exponent, enabled me to turn directly to the philosophy and
psychology of education, to problems of creative liberation and
growth, to democracy as a way of being in the world—matters
that again were commanding attention. By expounding his
instinctual critique of civilization, I was speaking to the
unfinished situations of our time. This was not particularly
noticed by reviewers, and only negatively by one who thought
that Sullivan's social ideas were insane. I never answered this
contention. Perhaps the past decade and the current crisis of
government have. Yet elsewhere it may have been noticed: by
Ullstein Verlag, publishers who had been put out of business
by Hitler and who had little reason on strictly architectural
grounds to reprint it, and by Jaico Publishing House, who
brought out an edition in India.

The reviews reprinted here indicate my continuing interest
in the Chicago School, in Frank Lloyd Wright, and in city
planning.

# VAN WYCK BROOKS'S
# ORDEAL AND PILGRIMAGE

AN AUTOBIOGRAPHY. By Van Wyck Brooks. Introduction by
Malcolm Cowley, foreword by John Hall Wheelock. Dutton.

Van Wyck Brooks never accepted the challenge of autobiography. His nervous breakdown, following his own strenuous self
examination in the literary case histories of Mark Twain and
Henry James, did not permit it. Thereafter, as he admitted in
the memoir treating this watershed of his life, writing was his
secret asylum and way of taking flight. His strict discipline of
reading and writing, the subjects of his subsequent studies
(Emerson, Howells, Helen Keller, and John Sloan), even his
monumental history of the writer in America and his memoirs
suggest that for Brooks writing itself had become a value and a
therapeutic exercise.

The memoirs, which he published in 1954, 1957 and 1961,
and which have now been issued as his *Autobiography*, are
reticent, even where Brooks, as in the chapter on his breakdown, seems most revealing. To one who knows from primary
sources the cultural periods of his work, the memoirs are un-
satisfactory, not because, like some recent memoirs by members
of his generation, an intimate knowledge is colored by current
scholarly interpretations of the past, but because so little, finally, is told. Brooks does for himself in the memoirs what he had

done for American writers in the five volumes of *Makers and Finders*—tells a story of literary contacts, weaves a tapestry of the literary life.

The memoirs, of course, have the charm of all of Brooks's loomcraft; he is, as he claimed for his alter ego Oliver Allston, "an artist himself." But they are almost entirely even in tone, as if (to change the metaphor) the ground note of memory had harmonized all the discords of his life. Perhaps the most truly *autobiographical* element in them is the lack of self-confrontation. This, and the few acerbities, tell us that the "literary life" Brooks lived was for much of his life not the "creative life" with which he associated it and to which he aspired. Had he chosen to write an autobiography its theme would have been the ordeal of the lost leader and the successful pilgrimage of the artist.

The creative life, as Brooks envisaged it, was a life of spiritual exuberance and social leadership; it made good socially the enfranchisement proclaimed by Emerson when he said in *The American Scholar* that "the one thing in the world, of value, is the active soul." Brooks was always a fierce partisan of the active soul, having early spoken for its needs in *The Malady of the Ideal* and having, in his own generation, fought successfully its principal enemy, puritanism.

During the years from 1909–1925, he was very much the "American scholar," or, since he himself had not yet recognized his place in the Emersonian tradition, a "great personality" such as he admired, one who dominated his age and transformed its character. This conception of the artist as prophet, whose obverse for Brooks was his notion of "failure," was part of his large nineteenth-century heritage. Whether he wrote studies of failure ("cautionary tales") or of success ("exemplary tales"), Brooks's single theme, as he himself announced in the title of his most vociferous book, was *Letters and Leadership*.

Not Harvard, where he was graduated in 1907, but his own extensive reading in literature and art history and travel to Europe, that "paradise of culture," awakened his sense of the grandeur of this role; and the times, to which in the memoirs he attributes his paternity, called him forth. He was part of the critical coming-of-age because, like so many of the sensitive young men of the time, he resented the preemption by business of all of our energies. The "acquisitive life" is Brook's polar term for the "creative life"; in their opposition, as we sometimes forget, is the real motive of American criticism.

So Brooks proposed, in lieu of expatriation, to make America another Europe. The pull of Europe defines what he wants: a tradition in which the intellectual is respected and by which he is sustained; intellectual centers where men-of-letters may shed their loneliness and by contact contribute to the friction of ideas that creates intellectual situations; schools—guilds of artists for instruction and headquarters (such as *The New Republic, The Seven Arts,* "291" tried to become) for the direction of cultural life. Europe in Brooks's view, has the "collective spiritual life" that America lacks. There one finds at play a "complicated system of critical and traditional forces"; and especially in France, "the most perfect example of a social organism the world knows," one finds the model of what Brooks means by national or organic culture.

Brooks is perhaps the last American writer to feel so intensely the American problem of Europe and America. It is understandable that the emotional difficulties of solving this complicated problem contributed both to Brooks's breakdown and to the conception of an organic New England community that flowered out of it.

One need only read *America's Coming-of-Age* (1915) and *Letters and Leadership* (1918), the books with which Brooks did so much to create a "resisting background," to see the quality of mind and way of thinking that as much as anything broke him. He did not need Herbert Croly, whose *The Promise of American Life* (1909) was *the* tocsin for criticism, to tell him to be "as uncompromising and as irritating as one's ability . . . will permit" and to tell him to abandon the ethics of statesmanship in a time of intellectual war. As John Hall Wheelock recognized in the tension of Brooks's restraint, Brooks contained "an extraordinary vehemence of thought and feeling." Gentle Brooks!

He was wonderfully so, and yet he remained aggressive to the end, even in the memoirs where, by offering himself as the representative man of his generation, he was able to justify himself and have the last word. In his tactics, at least, he never retired, as Paul Rosenfeld complained in the twenties, from the battle line.

The clue to Brooks's way of thinking may be found in his remark that "Allston liked to contemplate extremes and try to fill, imaginatively, the space between." So, for example, he gives us "highbrow" and "lowbrow," and the mediating term, "middlebrow." More often, however, there is no mediation but only opposition, as in the "creative life" vs. the "acquisitive life." Here, Brooks, a master polemicist, has followed his own advice to critics to find the deep, irreconcilable "opposed catchwords"; and in what follows we realize that his melodramatic way of seeing is supported by an equally melodramatic way of feeling. Brooks sounds his note when he says that "the happiest excitement in life is to be convinced that one is fighting for all one is worth on behalf of some clearly seen and deeply felt good against some greatly scorned evil."

This Brooks is still affectionately remembered by the associates he rallied. They remember the leader more often than the artist; and they have not, I think, seen in Brooks's breakdown and withdrawal the means which enabled him to shed the responsibilities of a public role that had become alien to him and to return to his proper personal course. For a few years during World War I, Brooks's personal needs and those of his generation were one, and he rose to leadership on the strength of his personal manifesto. But the new literary generation after the war, the "junior pessimists" as he first called the "coterie writers," did not respond to his suddenly old-fashioned summons. So Brooks, not without permanent rancor, returned by way of illness to take up the only feasible part of his program. In *Makers and Finders* he found his true calling and did true work; here is his finest work of art and his largest contribution to the usable past by the creation of which he hoped, finally, to redeem our culture.

The intellectual price Brooks paid for breakdown involved the repudiation of his vigorous early work and, as James T. Farrell noted, his transformation from a cultural nationalist to a cultural chauvinist. When Brooks first wrote of the critical resurgence of his time, he pointed out how much Americans were disposed to see the critic as a traitor. By the time of World War II, however, he himself, in the almost bottomless bitterness that accompanied his deposition by the modernists, had become a cultural patriot and national celebrant who attributed to other writers deathdealing motives.

To think melodramatically is finally to think conspiratorially, and from the moment in the twenties when he had begun to call names, Brooks was preparing for that ugly performance in the forties, when he came from cover and used patriotism to coerce assent to his views. Brooks's friends seldom mention this, nor the fact that the strongest book of this half of his career is *Opinions of Oliver Allston* (1941), where he took tactical advantage by playing dead. (In a critical sense he had been, and this "biographical" volume is his most autobiographical work.) Perhaps Brooks's friends prefer to remember the early leader because in this role Brooks represents the possibilities of renewing society, not by political means (his unacknowledged enemy was Croly), but by cultural means. Brooks believed in the "visionary leader"; artists were the pathfinders of society, and by means of literature they would meet the social and religious problems which he felt were at the heart of the civilized modern world.

Long careers have curious turns, though those of Brooks's turn about the same idea. One measure of his value, and of the period that entertained his ideas, is to compare him with a counterpart today, someone like David Riesman. Brooks's accomplishment is that of a visionary leader: to have suggested a new personality type and a new style of life. As the editors of the *Dial* said when giving Brooks its award, "He has believed that the creative life is the only life tolerable to intelligent men and women, that the life which is not creative is spoiled and stunted and unworthy." This creative life, assuredly, is not the "autonomous" life Riesman offers us.

Another measure, one that does justice to Brooks's entire career, is the fact that having made us aware of the high responsibilities of the literary vocation, he tried throughout a long life, as Edmund Wilson noted in its early phase for the instruction of his contemporaries, to keep faith with his profession. In a country where Brooks believed the writer seldom matures and most often goes down to defeat, he managed to drive on to the end.

*Author's
Note*
This is the fragment of which I spoke earlier—a condensation of my work on Brooks. His *Autobiography* provided the only occasion I had for writing about him, and I used it to get down the generalizations or headings of a book rather than to treat in detail the autobiography under review. I note this because I was interested in autobiography—*The Examined Self* by my friend Robert Sayre had excited me—and had already begun to consider it in my study of Sullivan.

Brooks was among the most generous of those writers to whom study introduced me. Once contact was established, he sent postcards with bibliographical information that he thought I might find useful, and when I inquired about his letters, he immediately dispatched, unregistered, fifty years of personal correspondence.

# RANDOLPH BOURNE

THE BRIEF career of Randolph Bourne began in 1911 when he published in the *Atlantic Monthly* a rejoinder to one of those perennial animadversions on the younger generation. In its February issue the magazine had featured "A Letter to the Rising Generation" by Cornelia Comer, a frequent contributor. Adopting a Roman sternness and a sarcastic religious voice, she censured the young men of good families for abandoning the ways of their fathers. She knew that new conditions would not produce the sort of men the old conditions had, that the rising generation had been "conceived in uncertainty [and] brought forth in misgiving"; to be "nobly militant" would be difficult for a generation victimized by educational experiments and the eroding belief and authority of the elders. Yet everything about these young men annoyed her: their "agnostic-and-water" religious viewpoint, their Whitmanian notion of Personality and Shavian delight in the liberation of the natural will, and especially their experimental approach to ethics and advocacy of socialism, which she indicted as justifications of irresponsibility. The younger generation, she believed, lacked force and fortitude, was "soft," was deformed by "mental rickets and curvature of the soul."

Mrs. Comer's annoyance indicates the extent to which com-    137 munication between fathers and sons had broken down. She accurately observes the postures of these "Whitmanshaws" but considers them "cheap"; she will not have them enjoy without a large outlay of pain. She says that "the final right of each generation to its own code [of manners] depends upon the inner significance of those manners," but she does not search—to the limit of an elder's sympathy and power—for that significance. This, to be sure, only the new generation itself can fully express, thereby declaring itself and adding its increment to human history. Meanwhile, failing to understand that she is disturbed by the role of youth—by the fact that change, as Erik Erikson says, is "the business of youth and . . . challenge the essence of its business"—she prophesies: "It may easily happen that the next twenty years will prove the most interesting in the history of civilization. Armageddon is always at hand in some fashion. Nice lads with the blood of the founders of our nation in your veins, pecking away at the current literature of socialism, taking out of it imperfectly understood apologies for your temperaments and calling it philosophy—where will you be if a Great Day should really dawn?"

In replying to Mrs. Comer, Randolph Bourne had one of the few advantages in the confrontation of generations: he understood her generation more fully than she understood his. Her viewpoint and tone were as familiar to him as Bloomfield, New Jersey, the old respectable middle-class town in which he was born (in 1886) and raised and which, all his life, bitterly attracted him. He confessed to a correspondent, whose small-town plight was similar to his, that he owed most of his political, social, and psychological education to Bloomfield, that "its Church, its social classes, prejudices, conservatism, moral codes, personalities—all furnish the background against which I throw all my experience, and in terms of which I still see life and suppose always shall." In his master's thesis he studied the effects of suburbanization on the social life of the town, explaining that the process was slower there than in nearby Glen Ridge and Montclair because the "Calvinistic religion was bred in the bone of the town, and it [would] take much urban sophistication to get rid of it." And, perhaps to find a purchase for himself and others after the war, he began an autobiographical novel of which only the chapter on his sixth year in Bloomfield was published—a chapter with which the monthly *Dial* was launched.

In everything except money, Randolph Silliman Bourne belonged to the "comfortable classes" for whom and to whom Mrs. Comer spoke. The quarrel between them was a family matter, an affair almost entirely of the middle class. He was, in fact, one of the "nice lads" of worthy native ancestry and good family whom she threatened with class-displacement and the rough discipline of "life." He, however, was already intimate with both. His birth, as he said, had been "terribly messy"; inept forceps-delivery had left his face scarred and misshapen. Then, in his fourth year, he had been ill with spinal tuberculosis, had been stunted and bent, "cruelly blasted," he once complained, "by the powers that brought him into the world." (According to his passport, he was five feet tall, had brown hair and a medium complexioned long face with blue eyes, a large nose, straight mouth, and receding chin. A close college friend reported that it was not his deformed back, which he learned to hide with a black cape and by carefully seating himself, but his malformed ear—"a rudimentary appendage"—that repelled people, and that Bourne himself disliked his "sloping chin.") He also knew a disability more common in his generation of writers: the failure of the father, itself a sign of the crumbling edifice of Victorian middle-class values. His father, Charles Rogers Bourne, had failed in business and had consented to leave home when his brother-in-law made this the condition of his support of Sarah Barrett Bourne and her four children. A cruel banishment! A martyrdom, Van Wyck Brooks might have said, to the "acquisitive life," and one that would have impressed the boy with the inexorable Calvinism of the household and with the belief, for which he said he "suffered tortures," that failure was always the result of moral weakness. Genteel impoverishment and depen-

dence is perhaps the worst affliction of the respectable—to have
to live constantly, as Bourne remembered, under the "awful
glowering family eye of rich guarding relatives," who also, as far
as he was concerned, remained "dumb and uninterested." An
aunt and grandmother were warm sustaining presences, but his
mother's unhappiness, a proper disposition in such circumstances, established the ground tone of what he called his
"doleful home."

Perhaps the absence of his father confirmed the gentility of his
upbringing. Like Miro, the fictive hero of "The History of a
Literary Radical," he found in his environment little genuine
cultural nourishment but much cultural devoutness. In his
home, as in many more, the classics, in Eliot's exact description, "Upon the glazen shelves kept watch"; only the metropolitan newspaper opened to him a portal to the world, and to it he
attributed his real education. He was a well-behaved boy whose
success as a student had been due, he admitted, to "my moral
rather than my intellectual sense." Indeed, in the few pages of
the diary he began in his fourteenth year, he reveals himself to
be the phenomenon he later thought appalling, the "good"
child. Here he records the eager steps of a culture-famished,
priggish youth intent on success and social acceptance: he and
his sister have joined the church ("Mamma wants us to very
much"); he has begun to excel in school ("Wonder of wonders! I
got 100 in a Greek exercise that I did tother day. I have never
gotten it before"); he has been elected class president, though
"not very popular in the school and very little known"; he has
begun to collect stamps and well-printed and -bound books—
Lowell's and Whittier's poems, *Ivanhoe* and *The Vicar of
Wakefield*—and to record his literary opinions ("I have just
finished reading 'Eben Holden.' It beats 'David Harum' by a
good deal. . . . The love story is about the prettiest and sweetest I
have ever read"); and he has discovered that babies are "cute,"
has sent his finest valentine to a girl named Grace Wade, has
gone to a "very dainty and lovely" luncheon, and has been taken
by his Aunt Fan to *Lohengrin*.

The career of respectability begun here might have continued had Bourne been able to enter college on graduating from high school in 1903. But his uncle was unwilling to provide this privilege, and he was turned out to work, learning, as he said in "A Philosophy of Handicap," that "the bitterest struggles of the handicapped man come when he tackles the business world." He worked for six years: in an office, as an accompanyist and music teacher (he was a competent pianist), and as a "factory hand" perforating music-rolls for player pianos, an indelible experience of the piecework system that he described in "What Is Exploitation?" Desperate to escape such lower depths, he finally practiced the "dodging of pressures" he preached to those similarly trapped: "I solved my difficulties only by evading them, by throwing overboard some of my responsibility [he was the eldest child]." At the age of twenty-three, he entered Columbia University on a scholarship, to discover, gratefully, that "college furnishes an ideal environment where the things at which a handicapped man . . . can succeed really count."

In 1909 Columbia was already a great metropolitan university and headquarters of modern thought. In many departments, its professors belonged to the vanguard: Franz Boas, in anthropology; John Dewey, in philosophy, psychology, and education; Charles Beard, in political science; James Harvey Robinson, in history—to mention only those most frequently considered in the history of American revolt against formalism. There, Bourne was befriended by his teachers, especially by his "great hero-teacher" Frederick P. Keppel, who helped him financially, and was surrounded by bright, sympathetic young men many of whom shared with him the editing of the *Columbia Monthly*. There, he declared, he found a spiritual home. The congenial intellectual world and the fresh atmosphere of ideas represented for him the valuable "college education" that then, as now, was overwhelmed by "college life." "What we all want the college to be"—he later wrote in "What Is College For?"—"is a life where for youth of all social classes the expressions of genius, the modern interpretations of society, and the scientific spirit, may become imaginatively real." Having quickly abandoned fusty literary studies for the "intellectual arena" of the social sciences, he got what he said a student should: "a fused and assimilated sense of the world he lives in, in its length and breadth, its historical perspective and social setting." Columbia, he told a prospective student, had revolutionized his life.

When he wrote this to Prudence Winterrowd of Shelbyville, Indiana, he was thinking mostly of the thwartings he had known in Bloomfield and the heady release Columbia had provided him. But it had revolutionized his thought and, in a more modest way, his action. He had a certain notoriety because he protested such things as the exploitation by the university of its scrub women and page-boys. If not a big man on campus, he was an older, notable one: a socialist, an editor of the highbrow literary magazine that in his time had repudiated *fin de siècle* symbolism for critical realism. On the magazine he had served a valuable apprenticeship, had found his vocation; and after his appearance in the *Atlantic Monthly*, he had the glamour that invests the undergraduate who arrives in the real world ahead of the rest.

Bourne's praise of Columbia was not extravagant because, with his inability to set himself in motion, he owed much of his achievement to its stimulus. In the struggle to get a foothold, he explained in "The Experimental Life," "the difference is in the fortune of the foothold, and not in our private creation of any mystical force of will." Columbia was a fortunate foothold, which he did not readily give up; it had awakened his capacity, produced activity and success. Dean Frederick Woodbridge, for example, had suggested that he reply to Mrs. Comer and had forwarded his essay to Ellery Sedgwick, the editor of the *Atlantic Monthly*, who served Bourne, for as long as he permitted, as literary counselor. Bourne acknowledged that the magazine was his "good angel" and "coddled" him. Sedgwick prompted several essays—some of Bourne's most significant essays and a large proportion of his best work were printed by him—and Sedgwick made the magazine another foothold. With his help, Houghton

Mifflin Company published Bourne's first book, *Youth and Life*
and so he established himself. Columbia postponed the crisis of
vocation and prepared him for it by enabling him to spend a year
in Europe; and when this crisis was again at hand, Sedgwick and
Charles Beard secured a place for him on Herbert Croly's new
liberal weekly, the *New Republic*.

To the psychological and intellectual weather of these exciting turbulent years, *Youth and Life* is excellent testimony—
"thoroughly and almost uncannily autobiographical," Bourne
ruefully admitted. Walter F. Greenman, a Unitarian minister
in Milwaukee, one of the many educated people (social workers,
ministers, teachers, and idealistic housewives) the book inspired, believed it to be "the truest interpretation of Youth to
itself" that he knew. It made him feel "as if my beloved Emerson
had had a reincarnation in the 20th Century," and he told
Bourne that it was "the most innocent looking sweetest stick of
dynamite anybody ever chewed." In these essays, which include
the reply to Mrs. Comer, is the full statement of the case for the
younger against the older generation. The reviewer in the *Columbia Monthly* praised them highly as a declaration but complained that the essay form had eliminated the poetry of youth.
Yet no other book of this time expresses so well, even while
making youth an ideology to which to be loyal, the precarious
condition and the virtues of this season of life. For all of its
faults, deriving mainly from reliance on the rhetoric of
uplift—a rhetoric, however, that in conjunction with candor
and fresh ideas effectively expresses the new idealism—it is an
irreplaceable book of this generation, like the war essays of
Bourne's *Untimely Papers*, and belongs with his best work.

The title itself brilliantly states the issues, which, because of
Bourne's fidelity to experience, address every younger generation as well as his own: the confrontation of youth, a new
generation, with "life"; the resources of life, which youth bears;
and the responsibilities it has for its replenishment. At the very
moment in Western history when Ortega announced that the

theme of our time was the restoration of life to its proper relation
with culture, Bourne called the young men and women of his
generation to life and showed them an open and daring stance
toward the world, one flexible yet resilient, that would enable
them to master and enjoy the "experimental life." Using these
essays as a form of self-therapy—they are continuous with his
remarkable correspondence—he investigated his identity crisis,
one of more than usual significance because profound historical
changes contributed to it. In doing this, he either anticipated or
confirmed the advanced thought of men like Ortega, Erikson,
and Paul Goodman, for he recognized the concept of the
generation and its historical, social, and psychological compo-
nents. He knew what it meant to grow up absurd and how much
absurdity was due to an older generation; he knew that life had
stages, each with its necessary virtue, and that in the cycle of
generations youth, having the regenerative function, was especially important; and he knew that for psychological and
social reasons the conflict of generations was as inevitable as it
was necessary, yet sometimes irreconcilable, because beneath
the rebellion over child-rearing and education, philosophies
and values, was the stark fact of power—that the older generation, as he said, wished "to rule not only their own but all the
generations."

The first three essays specifically treat these themes, although
the remaining essays, by way of exploring the thoughts and
solutions of youth, consider them too. The general case gives
way to particular applications, and the book concludes with the
most intimately personal essay, "A Philosophy of Handicap,"
which had stirred the readers of the *Atlantic*, and Sedgwick had
insisted Bourne reprint—an essay that now certified the book by
giving it a signature and fastened to the younger generation the
virtue of unassuming courage.

As Bourne describes it, youth is a condition, the result of a
profound psychological crisis and coming-of-age when one is
"suddenly born into a confusion of ideas and appeals and traditions" and enters a "new spiritual world." Whether or not this

144

crisis is fruitful depends on awareness and spiritual force, on finding release for oneself not in "passion" but in "enthusiasm." For the way of passion is not "adventurous"; it is the way of "traditional" youth, who, like most of those friends of Bourne's youth in Bloomfield whose social life excluded him, pass easily through the crisis by avoiding it, by following pleasure and settling for, as well as into, established routines. To seek security at the expense of consciousness is to forfeit youth, and Bourne does not speak for these young people but for those radical ones, like his Columbia friends, who have not been cautious and have exposed themselves "to the full fury of the spiritual elements." These adventurous youth discover the precious gift of life and become the responsive ones who, if they continue to seek and search, alter the sensibility of the age. Only the young, Bourne says, "are actually contemporaneous; they interpret what they see freshly and without prejudice; their vision is always the truest, and their interpretation always the justest." Not burdened with stock moralities, they follow the open road of experience, always susceptible to the new, eager for experiment, ready to let ideas get them. Their enthusiasm is for fresh ideals to which to give their loyalty, and nothing angers them more than the spiritual torpor and "damaged ideals" that, in this account, define old age.

The attack on the elders is directed to this condition. As in *Walden*, so here: "Age is no better, hardly so well, qualified for an instructor as youth," Thoreau says, "for it has not profited so much as it has lost." What it has lost, essentially, is the spontaneity of being—"the soul's emphasis," in Emerson's wonderful phrase—that sustains the virtue of each season of life and impels one's moral growth. Age has lost the very condition of youth, which Bourne believes to be the epitome of life. It has forsaken the "battle-ground of the moral life" to which childhood familiarization with the world opens and all subsequent stages of life, to be worthy, must contribute support. Just as toward children the duty of elders is to refrain from imposing moralities and, by permitting natural growth into the world, to

**Randolph Bourne**

prepare them for the vital morality of self-mastery, so toward youth the duties of middle and old age, respectively, are to "conserve the values of youth" by living up to them and then, in relinquishing power, wisely to understand "the truth and efficacy of youth's ideal vision."

The aim of this gospel of youth is "to reinstate ideals and personality at the heart of the world." Tested by this gospel, the older generation has failed. The older accuses the younger generation of being soft when, in fact, it is palpitant, for the virtue of all its virtues, the passion for justice, has been kindled by the kind of world the elders have given it. To them Bourne attributes the cardinal fact about the younger generation: that it has had to bring itself up and, accordingly, has learned to judge by its own standards. The education provided it has not fitted the needs of its freer social life and wider awareness of the world. The formulas of the elders have not been helpful, and their models of success have not been attractive. It finds distasteful the routine, chicanery, and predation of the business world to which they would guide it, regrets the lack of individual social responsibility in the increasingly corporate economy, and is hampered by the high cost of professional education. In every way the elders refuse it confirmation, deny it by evading with "nerveless negations" the issues raised by its "positive faith" in social reform. And so, at the pitch of his indictment, Bourne says, "the stupidities and cruelties of their management of the world fill youth with an intolerant rage."

What is hardest to understand about another generation is the very thing Bourne tried to explain in the body of his book: its way of being in the world. He begins, in "The Life of Irony," by defining its point of view, the "comic juxtaposition" it has adopted in order to revivify the world. Irony, to be sure, is deadly accurate and reveals the absurdity of many things; it has a negative power and, as Bourne's friends complained of his use of it, is often accompanied by "malicious delight." Yet for Bourne it was much more than a hostile critical weapon: it was a social mode of being, his way of embracing the world and finding in it a field for vital intelligence. He speaks of irony as the "science of comparative experience," as "a sweeter, more flexible and human principle of life, adequate, without the buttress of supernatural belief, to nourish and fortify the spirit." It is the foe of both "predestined formulas" and spiritual apathy, un-fixing things, restoring fluidity, and, at the same time, bringing "a vivid and intense feeling of aliveness." It admits to experience the "noisier and vivider elements" that the New Humanists wished to exclude, and is therefore "rich" and "democratic." Like Whitman's mode of acceptance, irony requires that one take another's position and contact the world. It is an "active way of doing and being" that confronts one with his own firsthand experience, occasions "surprise," and brings with it (in one of Bourne's favorite words) the "glow" of life.

Of greatest significance in this redefinition of irony is the fact that it weaves itself "out of the flux of experience rather than out of eternal values." But of greatest moment to Bourne is the fact that the experience he has in mind is social and that what he needs most to nourish it are friends. This relish for friendship is not merely the reflection of the life he was living at Columbia; it is also an affirmation of temperamental need. To the depriva-tion of everything else, he says, he is invulnerable; and Clara Barrus, a friend of John Burroughs and student of Whitman, when she read the essay on friendship was moved to send him Whitman's poem, "I Saw in Louisiana a Live-Oak Growing." Bourne used his friends, as Emerson did, to discover aspects of himself, but he did not demand of them, as the Tran-scendentalists did, a running together of souls. He asked much, but on a lower plane: the excitement that generates thought; not binding spiritual relations so much as lively intellectual occa-sions. His conception of friendship was social where their con-ception was personal; he was the least of solitaries, a thoroughly social being, and the sociality he required of friendship he required also of the great community. His personal need for friendship inspired his correspondence and, after the cama-raderie of Columbia, his search for another rewarding form of social life. But it also inspired, as a similar need had in Whitman, the vision of a pluralistic fraternal society that fired his generation.

Bourne's feeling for the possibilities of an intensely individual yet socialized life generated the gaiety of spirit that, in spite of his awareness of the world of fright, characterizes his book. He is familiar with the despair of naturalism, but he knows that the adventure as well as the precariousness and peril of life is grounded in this condition. To alleviate the sickness of scientific materialism, he proposes a new idealism, scientific in method but mystical in scope, such as he had found in Whitman, Maeterlinck, and William James—an idealism whose newness he suggests when he writes that youth "must think of everything in terms of life; yes, even death in terms of life." In addition, he limits responsibility to social rather than metaphysical evil, to those evils that human "interests" and "ideals" can remedy, and, by explaining the appeal of the "social movement," defends the radicalism of the younger generation while rousing in it his own desire to "ride fast and shout for joy."

In behalf of his generation, Bourne presents an objective that enlists loyalty, that satisfies the claims of both social action and religious sentiment; and, implementing it, he offers a new conception of success and strategy for achieving it. He treats success in "The Experimental Life" and finds its touchstone in the readiness of spirit that contributes also to the adventurous life of irony. "I love people of quick, roving intelligence, who carry their learning lightly, and use it as weapons to fight with, as handles to grasp new ideas with, and as fuel to warm them into a sympathy with all sorts and conditions of men"—this remark (and self-portrayal) in a letter describes the achievement of a way of being, the transformation of personality that for Bourne constitutes success. He detests the doggedness and prudence of planning one's life, for life is not plan and cannot be taken frontally. One must go roundabout, must consult his "interests" (the solicitations of the world) and stand "poised for opportu-

nity." Life is not a battle, as the elders believe, but an experi-

ment. "Life is not a rich province to conquer by our will, or to **Randolph**
wring enjoyment out of with our appetites, nor is it a market **Bourne**
where we pay our money . . . and receive the goods we desire,"
Bourne says, repudiating the notions of the older generation as
well as those of the still younger generation of Fitzgerald and
Hemingway. "It is rather [as Thoreau demonstrated] a great tract
of spiritual soil, which we can cultivate or misuse."

Bourne upholds the intrinsic success of self-culture. He believes as firmly as any Transcendentalist in the primary duty of
living one's own life—like Thoreau, he hugs himself. The
unpardonable sin is "treason to one's self," the easy self-betrayal
of letting outer forces arrest the development of one's inner
nature. He says that "convention is the real enemy of youth" and
advises them to dodge the pressures that "warp and . . . harden
the personality and its own free choices and bents." Of these
pressures, the most formidable and intolerable is the family, for
intimacy compounds its force. In a letter to Prudence Winterrowd encouraging her to leave home, Bourne writes bitterly of
the spiritual cannibalism of parents who demand that their
children sacrifice their lives for them. He tells her that he wants
"independent, self-reliant, progressive generations, not eating
each other's hearts out, but complementing each other and
assuming a spiritual division of labor."

Now Bourne does not incite youth to rebellion for light and
transient reasons. He is aware of their obsession with sex, but
mentions it only to set them the task of taming it; his advice is to
neglect rather than repress this desire. (He himself was disturbed
by desire because he felt debarred from its fulfillment and was
still Puritan enough, as "The Major Chord" indicates, to divide
the claims of soul and body and imagine them in the conventional terms of light and dark lady. In this unpublished dialogue,
the cool, luminous light lady stands for the pleasures of mind
and spirit—for the kind of intellectual relations Bourne actually
has with women. The dark lady, warm and naked, represents
the body, "the surge and passion of life," and the imperious
injunction to live in the body: "You must live, my poet, / And    149

the body only lives." The poet admits his sexual hunger, but
does not take the dark lady. Instead he confronts the light lady,
whom he notes resembles the dark lady, with his desire and
compels her to be both body and soul and to yield a safer passion:
"Not the smoky fires of passion," "Not the voluptuous
fumes. . . ." Certainly what Bourne told a confidante, Alyse
Gregory, was true: that the struggle with unrealized desire hampered him, yet colored "all his appreciations," motivated "his
love of personality," and filled his life "with a sort of smoulder-
ing beauty." And considered along with all Bourne said in
support of desires of other kinds, his solution to the problem of
sexual desire confirms Dorothy Teall's statement that the sexual
revolution of their generation was more a matter of "refreshment
of emotion . . . than a revolution in morals.") Bourne does not
treat this problem, except by sympathetic indirection in sketches
like "Sophronsiba." The liberation he preaches is neither sexual
nor an end in itself but a means to a new "spiritual livelihood."
Youth, he says, "must see their freedom as simply the setting
free of forces within themselves for a cleaner, sincerer life, and
for radical work in society." He asks youth to find socially
productive vocations, to contribute to reform *in their vocations*—by following journalism or art, medicine or engineer-
ing, not the law, ministry, or business. They must pursue their
self-culture in society and stake the fulfillments of self on social
reconstruction. He announces these ends in "For Radicals,"
his directive to the American Scholar, and calls the "idealistic
youth of today" to the work of reform that Emerson had spoken
of as "the conversion of the world."

The Reverend Walter Greenman wondered how long Bourne
would go on using the antithesis of youth and age, and told him
to guard against the assault of age and the drying-up of literary
material by finding a "new cleavage." The advice was needless.
*Youth and Life* was not quite the "charmingly immature book"
Norman Foerster, a New Humanist professor, thought it, for
youth and age, as Bourne used them, were exactly what Van

Wyck Brooks meant by opposed catchwords that correspond to genuine convictions and real issues. Bourne may have approached these issues youthfully, but they were issues of profundity and scope and, followed out, disclosed an abyss in American culture.

Two years before the publication of *Youth and Life,* Santayana had spoken of America, in "The Genteel Tradition in American Philosophy," as "a country with two mentalities, one a survival of the beliefs and standards of the fathers, the other an expression of the instincts, practice, and discoveries of the younger generations." These mentalities were represented, in Stuart Sherman's adaptation of Emerson's phrases, by the Party of Culture and the Party of Nature; and the battle between them, long in preparation, was the bitterest in our cultural history because the insurgent modernists were at last strong enough to attack the entire nineteenth-century orthodox inheritance. Since Emerson's time, the Party of Nature had returned to society; the *nature* in its title was merely a New Humanist slur-word designating its arch-foe, naturalism. This party was in fact Emerson's Party of Hope, inspired anew by the possibilities of social reform. Radical in its theories of education, socialistic in politics, cosmopolitan and urban, this party exuberantly embraced contemporary America. The Party of Culture, on the other hand, was what Emerson had called the Party of the Past, renamed in tribute to Matthew Arnold, and rightly, because it looked to "culture" to maintain its traditional social and religious values. It was predominantly eastern, Anglo-Saxon, professorial; it spoke for the good families of native stock, for the established and wealthy. To these parties Bourne fixed the distinctions of youth and age, for in the battle between them he saw "the struggle of the old to conserve, of the new to adapt"— that "overlapping of the generations, with their stains and traces of the past" that, instead of evolution, accounted for social change.

Ortega has said that a generation is not a succession but an argument. The truth of this observation is especially evident at those times when assumptions are exposed by loss of conviction and points of view alter radically. The Transcendentalists had engaged in such an argument about the nature of human experience and creativity and the ends of American life—an unfinished argument resumed in Bourne's time. He put the issue when he said that his generation wanted "a new orientation of the spirit that shall be modern." And Walter Lippmann, another spokesman for this generation, put it in another way when he wrote in *Drift and Mastery* (1914), a book Bourne greatly admired: "The sanctity of property, the patriarchal family, hereditary caste, the dogma of sin, obedience to authority,—the rock of ages, in brief, has been blasted for us. Those who are young today are born into a world in which the foundations of the older order survive only as habits or by default." Industrialization had changed precipitately the ways of economic and social life, and since the 1880s thinkers—a whole literature—had been assailing the modes of thought supporting the old order. Its guardians, however, seemed neither prepared nor willing to meet the challenge of "experience"—to fulfill new needs and, in Lippmann's phrase, restore the "moral texture of democracy."

The enemies of those who at every stage of our history have responded to the moral imperatives of democracy have been cowardice and complacency, the moral deficiencies Bourne attributed to the older generation. Here, it was most vulnerable because of its assumption of virtue, and Bourne, often with devastating lightness, continued to attack it. He drew its several portraits—caricatures, perhaps, when compared with his tender sketches of the young—in "One of Our Conquerors," "The Professor," and "The Architect."

The conqueror, barely disguised, was Columbia's president, Nicholas Murray Butler, one of the "sleek and successful elders" who was "against everything new, everything untried, everything untested." With his ideal of service and gospel of success, his Anglo-Saxon prejudices, absolute idealism in philosophy, and Republican political rectitude, he was the representative

public man of the older generation, an intellectual Horatio
Alger, the Captain of Learning who, in the *Columbia Monthly*,
had told the undergraduates, "Don't Knock! Boost!"

The professor, drawn appropriately with delicate irony, was
John Erskine, also of Columbia. This professor of English had
acquired from Henry Van Dyke and Charles Eliot Norton the
"ideals of the scholar and gentleman" and protected the "chalice
of the past." Himself free from "philosophic or sociologic taint,"
he deprecated (as Bourne personally knew) "the fanaticism of
college men who lose their sense of proportion on social questions."

The architect, an American whom Bourne had met in Italy,
shared the professor's gentility and cultural colonialism, for he
was an exponent of the Gothic style and a devotee of art for art's
sake. Both belonged with the Arnoldians treated in "The Cult of
the Best" and "Our Cultural Humility"—those, Bourne said,
who believed that "to be cultured . . . mean[s] to like master-
pieces" and whose reverential, moralistic attitude toward art
closed their eyes to the "vital." Of their company—indeed, with
Irving Babbitt, one of their spokesmen—was Paul Elmer More,
whose *Aristocracy and Justice* prompted one of Bourne's sharp-
est replies to the older generation. More, he claimed, not only
completely misunderstood modernism and was out of touch
with "the driving and creative thought of the day"—was derelict
as an intellectual—but was an intellectual partisan of plutoc-
racy, a defender of class exploitation, a judgment More never
lived down.

The common want in all of these members of the older
generation is the social conscience, which, Bourne said, was
"the most characteristic spiritual sign of our age." His generation, he believed, had shifted its spiritual center from the personal to the social. It sought social rather than individual
salvation—did not, as he trenchantly explained the religious
motives of the older generation, accumulate personal virtue by
morally exploiting others and condone social evil as a foil for
individual goodness. The older generation believed "in getting

all the luxury of the virtue of goodness, while conserving all the advantages of being in a vicious society." Its ideals were selfish and did not appeal to the young who, Bourne said, had begun to "feel social injustice as [their] fathers felt personal sin" and had been converted to a belief in "the possibilities of a regenerated social order."

Youth could no longer be contained in a world "all hardened and definite," by "tight little categories," as he said of More. For More's ethics of repression was the ethics of a "parsimonious" world and had no place in a new world of "surplus value, economic and spiritual." The young had responded to the appeal of a more abundant life, and their response was complete—economic, spiritual, aesthetic. Like More, however, the elders were as insensitive to aesthetic as to moral experience. They did not see that the vision of the social movement was very much an aesthetic one, and their deficiency of social conscience was compounded by "genuine anesthesia," an inability to respond to the petitionings of life and deliver themselves, as Bourne claimed he had, "over to the present."

Bourne's generation had been able to do this because it had acquired from the pragmatists a "new philosophical vista," as Santayana said of the thought of William James, one "radically empirical and radically romantic." Ralph Barton Perry, in *Present Philosophical Tendencies*, an excellent review of contemporary systems that the bright young men of the *Columbia Monthly* considered elementary, treated pragmatism as an especially significant sign of the spirit of the age. Negatively, he wrote, pragmatism represented a "reaction against absolutism, long enthroned in academic and other orthodox circles"; positively, it represented the "biological" imagination," the conception of an exigent naturalistic environment from which, in the need for adaptation, knowledge and religion themselves arise as "modes of life." Pragmatism, however, was not a philosophy of renunciation or despair, but an enabling melioristic philosophy of collective human effort: "It teaches that the spiritual life is in the making at the point of contact between man and . . . nature" and that knowledge is instrumental, a power that, guided by

desire and hope, may "conquer nature and subdue the insurrec-
tion of evil." Santayana said that this philosophy was "a
thousand times more idealistic than academic idealism" and
observed that it was the "philosophy of those who as yet had had
little experience"; Perry concluded that it was the philosophy of
"impetuous youth, of protestantism, of democracy, of secular
progress—that blend of naïveté, vigor, and adventurous courage which proposes to possess the future, despite the present and
the past." Such, in any case, was the philosophy which, Santayana announced, had "broken the spell of the genteel tradition, and enticed faith in a new direction."

Bourne had discovered pragmatism at Columbia, where, he
told Prudence Winterrowd, "we are all instrumentalists." To
her, in fervent letters explaining this "most inspiring modern
outlook on life and reality," he also related the story of his
conversion. He had moved from Calvinism ("I began in the
same way as you") to Unitarianism ("mild and healing") to rank
materialism ("I... took great delight in lacerating a rather
tender and green young man whose delights was in Emerson
and Plato, whom I despised"). Then, in 1911, in a course with
Professor Woodbridge, the "virus of the Bergson-James-
Schiller-instrumental-pragmatism" got into his blood; and now,
two years later, he preached James as a prophet. In view of his
later relationship with Dewey—his discipleship and
apostasy—it is interesting to note in these letters Bourne's failure to mention Dewey and, in other letters, his low opinion of
Dewey's courses. He was not fired by Dewey; James was his man
because he had what Bourne missed in Positivism—"the verve,
the color, the music of life." He told Miss Winterrowd that
James kept alive for him "a world where amazing regenerations
of the vital and spiritual forces of man take place... [a world at
once] so incorrigibly alive and so incorrigibly mystical." James's
world was one of "fluid, interpenetrating, creative things," and
Bourne described its appeal when, in a letter to Brooks, he
distinguished between mere intellectualism and the "warm area
of pragmatic life."

Pragmatism satisfied both the old, now bereft, religious sentiment and the new clamorous scientific spirit. It mediated the extremes of idealism and naturalism. It provided scope for faith and action—and for faith in action. Grounding everything in experience and toward everything proposing an experimental attitude, it upheld the prerogatives of personality at the same time as it encouraged social reform. Itself a product of the biological imagination—a life-philosophy—it stimulated the sociological imagination and the faith in salvation by intelligence that were then characteristic of liberal thought. It inspired men to master social drift in the way that the votary Lippmann suggested, by substituting "purpose for tradition," by deliberately devising means for achieving chosen social ends. And to those who adopted its method, it also imparted a democratic vision—it laid, as Bourne said of the new social sciences, "an inexpugnable basis for the highest and noblest aspirations of the time."

How fortunate for Bourne that, finding at home no work for himself equal to these aspirations, he was able to nourish his social imagination elsewhere. Having been awarded a Gilder Fellowship, a handsome patent for sociological investigation, he embarked on July 5, 1913, on the *Rochambeau* for a year's stay in Europe. There he did not follow a course of intensive study so much as a course of extensive travel; he allowed himself a true *Wanderjahr*, rushing over the Continent during the first summer, settling in England and France for most of the autumn and winter, and resuming in the late spring the travels that ended, on the eve of war, with a midnight escape from Berlin to Sweden.

"Impressions of Europe, 1913–1914," the report he reluctantly wrote to satisfy the terms of his grant, is the summary account of this year, the year in Bourne's life, however, for which his correspondence, diary, and articles provide the fullest record. In contrast with the amplitude and immediacy of these materials, the "Impressions" seem thin and belated. Bourne had by this time told his story too often, and he now chose to tell it differently (for which it is valuable), from the perspective of war and in the light of "the toddlings of an innocent child about the edge of a volcano's crater." "Impressions," in any case, was the right word because he was honest enough to claim no more for his researches and, in a genuine sense, had been another Irvingesque saunterer. He called his travel articles to the Bloomfield *Citizen* "Impressions of a European Tour" and told a friend that he liked "to go sauntering about the streets, looking at all sorts of charming and obscure scenes." He enjoyed the picturesque, as on his journey from Paris to Italy, appreciated the formal achievements of European culture, and knew how to extract the flavors of experience. But he also knew how to grasp a city as a living form by searching out the close textures of its actual social life. He knew that culture was not only the artifacts to which Baedekers were guides, but a process, a present way of life, with which he must make contact. His vision was seldom indolent and, whether sauntering or rushing about, he saw sharply with the eye of a social psychologist.

For Bourne this year abroad was especially formative. He considered it a good test of the experimental life and admitted that at times he was not up to its demands. He missed most his close little world of friends, and to some extent the degree of his success in finding similar groups colored his judgments of England and France. His need and tenacity—and his range of response—are evident in his voluminous correspondence. To Arthur Macmahon and Carl Zigrosser, former roommates at Columbia, he wrote, respectively, of political events and art; to Henry Elsasser, reputedly the most brilliant of his Columbia friends, he sent his profounder speculations; and to Alyse Gregory, whom he had met shortly before his departure, he wrote about socialism and suffragettism—and about himself, for during this period of his life, she was the woman in whom he had chosen to confide.

One of the books that he read with appreciation at the beginning of his travels and soon felt confirmed his European experience was James's *The American*. For Europe immediately forced him to measure his personal resources and those of America, and offered the occasion of a slight, which, one suspects, was more damaging to Bourne than he let on because he never "literized" it as he usually did his experiences. He had been rudely turned out of the country house of S. M. Bligh, a Welsh psychologist to whom he particularly looked for sponsorship in intellectual circles. The smart set he met there did not, it seems, delight in his kind of irony. "My prophetic strain would come out," Bourne wrote Elsasser, "and my Socialism appeared as wild and hairraising, if not actually mad, in that society of tough British and class-prejudice." His values were turned upside down: "Ideals of militarism, imperialism, moneymaking, conservation of old English snobberies and prejudices, all swept before me in an indescribably voluble and brilliant flood, and I was left, as you may surmise, stranded like a very young Hosea or Amos at the court of some wicked worldly king." To another correspondent he confessed that he had had "a hell of a time emotionally"—he had indeed been shocked and wounded, and nothing he later experienced in England mollified him. He made his way eventually, meeting the Webbs and Wells, listening to Shaw and Chesterton, studying garden cities, visiting at Oxford, attending the meetings of suffragettes at Knightsbridge. But England made him feel "just about ready to renounce the whole of Anglo-Saxon civilization." The only live thing, he told Carl Zigrosser, had been the suffrage movement. Otherwise, he found "the whole country . . . old and weary, as if the demands of the twentieth century were proving entirely too much for its powers, and it was waiting half-cynically and apathetically for some great cataclysm." By contrast, he exclaimed in a letter to Alyse Gregory, "How my crude, naive, genial America glows!"

Although Bourne had reason to feed his grudge on England, his attitude was characteristic of the younger generation, which discovered in England and France the cultural representatives of the battle it was waging at home. What better example of the Victorianism it had rejected in the Genteel Tradition than old

Anglo-Saxondom itself, with its "fatuous cheerfulness" and "incorrigible intellectual frivolity" and "permanent derangement of intellect from emotion"? What better example than France of its youthful modernism—of its delight in quick intelligence, its ardent fraternal sentiment, its responsiveness to social issues and capacity for social change, its pleasure in the taste and color and movement of life? When Bourne turned from London to Paris in December, he entered, he said, "a new world, where the values and issues of life got reinstated for me into something of their proper relative emphasis." To this world the reading of Rousseau's *Confessions* had been his introduction, for it had, he wrote Alyse Gregory, "cleared up for me a whole new democratic morality, and put the last touch upon the old English way of looking at the world, in which I was brought up." It had opened to him the culture of France, which, within less than a month, he felt had completed the "transvaluation of values begun ten years ago when my Calvinism began to crack."

Kept from much about him by his poor command of French, Bourne, nevertheless, established a more satisfactory life in Paris than he had in London. He settled near the Sorbonne, whose greatness he contrasted to "poor little Oxford." The intellectual orientation was agreeably sociological and psychological, and he read sociology in the Bibliothèque Ste. Geneviève and attended the lectures of Bouglé, Delacroix, and Durkheim. He associated with students who were as representative of Young France as he was of Young America (at this time, Youth was an international movement) and he was invited to speak to them about their ideals, the philosophy of William James, and the poetry of Whitman, who had influenced Jules Romains, the author of *La Vie unanime*. Although he had complained at first of the lack of feminine society and in desperation took tea with a silly married American woman—his description of her in a letter to Alyse Gregory is choice—he eventually found a French girl with whom he enjoyed an "intellectual flirtation," the girl of "Mon Ami," his most radiant portrait of youth. The campaign for parliamentary election aroused his political sympathies where the weary Liberal politics of London had not, and, if what and how much he wrote is any measure, the culture of France stimulated him more profoundly than that of any other country.

After France, he did not settle long anywhere because the pace of his travels increased and European life itself was unsettled. In Italy the political activity was as coruscating as the light, as clamorous as the marketplace. Bourne attended most to the mind of Young Italy through which, it seemed to him, "Nietzsche was raging": to the students demonstrating for Italia Irredenta, to the futurists in art, to the signs of modernism that, he believed, promised for Italy a "new renaissance of the twentieth century." He witnessed in Rome the violent three-day general strike of June—his taste of revolution—and was pleased with the solidarity of the radical classes; and he observed election night in Venice, which, he noted in his report, perhaps with mischievous intent, confirmed "the economic interpretation of politics." Working northward, he returned for the Bern Exposition to Switzerland, his land of delight, "a country . . . that knew how to use its resources for large social ends!" And then he went to Germany, where he studied enthusiastically its planned towns and housing schemes, its new architecture and decorative arts—the evidence of an efficient municipal science that was curiously "undemocratic in political form, yet ultrademocratic in policy and spirit"—but was troubled by the people, by their "thickness and sentimentality and . . . lack of critical sense." There his travel plans were altered and much that he hoped for came to an end. On July 31, he arrived in Berlin, where he experienced the hysteria and outbreak of the war under whose shadow he was to live for the remainder of his life.

The most important result of Bourne's travels was a clearer awareness of the nature and diversity of culture. This was the very thing he emphasized in his report as a corrective to the American tendency (especially dangerous in time of war) to consider the picturesque aspects rather than the fundamental emotional and intellectual differences of foreign countries. "My

most striking impression," he said, "was [of] the extraordinary **Randolph**
toughness and homogeneity of the cultural fabric in the dif- **Bourne**
ferent countries. . . . Each country was a distinct unit, the parts
of which . . . interpreted each other, styles and attitudes, literature, architecture, and social organization."

The three essays that he published in the *Atlantic Monthly*
during the summer and fall of his homecoming probe this
theme. "An Hour in Chartres" is an essay on cultural style—on
"the way things hang together, so that they seem the very
emanation of a sort of vast over-spreading communal taste."
"Maurice Barrès and the Youth of France" considers the cultural foundations of nationalism and the role of youth in its
preservation and advancement. In this essay, Bourne expresses
admiration for what Brooks, in *Letters and Leadership*, would
call "the collective spiritual life." He knows the evils of
nationalism, yet seeks the "intimate cultural fabric" so lacking in
America; and he offers a conception of nationalism, emotionally powerful but still somewhat vague, that enhances the
quality of life by satisfying social and mystical needs. Although
he understands the origins in French military defeat of Barrès'
idea and recognizes its essential traditionalism, he finds it over-
whelmingly attractive: "the nourishing influences of a rich
common culture in which our individualities are steeped, and
which each generation carries on freely, consciously, gladly the
traits of the race's genius,—this is a gospel to which one could
give one's self with wistfulness and love!" Here, for Bourne—
and youth—national culture has become an object of loyalty.

Finally, in "Our Cultural Humility," he applies the idea to
America, where the very appreciation of European culture
(Arnold's "the best") keeps us from engaging in the vital process
of our own culture and from producing indigenous art. He asks
us, therefore, to foster a national culture of our own: "This
cultural chauvinism is the most harmless of patriotisms; indeed
it is absolutely necessary for a true life of civilization." We have
already, as he himself had been learning, an indigenous tradition of great artists; he mentions here and in letters Emerson,

Thoreau, Whitman, William James, Henry James, Edward
MacDowell, and Augustus Saint-Gaudens. (Brooks, whose
*America's Coming-of-Age* would be more influential in forming
this generation's sense of the past, mentions favorably only
Whitman.) Now all we need do, he advises, is "turn our eyes
upon our own art for a time, shut ourselves in with our own
genius, and cultivate with an intense and partial pride what we
have already achieved."

The substance of this culture is conveyed best in another essay
of this time, "A Sociological Poet," where Bourne speaks of
Unanimism as Whitman "industrialized" and "sociologized."
He advocates the larger collective life of "democratic cama-
raderie," the replacement of the old individualistic life by a
new "mass-life" to be lived in the city; and he carefully distinguishes the emergent group feeling he desires from the herd
instinct, which fear rather than the warm social conscience
feeds. Bourne considers the metropolis to be the "human"
milieu and maintains that "the highest reality of the world is not
Nature or the Ego, but the Beloved Community"; and he
believes, as he wrote later in "American Use for German Ideals,"
that the pragmatism of James and Dewey and the social philosophy of Josiah Royce strengthen the possibility of such a democratic socialized life.

Bourne derived the functions of this culture from his experience in France and its form from his study of the civic art of
Germany. Whenever he defends German ideals or culture, as
in the essay cited above and in "A Glance at German 'Kultur,' "
he has in mind the civic art that he once told Carl Zigrosser was
"the king of the arts, because of its completely social nature." He
placed Hampstead Garden Suburb above any planned town in
Germany, but he placed Germany above all other nations, "in
the very vanguard of socialized civilization." In this respect,
Germany epitomized the twentieth century, which explained,
Bourne thought, American hostility toward her: she challenged
our attitudes and social habits, and, in repudiating her organization and collectivism, we were repudiating the "modest collec-

tivism" of our own progressive movement. Wherever he went in America—to the Midwest, for example, whose urban chaos he described in "Our Unplanned Cities"—he appreciated anew the achievement of Germany: "I love with a passionate love the ideals of social welfare, community sense, civic art, and applied science upon which it is founding itself. . . . I detest . . . the shabby and sordid aspect of American civilization—its frowsy towns, its unkempt countryside, its waste of life and resources."

Fed by subsequent experience and urged by the intense pressures of wartime, the lessons of the European year took form in Bourne's most important essay on American culture. "Trans-National America" (1916), which the admirably tolerant Sedgwick accepted for the *Atlantic*, was at once Bourne's most incisive analysis of the failure of the older generation and his clearest, most challenging directive to the younger generation. It presents his vision of the kind of culture to which America should aspire and the redeeming role such a culture would enable America to play in the debacle of European nationalisms; and when set up as an alternative to participation in the war ("the war—or American promise" of Bourne's "A War Diary"), this vision of culture provided the test of pragmatic sociology. Bourne's vision anticipated the program of *The Seven Arts*, the magazine that Robert Frost said died "a-Bourning," and first disclosed the landscape described in books such as Waldo Frank's *Our America*.

This deeply personal vision has collective sources. In *The Promise of American Life*, Herbert Croly had spoken of "an over-national idea" and had cited Crèvecoeur's account of the melting process that made the American a new man. To this notion of Americanization, Israel Zangwill's play *The Melting-Pot* had given currency and approval; but Horace Kallen, whom Bourne knew, had repudiated it and proposed instead a "federation of nationalities," or "cultural pluralism," as he subsequently called it. During these years, cosmopolitanism, associated with the city and its immigrant populations, was a cultural stance toward America as well as Europe. H. W. L.

Dana, a teacher at Columbia whose dismissal during the war
Bourne protested, wrote him, in 1914, that Columbia was
"more than national," more than "Anglo-Saxon"; and writing
from Europe to Edward Murray (a friend described in "Fergus")
Bourne had observed that "the good things in the American
temperament and institutions are not English . . . but are the
fruit of our far superior cosmopolitanism." As a child, he had
been offended by the unattractive Polish girls who worked in the
kitchens of Bloomfield; but now he appreciated immigrant life,
the Italian settlement, for example, at Emerald Lake (similar to
the Guinea Hill district of William Carlos Williams' nearby
city) which, he said, injected "sudden vitality into our Puritan
town."

"Trans-National America" faced directly the problem of immigration and the making of Americans that had become a
conspicuously serious issue of our culture when the show of
loyalties provoked by the war revealed our cultural diversity.
Sedgwick disapproved of the essay—he called it "radical and
unpatriotic" when informing Bourne of the many commenda-
tions it received—and insisted that America was "a country
created by English instinct and dedicated to the Anglo-Saxon
ideal." One recalls another editor of the *Atlantic*, another
"hereditary American" (the phrase is Van Wyck Brooks's) who
warned us to guard the gates; and Brooks put their fears very well
when, in *America's Coming-of-Age*, he retold the story of Rip
Van Winkle, the story of an innocent old America that hears in
its sleep, not Henry Hudson's men, but "the movement of
peoples ["Jews, Lithuanians, Magyars and German socialists"],
the thunder of alien wants." Bourne, speaking, he said, as an
Anglo-Saxon, threatened the Anglo-Saxon hegemony by announcing that "America shall be what the immigrant will have a
hand in making it, and not what a ruling class . . . decides that
America shall be made," by questioning the efficacy of
Americanization and redefining the meaning of Americanism.

Bourne's most damaging charge is twofold: that the Anglo-
Saxon has not transformed the "colony into a real nation, with a

tenacious, richly woven fabric of native culture" and that its theory of Americanization is destructive of this very possibility. For Americanization has not produced socialized men but insipid mass-men, "half-breeds," he says, who have been deprived of their native cultures and given instead "the American culture of the cheap newspaper, the 'movies,' the popular song, the ubiquitous automobile." In this way, Americanization contributes to the wreckage rather than creation of culture:

"Just so surely as we tend to disintegrate these nuclei [various immigrant cultures] of nationalistic culture do we tend to create hordes of men and women without a spiritual country, cultural outlaws, without taste, without standards but those of the mob. We sentence them to live on the most rudimentary planes of American life. The influences at the center of the nuclei are centripetal. They make for the intelligence and the social values which mean an enhancement of life. And just because the foreign-born retains this expressiveness is he likely to be a better citizen of the American community. The influences at the fringe, however, are centrifugal, anarchical. They make for detached fragments of peoples. Those who came to find liberty achieve only license. They become the flotsam and jetsam of American life, the downward undertow of our civilization with its leering cheapness and falseness of taste and spiritual outlook, the absence of mind and sincere feeling which we see in our slovenly towns . . . and in the vacuous faces of the crowds on the city street. This is the cultural wreckage of our time . . . America has as yet no impelling integrating force. It makes too easily for this detritus of cultures."

This eloquent passage arises from the deepest tensions of Bourne's social imagination: "I must be interpreting everything," he once said, "in relation to some Utopian ideal, or some vision of perfection." It suggests some of the values he hoped to restore by means of "an enterprise of integration." The new peoples were "threads of living and potent cultures, blindly striving to weave themselves into a novel international nation." Having at their disposal the very agencies that had transformed

Bourne and enabled his vision, they might, with its help and practical civic measures of the kind he outlined in "A Moral Equivalent for Military Service," someday achieve it.

"Trans-National America" was not published in the *New Republic* because its editors, as Sedgwick recognized, never gave Bourne space enough to work out his ideas and because, from the start, as Bourne complained, they never gave him any say in policy. When he returned from Europe, the *New Republic* was being organized and staffed; it was the forum he had been seeking, and it gave him a place at a thousand dollars a year. These wages, he felt, were minimal; he was, so he told Alyse Gregory, "a very insignificant retainer." Though he attended the weekly luncheons of the editors, he found his relations with them uncomfortable and remained outside their circle. Sedgwick had warned him of the dangers of magazines—that most are not "loyal to ideas" and are "treacherous to taste" and that radical ones often "set their sails to other breezes." Of Croly and crew, he said: "they are the solemnest procession that ever marched. . . . They can celebrate a Puritan Thanksgiving, but whether they will make the Fourth of July hum, remains to be seen." When Bourne expressed disappointment at Croly's reluctance to "go in instanter for smashing and quarreling," Sedgwick counseled him to give the magazine time to develop a soul. He did, maintaining a connection with the *New Republic* until his death, but he was dismayed.

On coming home, he had tried to reestablish his Columbia life. For a time he lived with Carl Zigrosser at the Phipps model tenements on East 31st Street and socialized—and fell in love—with Barnard girls. But eventually his center shifted. The *New Republic* set the boundaries of his intellectual world: the Public Library, the Russell Sage Foundation, and Greenwich Village. And there he began to meet other people, Elizabeth Shepley Sergeant, for example, who introduced him, in the summer of 1915, to the elite New England summer colony at Dublin, New Hampshire. ("Housekeeping for Men," a light essay, describes the cabin life that was sustained by dinners and evenings with worthies like Amy Lowell and the Abbott Thayers, the latter of special importance to Bourne because through them he met Scofield Thayer who tried to promote his interests in the *Dial*.) He also met Elsie Clews Parsons, a vigorous, intelligent anthropologist and sociologist, who offered him a haven at Lenox, Massachusetts. His typically full social life is recorded in a datebook for 1916, where one now finds the names of Agnes de Lima, a social worker, and Esther Cornell, an actress, the one the guardian spirit of his life and legacy, the other, her friend, the beautiful girl who would have married him and with whom, at last, he entered a mature emotional life. With them, and Frances Anderson, he shared a house at Caldwell, New Jersey, during the summer of 1916. Agnes de Lima recalls that "it was a delicious setting for R., the center of attention with three devoted and high spirited girl companions paying him obeisance"; and she conveys the quality of devotion that still enshrines Bourne's reputation when she writes that "we all adored him of course, fascinated, stimulated, enormously fired by his brilliant intellect, his thrilling range of interests, his unique flair for personal relationships." (One is grateful for Edward Dahlberg's not so foolish surmise, that Bourne was "a sensual gypsy Leporello with [to?] women." All remember his piano-playing—music, he once approvingly noted in a book review, was an emotional equivalent for otherwise unexperienced raptures.) Of male friendships he said very little, but one sees, in his relationships with Paul Rosenfeld and Van Wyck Brooks, that they were strong and good, founded on the conviction of a common intellectual enterprise.

For the *New Republic* Bourne wrote almost one hundred pieces, nearly half of them reviews, the remainder articles, portraits, and editorials. Occasionally he was permitted to write about war issues, but he had been recruited to write about other matters, and most of his work was confined to education and a small but significant amount to city planning. Many of his essays on education were reprinted in *The Gary Schools* (1916), a study of the work-study-and-play schools that William Wirt, a disciple of Dewey, had organized in the new steel town and was proposing for New York City, and in *Education and Living* (1917), a general collection held together by Bourne's insistence that the long process of education be a living now, not a postponement of life. These books contributed to Bourne's reputation as (to cite one reviewer) "the most brilliant educational critic of the younger generation," but neither has the solidity of achievement that makes reputations permanent. In the first, he was encumbered by the publisher's demands that he write for teachers and superintendents and subdue his enthusiasm for Wirt; in the second, repetition drains away the force some of the essays have singly. These books, however, represent the mastery of a field. They develop the primary themes of *Youth and Life* and bridge Bourne's personal and social concern for human fulfillment. And in them one begins to appreciate the extent to which Bourne has become a publicist of the kind he admired in J. A. Hobson—a man with "immense stores of knowledge, poise of mind, and yet radical philosophy and gifts of journalistic expression."

In retrospect, Agnes de Lima depreciated these books, remarking, however, that Bourne was finely perceptive about the needs of children, a truth confirmed by "Ernest: or Parent for a Day," a charming *Atlantic* essay that readers may find sufficiently representative of this strand of his thought. Yet there is value (and pleasure) in reading more: the realization of the alliance of educational with modern thought, of the place of education in democratic society as an essential and democratic process, as a revivifier of its faith and instrument of its reform. *Democracy and Education*—such was the title of Dewey's challenging book of 1916, when education had become an urgent domestic issue and no other social enterprise seemed to partisans like Bourne so hopeful, rational, and democratic. "To decide what kind of a school we want," he said, "is almost to decide what kind of society we want"—a disclosure of faith that may

explain the presence among his unpublished papers of an essay

(of 1918) extolling the efforts of the British to prepare for social
reconstruction by initiating educational reforms during the war.

Much of Bourne's work before and after America entered the war was educational, either about education or in the interest of overcoming what, in 1915, he called our "mental unprepared-ness." War had been the means, he explained, of shocking even his up-to-date generation into an awareness of a world where war happens, and it had given the intellectuals the task of replacing the "old immutable idealism," no longer credible, with a "new experimental idealism." "We should make the time," he told them, "one of education." Instead of military preparedness, our need, he said, was "to learn how to live rather than die; to be teachers and creators, not engines of destruc-tion." Before war was declared, he had worked for peace, the essential condition of democratic reform; for the American Association of International Conciliation he edited a sym-posium of peace proposals and programs, *Towards an Enduring Peace* (1916). And he had been a leader of the Committee for Democratic Control, which tried to halt the descent to war by publishing in the newspapers (and the *New Republic!*) antiwar advertisements and appeals for popular referendums. With war declared—"the effective and decisive work" that the editors of the *New Republic* claimed had been accomplished "by a class which must be . . . described as the 'intellectuals' "—Bourne took on the role for which he is most often remembered: he became the critic of the war strategy and, especially, of the intellectuals who had broken faith with pragmatism and had closed out the promise of American life by eagerly joining "the greased slide toward war."

It is fashionable now to admire Bourne's unyielding spirit and intellectual rectitude but to pity him for assuming that the drift of things is susceptible to human mastery. When depressed by the penalties of lonely opposition, he also indulged himself in deterministic views (see "Old Tyrannies"). Yet however much in a metaphysical sense drift may be a true account of things, it is not a true account of the diplomacy that led to war. Here events seemed to have their own way but were actually chosen and, as Bourne maintained (see especially his comments on the presidency in "The State"), other choices might have prevailed. The question seldom raised by those who, curiously, speak up for intellectuals but impugn their force is the one with which Bourne in effect challenged the boastful intellectuals of the *New Republic*: had the intellectuals taken Bourne's position, would the outcome have been otherwise? By assuming that it would, one grants Bourne the condition of justly understanding him.

The wayward course of the war strategy and the policy of the *New Republic*, which Bourne cogently analyzed in five essays published in 1917 in *The Seven Arts* (collected in *Untimely Papers*, 1919), is now of less interest than his assessment of pragmatism and inquiry into the motives and roles of intellectuals. War taught Bourne that pragmatism was not so much a philosophy for fair weather as one requiring for its survival an open world of alternatives. Where choice is impossible, pragmatism ceases to exist, for intelligence ceases to have a function; in "total" or "absolute" situations like war, it is without leverage. This was the point Bourne directed specifically to John Dewey, whom he had once petitioned in an essay of praise to become an intellectual leader in "the arena of the concrete," and who, since 1916, had done so by becoming the philosopher-statesman of the *New Republic* and *The Seven Arts* (until July 1917, when Bourne and Brooks replaced him) and of the *Dial*.

To read Dewey's essays is an uncomfortable experience, wholly justifying Bourne's judgment that the philosophy of Dewey "breaks down . . . when it is used to grind out interpretations for the present crisis." Dewey speciously justified the use of force and was concerned more with winning intellectual assent to participation than clarifying the values for American national life that he claimed would come of it. Once committed to war, he wished only to get the job done in a "business like way." He insisted that "an end is something which concerns results rather than aspirations," and considered pacifists, including Bourne, "passivists," victims of "moral innocency" and "futility." Yet aspirations were the issue. For Dewey, father of a noble concep-

170

tion of America and leader of the educational work to be done, had himself chosen war, had turned from his own best vision and had become, as Bourne, feeling betrayed, said, a fatuous instrumentalist who believed naïvely that he was controlling the "line of inevitables" war brings. "It may be pragmatism to be satisfied with things that work," Bourne wrote in an unpublished essay, "but it is a very shallow one." Pragmatism was always for him a philosophy in which ends count, and he remained true to it by demanding alternative courses of action and by keeping in view the "American promise"—and nowhere so demonstrably as in these *timely* papers, where, in the exercise of intellectual responsibility, he mastered his materials, argument, and tone in writing of unusual incandescence.

As Dwight Macdonald recognized (in *Politics*, his personal attempt to propose courses during another war), Bourne had "continued along the way [the pragmatists] had all been following until the war began." They, however, took the path Bourne describes in "The War and the Intellectuals." Feeling that to be out of the war was "at first to be disreputable and finally almost obscene," they assumed "the leadership for war of those very classes whom the American democracy has been immemorially fighting." Joyfully they accepted this leadership and willingly abandoned criticism for propaganda, "the sewage of the war spirit." Neutrality had put the intellectuals under the strain of thinking; it was easier to act; and action brought relief from indecision. So the thinkers, with their "colonial" (Anglo-Saxon) sympathies and their eagerness to be responsible for the world, with their "emotional capital" idle for want of domestic spending but ready for investment in Europe, "dance[d] with reality." And this reversion to "primitive" ways, though understandable, was not only costly beyond measure ("the whole era has been spiritually wasted") and supremely ironic (for how can war and democracy be coupled?) but especially shameful because it led the intellectuals to repudiate everything that becomes the intellectual and to impugn the work of the few who were peaceminded. Included in their company, moreover, were those younger intellectuals of a different kind whom the elder prag-

matists had trained: those "experts in the new science of administration" hailed by Lippmann in *Drift and Mastery*, whom
Bourne now found "vague as to what kind of society they want,
or what kind of society America needs, but . . . equipped with all
the administrative attitudes and talents necessary to attain it."

Bourne himself accepted the role of the "excommunicated,"
of an "irreconcilable." He tried to make his apathy toward the
war "take the form of a heightened energy and enthusiasm for
the education, the art, the interpretation that make for life in the
midst of the world of death." But the role, which he defined in
such therapeutic essays as "Below the Battle" and "The Artist in
Wartime" (unpublished), was a very hard one, requiring, as
Croly long before had warned the intellectuals, "sharp weapons,
intense personal devotion, and a positive indifference to consequences." In a sense, Bourne was a war casualty, unwounded,
he bravely said, by "all the shafts of panic, patriotism, and
national honor," yet deeply dispirited. He suffered—more,
according to Elsie Clews Parsons, from the renegation of the
intellectuals than from personal exclusion—and he was hurt by
the bitterness that he predicted would grow and "spread out like
a stain over the younger American generation." He frequently
expressed the wish to escape to the "great good place" and, as if
desperately fighting to attain it, struck out, in the book reviews to
which he was limited in his last year, at those who seemed to
stand in his way: he quarreled with Dewey over a disciple's book;
discredited Sedgwick's judgment by slashing at Paul Shorey's
strident defense of the New Humanism; turned on Dean Keppel, who was currently working for the War Department, by
gratuitously pointing out that "his mind is liberal and yet it
serves reaction"; and needlessly punished Brander Matthews in
order to express his misgivings over wartime Columbia.

Yet what is impressive in Bourne's career, finally, is the
attempt to master disillusionment and despair by recovering the
very history of his generation, by learning the lessons it had to
teach and plotting the course it might take. Bourne never
shirked the responsibility of thought and began the "anxious
speculation" that he told Brooks "should normally follow the

destruction of so many hopes." The most ambitious project of this kind was the long unfinished essay, "The State," in which he vented the "scorn for institutions" that had once combined "with a belief in their reform." This essay, overrated by those who consider it an especially prescient political treatise, has the frantic quality of one whom events have forced back on himself—its companion work was the unfinished autobiographical novel. Bourne did not write it because the state, as legend claims, coerced him, but because he needed to understand the social behavior of the time: why, for example, an apathetic nation goes to war and centralization of power contributes not to the creation of social wealth (as Croly had once said it would) but to its spoliation in war. The essay exhibits a sharp analytical power but also a conspiratorial mentality: Bourne makes the Anglo-Saxons the betrayers of democracy throughout American history and explains the failure of reform in his "ephemeral" time by ascribing it to an evil power which he thinks simply awaited the war to make itself known. The cynicism of the essay is protective and, like its bitterness, was accepted too uncritically by the next generation. Bourne appeared to put too high the odds against idealism, ruling out the very agency that he still believed to be necessary and efficacious.

"Bourne was keenly conscious of lost values," Elsie Clews Parsons wrote, "but he was resourceful in compensations." And by way of exemplification, she noted the suspect but important strategy of his essay: "In his essay on the State he had begun to battle for distinctions between State, Nation, and Country, in which the State became the conceptual scapegoat for the sins of patriotism, leaving Nation and Country immaculate and worthy of devotion."

Bourne's goal had not altered, only the way. War taught him what any crisis may teach a reformer: that society is not as plastic as the ideas in our minds, that freedom runs into limitation, that wholesale social reconstruction must submit to the slower processes of education. It did not destroy his faith in political action, although it made him distrustful of the "cult of politics" and increased his appreciation of the social uses of personal expression—of the resources "malcontents" might find in art and criticism. His own essays in criticism such as "The Art of Theodore Dreiser" and "The Immanence of Dostoevsky" reveal a maturing critical sense and represent the kind of criticism he defined in "Traps for the Unwary" and in the closing pages of "The History of a Literary Radical." As he had pointed out earlier in a review of H. L. Mencken, puritanism was no longer a significant cultural issue; criticism had work to do more important than moralizing. For the real enemy of art was the widening, responsive, but still genteel public that wanted "the new without the unsettling."

A "new criticism," accordingly, was needed to rectify "the uncritical hospitality of current taste" and to give the artists, who promised, he believed, "a rich and vibrant literary era," an "intelligent, pertinent, absolutely contemporaneous criticism, which shall be both severe and encouraging"—the latter to be obtained only when "the artist himself has turned critic and set to work to discover and interpret in others the motives and values and efforts he feels in himself." This criticism, Bourne explained to Harriet Monroe, editor of *Poetry*, was not aesthetic in the sense of being merely appreciative or of providing "esoteric enjoyment" (what she called "pink-tea adulation"), nor did it treat art wholly in terms of itself or move "hazily in a mist of values and interpretations." He insisted that it also be social criticism—that it take into account "ideas and social movements and the peculiar intellectual and spiritual color of the time." To have conceived of these requisites of criticism and of a "new classicism" demanding "power with restraint, vitality with harmony, a fusion of intellect and feeling, and a keen sense of the artistic conscience" is evidence of Bourne's unfailing sensitivity to the direction of his culture and, although the critic he seeks had need of the strengths of an Eliot, Pound, and Edmund Wilson, evidence of his awareness that the work he set himself should be less prophetic (not like that undertaken by Brooks and Waldo Frank) and nearer to his developing capacities.

174    In an autobiographical essay "The History of a Literary

Radical," he called himself a literary radical chiefly to distinguish the intellectual type of his generation from that of the
older generation. The literary radical possesses an imagination
at once aesthetic and sociological. He wishes to nurture his art
in society and to use it to reform and enhance social life. His
most common difficulty is the adjustment of aesthetic and social
allegiances. In his own case, Bourne told Elizabeth Shepley
Sergeant, "the reformer got such a terrific start in my youth over
the artist that I'm afraid the latter is handicapped for life." But he
knew, as he said with respect to his friend John Burroughs, that
the "eternally right way and attitude of the intellectual life" is to
look at the world with "the eye of the artist" and to employ one's
science to "illumine . . . artistic insight"; and this he always tried
to do by being radical in another sense: by going back to the root
of perception. For all of his science, Bourne remained an
essayist who addressed the world in the first person and in his
writing attempted to reproduce the atmosphere of discussion
that he valued so much, and whose style, as Alvin Johnson
noted, possessed "warmth with light [and] logical straightfor-
wardness combined with charm and sympathy." He had, to
borrow a phrase from Santayana's applicable discussion of
romantics and Transcendentalists, "a first-hand mind." Autobiography was the mode he cherished, the staple thread of all
his work, his way of being true to himself and his circumstances
and of bearing witness, which makes his true inheritors not so
much those who took over his topics as those who discovered for
themselves the necessity and resources of an autobiographical
method. The autobiographical novel upon which Bourne was
working at the time of his death is not of interest as a novel but as
an example of what, at the beginning of his career, he said was
needed: "true autobiographies, told in terms of the adventure
that life is."

Bourne began "An Autobiographic Chapter" by telling how,
when he was six, his family had moved from a house on a back
street to another house offering a life more spacious: "And his
expanding life leaped to meet the wide world." This characteris-

tic fronting of the world with "its new excitements and pleasures" was, he wrote, "like a rescue, like getting air when one is
smothering." This image was perhaps more premonitory than
he knew when, in the last dismal months of his life, he used it to
describe the sense of relief he had felt on the occasion of his first
rescue; for on December 22, 1918, in his thirty-second year,
with the war over and new prospects before him, he succumbed
to influenza.

The legends about Bourne that almost immediately arose
created the impression of martyrdom that his example of intellectual courage neither sustains nor needs, and hindered a just
appreciation of his work. He deserves the prominent place he
has acquired in the history of his generation and, because his
actual literary achievement was small, a modest place in the
literary tradition that in his time he was one of the few to value.
At the end of "The History of a Literary Radical," he speaks of "a
certain eternal human tradition of abounding vitality and moral
freedom" that may be found in such American writers as
Thoreau, Whitman, and Mark Twain. This is the tradition he
served.

Bourne, yes; but first Wilson. Edmund Wilson is too important to me to be passed over because I have nothing to place
here as a token of the book I wrote about him. He follows
Sullivan and precedes Bourne—is so much the central figure
in a sequence of thought and feeling that to fail to mention
him now would distort the record.

The early years of the 1960s during which I worked on him
were the birth years of the New Left, a time of teach-ins and
civil rights and peace demonstrations, a time of public and
private crises (public and private are inextricable, as Wilson
knew), crises that for me were almost entirely matters of the
generations: of parent and children, teacher and students,
younger scholar and older colleagues. With the coming of the
new decade these relationships were disruped and acerbated,

and my total human environment became chaotic and convulsive. The difficulties of teacher and students were not as great as the others because I was able at last to teach face-to-face, to direct theses and give seminars (Edmund Wilson was the subject of the first of these). The difficulties of the others were extreme, not unusual but nevertheless devastating.

I do not remember these years with pleasure. For me, they were a dark time, a discontinuity not unlike those that threatened Wilson with disintegration. My stay was writing—and writing about him. He was to me what Justice Holmes was to him, a phenomenal man whose example is sustaining. Not only did he practice the kind of criticism I wanted to write, he defined, as his own use of "practice" indicates, a literary vocation, the kind of professionalism, opposed to careerism, of which I approved. He had intellectual endurance and persistence, qualities whose importance I now recognized and appreciated; and his work spoke to me of matters of immediate concern—of continuity and survival. It may be that this shows the extent to which I had become middle-aged. Perhaps I so readily identified with him at this time because his own attitude toward the present secured my ambivalence. I was a partisan of change—of the kind that conserves humanity—but I also felt defensive and hostile toward the young and the old who, in unsettling my world, were asking me to change.

My situation at the time of writing about Wilson (and, for that matter, Bourne and William Carlos Williams) may be considered a "descent," to borrow Williams' word for the necessary journey to chaos—and renewed contact with feelings and things—that quickens the imagination and restores the self. To write anything is to take that journey and to know its terrors, even, since this is a condition of work to which we accustom ourselves, to find the risk pleasurable. Yet the journey we take is not quite the same as the one we are forced to take; the risk of the latter is not calculated or limited, and the journey is longer—farther, deeper—and more terrible. In the former, we undertake the journey in order to write; in the latter, we write in order to endure and surmount the journey itself. In what I wrote at this time I chose the former journey, but found myself writing in order to overcome the exigencies of the latter. This explains not only my immediate attraction to these courageous writers, but both the personal and formal elements of the writing—the more than usual degree to which I am present (and introduce the present) in it and the more conspicuous shaping of the composition. These books— necessarily, I feel—were *written*, written in the awareness that one could not be careless. Their forms also address the times.

That I lived in my situation is evident in the themes of these books. That I lived through it is evident in their equanimity and in the restoration of good will toward the young. I dedicated *Edmund Wilson* to my children—to the new generation—because it was doubly a testament. And in the little book on Bourne, written in 1965, I renewed my defense of the young, of the Party of Hope, by way of repossessing the generous transcendental-pragmatic spirit that underlies so much of contemporary radical thought. I rehearsed a generational conflict comparable in severity and range of issues to that of the present—that it tallied in respect to so many things, in particular the repudiation of WASP culture and the adventurism of war, sharpened its edge as well as demonstrated the uses of the past and its continuity (the issues were its legacy), ideas that I wanted the younger generation neither to overlook nor disdain. This was also true of the university, whose uses, as Bourne found, were not wholly contemptible.

# AN INTRODUCTION TO WILLIAM CARLOS WILLIAMS

AT THE close of *Paterson IV* (1951), William Carlos Williams' epic poem of a poet and his culture, a man, presumably young, emerges from the sea, rests on the sand, puts on his faded overalls, climbs the bank, samples a beach plum and spits out the seed, and then, followed by his dog, heads inland. This episode—a representative anecdote of Williams' work— expresses an indomitable faith in the renewal of culture: the faith of a poet who, with great difficulty, had followed a similar course and, at least in the account of the poem, where persona and poet eventually merge, had failed his culture by failing to realise his "dream of / the whole poem," the poem that gives us our whole culture by "lifting . . . an environment to expression," by bringing it to form. He acknowledged during the composition of the poem that it was "an experiment, a failing experiment, toward assertion with broken means but an assertion, always, of a new and total culture."

The poem itself had tested his faith, for in it he had traced American history in the movement of the Passaic River to the sea, the "blood dark sea" of the violent, decadent present, and, like the poet in the poem, had wondered at the wonder of his faith:

                                              —you cannot believe
                                      that it can begin again, again, here
                                          again        here

Yet having faith also in the virtue of seeds ("the seed that floats to shore, one word," he told José García Villa, ". . . is that which alone can save us"), he believed that it would begin again, that the "Seed / of Venus" would return and he would see (again) "a girl standing upon a tilted shell, rose / pink." This girl, the Venus of his vision, is the "Beautiful Thing" he had always pursued. She is the rare presence of both the self and the environment, the very being of himself the poet wishes to reveal and the spirit of his place; and she is best discovered in the unity of self-and-environment, the flowering that art and genuine culture achieve. "Rigor of beauty is the quest"—these words prefacing the poem summarize a lifetime's work.

In his *Autobiography* (1951), Williams ends the narrative of his career as a poet by commenting on *Paterson* and speaks again, conspicuously, of this episode: "The man rises from the sea where the river appears to have lost its identity and accompanied by his faithful bitch, obviously a Chesapeake Bay retriever, turns inland toward Camden where Walt Whitman, much traduced, lived the latter years of his life and died." In a publisher's release, Williams called the man from the sea "Odysseus," thereby naming his awareness of the Greek epic against whose triumphant cultural achievement he tried his own work as well as his awareness of his celebrated contemporaries, Joyce and Pound, who had used the *Odyssey* to literary ends and against whom he was trying himself. But Odysseus named another, profounder motive: he was a wanderer and his emergence from the sea reminded Williams of his own emergence, of his homecoming and initiation as an American poet in "The Wanderer," the long poem first published in *The Egoist*, in 1914, along with work by Joyce and Pound. This poem, he said, took the place of the *Endymion*-like poem he had worked on during the years of his medical studies and 180 internship—took the place but did not wholly replace that romantic poem which was now recast under the influence of Whitman. Now—

> crossing the ferry
> With the great towers of Manhattan before me,
> Out at the prow with the sea wind blowing

—he set himself his task ("How shall I be a mirror to this modernity?") and to undertake it finally submitted to a baptismal death and rebirth of poetic consciousness in the native waters of the "filthy Passaic." Williams explained in the press release that "Odysseus swims in as a man must always do, he doesn't drown, he is too able, but, accompanied by his dog, strikes inland (toward Camden) to begin again." The ending of *Paterson* reenacts "The Wanderer" and proposes the same inward path of poetic discovery.

But the man from the sea is not the poet of the poem, now old. He is the poet of another, a new generation, and may belong to the generation of Allen Ginsberg, whose letters are included in the poem not merely to record the recognition Williams was beginning to receive from younger poets but the generous response with which he had always met them and the willingness with which he now relinquished to them his great poetic task. The poet in *Paterson* (both Williams and for much of the poem a genteel man of letters of the type of Eliot's Prufrock) is especially troubled in his poetic quest by what a new generation of poets, partly because of Williams' example, finds easier—the acceptance of the immediate environment, the direct approach, contact. Like the man in the sea and the poet of "The Wanderer," they risk descent into the chaos of self and world, the primal ground of art, and by means of art "rise" from the sea and accomplish the ascent to order and form that, in Williams' description of the creative process and its saving work, is its hopeful rhythmic accompaniment.

The man from the sea, moreover, is a prototype of the true discoverer of America. He is a hero of the kind depicted by Williams in *In the American Grain* (1925), the classic study of contacting the American environment praised by D. H. Law-

181

rence, who also recognized in touch a new adventurous way of
being an American. For the true discoverer (in his overalls)
strikes inland, meets erotically the expectation of the land, finds
nurture in it, seeds it, and, like his dog, searches it closely,
particularly, sensuously. He is a "voluptuary" of the landscape
like Boone, has the "Indian wisdom" of the senses advocated by
Thoreau; and he goes inward by following Whitman's advice to
the poet to study out the land, "its idioms and men." By turning
inward he also emulates Poe, whose greatness, according to
Williams, was grounded in this American gesture of repudiation
("he turned his back and faced inward, to originality, with the
identical gesture of a Boone"). Now, coming to Camden, he
finds a source of the American tradition, finds Whitman, who,
Williams said, began the necessary work of the new culture by
breaking "the dominance of the iambic pentameter in English
prosody." And further inland still, at Rutherford, he finds
Williams, who felt that his addition to this tradition, his greatest
achievement, had been the very measure, a new measure flexible enough to both articulate and order American experience,
that he had discovered in the writing of this poem. [1]

Van Wyck Brooks, a contemporary critic of culture whose
diagnosis of American barrenness contributed to Williams' conception of his task, might have found in the poet's life and
determination to strike up for a new world the material of an
"exemplary tale." Brooks's "cautionary tales"—*The Ordeal of
Mark Twain* (1920) and the *Pilgrimage of Henry James*
(1925)—told stories familiar to Williams. He knew the incubus
of puritanism: the suburban, middle-class, Unitarian boy who
wrote his mother that "I have done things against my own
feelings and convictions because you wanted me to" later told
Valéry Larbaud in *In the American Grain* that "you have never
felt it [puritanism] stinking all about you." He knew also the

---

1 Williams always acknowledged Pound's large contribution to a new measure. Pound fulfilled his pact with Whitman: "It was you that broke new
wood / Now is the time for carving." ("A Pact")

dismal state of cultural things that had alarmed the generation of America's coming-of-age: "*Lohengrin* in ITALIAN, SUNG AT MANHATTAN"—this was one sign of the times he noted in *The Great American Novel* (1923). And his earliest confrere, Ezra Pound, whose influence he humorously acknowledged by saying "Before meeting Ezra Pound is like B.C. and A.D.," had followed James by going to Europe. "Pound ran to Europe in a hurry," Williams said in *Contact*, the little magazine that he and Robert McAlmon edited in the early years of the twenties in order to countervail this centrifugal tendency ("We lack interchange of ideas in our country more than we lack foreign precept"). Pound's expatriation, he felt, was understandable, but consequently "he had not sufficient ground to stand on for more than perhaps two years." As late as the writing of *Paterson*, which once more tested the value of his own decision to stay, he recalled "the men that ran / and could run off." But Brooks, it seems, did not know or sufficiently appreciate Williams' early work. Later on, he wrote a preface to the poet's collected stories and treated him as an example of his own theory of localism, but that was after Williams himself had used *The Autobiography* to tell the exemplary tale of an American poet.

Williams was probably the last important American poet to insist on seriously playing out the drama of cultural allegiance that had so much concerned the writers and artists of the nineteenth century. This issue, at least in its old terms, is no longer of moment, and we are now likely to consider it, as Randall Jarrell did in a review of *Paterson*, a "dreary imaginary war in which America and the Present are fighting against Europe and the Past." It was never that simple, though in depicting it even Williams followed the old melodrama by casting himself as an American village innocent and T. S. Eliot as a cosmopolitan sophisticate. His allegiance, however, was a matter neither of patriotic nationalism nor of sentimental infatuation, and it is not adequately accounted for by Pound's explanations: the poet's resentment of his father's English nationality, and the special advantage of his diverse immigrant

background (he did not have "in his ancestral endocrines the
arid curse of our nation").

Williams' allegiance is better assessed if one remembers that
his own emergence as a poet was part of the American literary
renaissance of the years of renewed cultural aspiration just
before and after the First World War. He was one of the group of
cosmopolitan cultural nationalists who recognized in the revolutionary crisis of society and sensibility called "modernism" a
challenge to seek again on native grounds the promise of American life. America and modernism, he believed, were equatable,
issuing in the new, and in a liberating conception of culture—
that "culture of immediate references" of which he wrote so
brilliantly in the essay "The American Background." For him
the stake was freedom of self-origination: the recognition and
sovereignty of the organic impulse that moves all living things
(the "it" of "if it does not drive us, / it is vain," as he said later in
"Deep Religious Faith"). Culture, he maintained, "isn't a thing:
it's an act"; it is "the realization of the qualities of a place in
relation to the life which occupies it . . . the act of lifting these
things into an ordered and utilized whole." And it is relative, a
vital order of the immediate, a local labor of the imagination,
what he called elsewhere "an open formation," not the arbitrary
imposition of order by anything extrinsic, distant, abstract, the
kind of absolute order that he believed had been the profound
cause of the American Revolution and of our cultural colonialism. Defined in this way, the cultural issue goes beyond a
conflict of nationalities and becomes a fundamental issue of our
time: the restoration of primary culture, the adjustment of
Culture, the secondary culture bequeathed by the past, to the
vital needs it has displaced. Ortega called this, in 1923, "the
modern theme"—"culture, reason, art and ethics . . . must
enter the service of life." And Kenneth Burke, reviewing
Williams' work in 1922, formulated it well when he said that
"contact might be said to resolve into the counterpart of Culture."

184  The necessity of a culture of contact is what Williams' life and

work confront and exemplify. The conception of a dynamic, vital, relative (relative to us: related) culture underlies his art, which may be considered a flowering in imaginative forms of his perception of the particular and the local—a flowering of universal significance, he claimed, just because of this. This conception of culture required that he stay put (the practice of medicine helped), that he enter into immediate life (again by way of his "medicine" and the "*tactus eruditis*" of a physician), and that he discover the ground under his feet (historical America in *In the American Grain*, the recent past in the novels *White Mule* and *In The Money*, the present American scene in *The Great American Novel* and *Life Along The Passaic River*— ranges of history that *Paterson* brings together). And it forced him to reconsider his art, its materials and formal means, the agency of imagination in its making, its personal and social ends.

One first encounters in Williams' work the familiar modernism of most of his contemporaries in literature—the antimodernism provoked by the great industrial, scientific and democratic revolutions of the nineteenth and twentieth centuries. In "An After Song," a poem that characterizes *The Tempers* (1913), it is represented by a disquieting "modern twilight." This carefully executed poem belongs to the period when Williams was still in tutelage to Pound, still treating the conventional "poetic" subject matter of poetry in conventional ways. In the same volume, however, "Contemporania," its title taken from some of Pound's recent poems, shows Williams already aware of the "flower devices" by which he would people "the barren country"; and "The Wanderer," the poem announcing his vocation as a poet, published in the following year and used in later collections to preface his work, shows his readiness to mirror "this modernity"—such common aspects of contemporary metropolitan America as the Paterson strike, flamboyant Broadway, and the abject countryside—the vulgar or the "anti-poetic," as Wallace Stevens called it, noting also that it was Williams' "spirit's cure." In *Al Que Quiere!* (1917), the defiantly titled major book of poems in which a poet of originality and force first clearly speaks, he asked in "Sub Terra" to be joined by other poets with "earthy tastes" ("You to come with me / poking into Negro houses"), mocked middle-class respectability and success, exhibited some of the things that had made him want to subtitle the book "the pleasures of democracy"—the Negro of "Canthara," for example, and the girl of "The Young Housewife"—and demonstrated in "To a Solitary Disciple" some of the lessons of modern painting that had begun to inform his art.

Williams' mother had studied painting in Paris, and he, as he said, had been "hipped on / painting." He had done some painting during his student days at the University of Pennsylvania, where he met the poets Pound and Hilda Doolittle and the painter Charles Demuth. During the formative years of his poetic career—the years in which cubism radically transformed art—he had followed the modern movement at the Armory Show and Stieglitz's "291," at the studio of Walter Arensberg, an important collector (and the sponsor of *Others*, the most experimental of the avant-garde magazines to which he contributed), and in the work of his friends Marcel Duchamp and Marsden Hartley. Knowing French—he had spent a year in a Swiss school, and French was one of the languages of the household—he had access to the literature of cubism, both, as in the case of Apollinaire, that written to explain it and that exemplifying it. He carefully attended to the new work of writers like Joyce and Gertrude Stein, and listened to Pound, that vigorous teacher and guide always responsive to the developments of art, who in vorticism had worked out an application of cubism. Painting, accordingly, as much as, perhaps more than literature, was the immediate inspiration of his modernism, and in "To a Solitary Disciple" he appropriated for poetry the primary formal values that in painting had so dramatically replaced the conventional values of representation and sentimental association.

The painting that he asks his solitary disciple to notice may be one by Demuth—it has his characteristic force lines—and he is to observe in it not the subject or the colors, however worthy or exact, so much as the spatial relations and dynamics of the composition. What matters is the form of the imagination: the movement in (of) the painting itself, the way its rhythms strain toward flowering, flower, and, attaining mobile equilibrium, accomplish the work of imagination. But the poem is a work of art also, exemplifying the lessons it teaches; it too is a movement of perception in which poetry flowers ("the eaten moon / lies in the protecting lines") and the imagination surmounts—such is the triumph of art—the "oppressive weight" of things.

Such flowering, the interior drama of imagination, is the organic expression of Williams' art as it is of his idea of culture. Like the emerging life of "By the Road to the Contagious Hospital," art and culture are initially of the ground, and the imagination, whose forms they are, must "grip down" in order to "awaken." Perception, their vital movement, is temporal, a process of growth, each instant quick with the "transition" that Emerson supremely valued, pressing them toward the revelation of their complete forms. Nothing is more characteristic of Williams than this aspiration to form—an aspiration evoked in "Chicory and Daisies," where he petitions the chicory to lift its flowers "out of the scorched ground" because "the sky goes out / if you should fail."

The imagination overcomes chaos by ordering it, by this ascent finding release and freedom in a world of its own making. (The art-work is rewarded by a work or world of art.) Because its agency is threefold it performs this difficult work. By sensuous contact with things it avoids the estrangement of dualism; by perception it comes into the hidden perfections of things, discovering their inner rhythms and dancing with them; and by constructing the poem it raises things to its own plane and there disposes them according to its own intrinsic necessities, those necessities of art that are its forms.

Though the poem created in this way is an independent

object, as much a new reality as any modern painting, it is not objective but profoundly subjective in its revelation of the poet's act of imagination. These qualities, of course, belong to the dualistic apprehension of things that Williams' practice of imagination denies, and, having used them only to clarify, one might cite, as a more exact description of his practice, Kenneth Burke's remark that it "inordinates us into the human nature of things." And this is to be radically modern: to realize the perspectival nature of truth and the need to see an object in "all of its three hundred and sixty degrees of reality," as Charles Sheeler said in appreciation of Williams' art. Williams is deservedly praised for the things—or better, the thisness of things— he presents so exactly, but this is not the result of descriptive power. It follows instead from the "dynamization" he speaks of in *Spring and All* (1923), the process of imagination by which the truth of the independent natural object is transferred to the equally independent object of art. A poem like "Queen-Ann's-Lace," for example, is both true to the thing and the poet's erotic perception of it because both belong to the same perceptual space—the perceiver himself is part of the thing perceived— and the movement of perception by which it is intimately known and fully revealed also determines the prosody, the total movement and shape, of the poem. In this new world the poet is a measurer: every relation of poet and thing has its measure, the line, the controlling unit of the poem's formal order.

Most illustrative, perhaps, of Williams' modernism is the poem celebrating Einstein's first visit to America in 1921, for "St. Francis Einstein of the Daffodils" presents the modern view both in its content and form. The technique, by now, is familiar: a spatial ordering of seemingly unrelated things that at various depths have meaningful connection. The title itself exemplifies this by conjoining St. Francis, Einstein, and daffodils—a saint, a scientist, and flowers (recalling Wordsworth's "The Daffodils," may also stand in for poet). St. Francis, one learns elsewhere in Williams' writing, was his adopted patron saint, a gentle saint of the word, an artist who, to borrow from

"A Sort of a Song," through "metaphor . . . reconcile[d]/the people and the stones." Einstein, the discoverer of relativity, was truly a discoverer of a new world, as much as others, un-named, who contributed to the method of the poem; and, like Mme. Curie in *Paterson*, his discovery is associated with Columbus', even with the advent of Venus, a birth of beauty which, related to images of the Statue of Liberty and of spring-time, is also, as every coming to America was supposed to be, a rebirth of freedom. The daffodils, of course, are signs of spring, early flowers of Williams' favorite season, tokens of nature and the organic process of her renewal, and they are introduced, along with other portents of seasonal change, be-cause, as Williams explained in summary, "It is always spring time for the mind when great discoveries are made. Is not Einstein . . . saintly in the purity of his scientific imagining?"

The original version of the poem, published in *Contact* (1922), is considerably longer and more exuberant, but less decisive in form. Williams improved it, as he did early versions of other poems, by stringently cutting it to its essential structure. Einstein is only the occasion of the poem—a "violet" whose height is relative to its place but, for all that, a force of life equivalent to the "blossomy peartree," the winds, the sun; and in the field of meaning created by the poem, his idea is generative, a natural force. The poem itself is concerned with change—is itself both a product of change and a stimulus to it. It depicts some of the changes or new relations that occur as a result of such forces of life.

The poet, for example, is himself consciously affected and ponders the relation of past and present so crucial to the modern sensibility. Not without reluctance, he decides to sing of the past no longer—to sing instead, as he does in a later stanza, of the vulgar present, of the chickenyard and the old Negro, who, moved again to secure his survival, has poisoned "Lesbia." Meanwhile the sun of spring has united man and nature—young and old, trees and flowers—in fraternal embrace; and the southeast wind, another force approaching from the sea, has

moved the sleeping owner of the blossomy peartrees, all uncon-
sciously and yet inevitably, to respond by throwing off the covers
and again becoming new and naked. Within the simultaneity of
this order there is significant movement and tension, for though
the poem celebrates change and its benign effects, it does not
neglect the destruction and death accompanying them ("the
quietness of flowers is perhaps deceptive," Williams said in "The
Birth of Venus"). In its development, it moves through phases of
death and life, and even when it speaks for life reminds us of the
"tearing wind" and the dark night. Williams tells us, in "By the
Road to the Contagious Hospital," how things "enter the new
world naked, / cold, uncertain." He never minimizes the terror
of that "profound change"—in "Portrait of the Author," he is
almost overcome by it. In "St. Francis Einstein of the Daffodils," however, he accepts the hazards of change in the spirit
that later prompted "Rogation Sunday": "O let the seeds be
planted / and the worry and unrest be invited!" For he believed
that modernism opened a new, exhilarating prospect, one best
defined in organic terms. It was the issue of the good, the true,
and the vital, as the title of the poem suggests—energies that had
set in motion the natural elements, the earth, air, fire and water
of the poem, and promised the awakened orchard-owner (a new
Adam?) a new world.

The literary events that figure most prominently for Williams in
his *Autobiography* are the publication of Eliot's *The Waste Land*
in 1922 and the completion of *Paterson* in 1951. Eliot, he felt,
"had turned his back on the possibility of reviving my world";
*The Waste Land*, with what he later called atomic force, had
wiped out the resurgence that in *Paterson* was only again becoming evident. The dates of publication of these poems conven-
iently mark the period of Eliot's dominance and the beginning
of Williams' increasing influence, and Williams' account of
Eliot's impact, though exaggerated in respect to his own literary
production, is true to his profound emotional response.

His antipathy to Eliot antedates *The Waste Land. Prufrock*

and *Other Observations*, published in 1917, had overshadowed Williams' *Al Que Quiere!*, and he had already fixed his criticism of Eliot in "Prologue to *Kora in Hell*" (1920), his survey of the literary situation of the time, by putting Eliot down as a "subtle conformist"—a criticism comparable to Poe's attribution of plagiarism to Longfellow. Eliot was recognized more quickly than Williams and achieved an impressive literary position. But Williams did not go unrecognized as he tried to make out in dramatizing his slower arrival. He himself recorded (in *In the American Grain*, *A Voyage to Pagany*, and *The Autobiography*) his reception in Paris in 1924, where, in the company of Joyce, he had been feted; and although F. R. Leavis, understandably, did not mention him in *New Bearings in English Poetry* (1932), a study chiefly of the work of Pound and Eliot in altering the tradition of English verse, René Taupin, in *L'Influence du Symbolisme Français sur La Poésie Américaine* (1929), placed him with them and, in knowledge of the ways of the imagination, above them.

With Robert Lowell's help, Williams eventually accepted Eliot's contribution to the enterprise of modern verse. "He is a 'strong man' of letters," he said, "unrelated to the scene"— praise still somewhat grudging and pointing to a distinction Williams insisted on, that he had lived on the scene, "seventy years deep," as he noted in the title of an autobiographical essay. Eliot, of course, was his proper antagonist, as much the complete man of letters as he was. But, more important, they lived in radically different poetic worlds. Eliot lived in a world haunted by the terrifying loneliness of the egocentric predicament; he was fearful of personality and needed to contain it within the more inclusive and ever-tightening traditions of literature, culture, and religion. Williams lived in an ever-opening world whose spaces, as J. Hillis Miller has observed, he was able to fill, by imagination, with the bounty of his life and love.

In creating this poetic world, Williams brought together the two poets whose work defines the American traditions in poetry. Like Poe, he was concerned with craft, with the making of poems, and with the quest of beauty; like Whitman, he was concerned with the fulfillment of self, wanted to "tally" his environment, and had an enabling projective sympathy. In seeking beauty, however, he was not a visionary. His imagination was not "angelic" and its erotic energy was not attached to death. The perpetual journey he tramped was a "journey to love"—the title, adopted from Forster's *The Longest Journey*, of a late book of poems. And it was a journey of love, prompted throughout by a moral concern, as Alan Ostrom says, for "the propriety of all things as they exist naturally."

Williams had the necessary egoism of poets, but also an overriding concern for the work. "I am not driven by the search for personal distinction, I don't want to appear in person," he told Lowell in a letter on Eliot. "But I want to see the unknown shine, like a sunrise." With him modernism incorporated organicism and expressed again the American wonder.

With Williams, I rediscoverd poetry.

When I was an undergraduate, I wrote and published poems and read some once with Robert Penn Warren at a meeting of the Iowa Poetry Society—read nothing, of course, that would have merited Williams' warning in the introduction to Allen Ginsberg's poems: "Hold back the edges of your gowns, Ladies, we are going through hell." In keeping with what I had been taught and read, my poems were "metaphysical"; all I remember of Robert Frost's instruction—we spent some summer afternoons in a darkened room in University Hall—was his mockery and admonishment. At Iowa, where one is encouraged to be a poet and sometimes becomes the real thing, I was a "poet." I wasn't poet enough to take the necessary risks— that's how I see it now. My poetry didn't weather the war or graduate school or the round of teaching. I like to think that it didn't perish because of other publication, that in this work, too, its presence is detectable. Yet that is not the same thing as writing poems; it is not the same way of being in the world.

Twenty-five years later, when the conjunction of public and
private events was auspicious, I began to write poems again. By
this time, I had found Williams and a way to begin to begin
again. And soon—it makes the turn complete, poetically
right—we moved to Iowa City, where Kim Merker taught me
the elementary skills of his exquisite craft and helped me print
*And Four with Birds*, a pamphlet of some of my recent poems.

This does not make me a poet. I do not pretend to be one. It
only accounts for a deepening awareness of the vital necessity
and therapeutic uses of poetry—of the imagination. In writing
*The Music of Survival: A Biography of a Poem by William
Carlos Williams* (1968), I focused on one occasion in the life of
the poet, a time of extremity, when the making of a poem was
actually a matter of survival. Williams not only taught me
(again, again) how essential imagination is in surmounting the
various orders we impose on life, but how much its play is life
and the means to new life. Art is necessary: it is an act of life,
an action that mediates self and world; and it is a leap, the risk
itself that makes survival possible—the abandon Emerson acknowledged in "Circles" when he said that "the way of life is
wonderful; it is by abandonment." Art restores: the poems I was
writing and the writing of *The Music of Survival* were restora-
tive. This small book, with *Hart's Bridge* (1972), which it
proposed, is my defense of poetry, of what, finally, is radically
deepest in the Emersonian tradition.

I had always wanted to write a small book out of the riches of
a large subject. In writing a paper to accompany the seminar
papers my students were writing, I found the germ in a paragraph on Williams' trip to Juarez in *The Autobiography*. I treat
the writing of *The Autobiography* almost as much as that of
"The Desert Music," and I called the book "a biography of a
poem" in order to emphasize an idea whose validity I felt I had
demonstrated: that poems cannot be fully explicated or appreciated without attending to them as occasions, events in the
life and work of the poet. The poem is part of the book, placed
in the poet's and the reader's experience; and the reader, whose

way into the book is impeded by it, is asked to measure his initial response to it by what the rest of the book discloses to him.

I wrote this "Introduction" for a revised edition of *Masters of American Literature*, an anthology published in 1959. The inclusion of Williams would have appreciably brought it up to date and given symmetry to a volume beginning with Whitman and including Frost and Eliot. I print it here for the first time—and suggest that the reader interpose the texts of the early poems referred to in it.

# FROM LOOKOUT TO ASHRAM: THE WAY OF GARY SNYDER

I KNOW of no one since Thoreau who has so thoroughly espoused the wild as Gary Snyder—and no one who is so much its poet. His root metaphor, the "back country," covers all that Thoreau, explicitly or implicitly, meant by the "wild." " Poetry and the Primitive," one of the recent essays collected in *Earth House Hold* (1969), is his most important statement and the resolution of much of his work, an essay comparable in import, though not in distinction of style, to Thoreau's "Walking." Thoreau's essay, originally a lecture called "The Wild," is testamentary, and so is Snyder's, though his is not terminal. It does not conclude a life but draws a phase of life to conclusion and, in this way and by the affirmation of writing, announces a new departure at a deeper depth of realization. The two essays that follow it, "Dharma Queries" and "Suwa-no-Se Island and the Banyan Ashram," record his vows and practice, and the latter begins his life anew with his marriage to Masa Uehara, whom he celebrates in *Regarding Wave* (1969), his latest book of poems.

    *Earth House Hold*, spanning the years 1952 to 1967, provides an excellent introduction to a poet whose poetry, because of its autobiographical nature and allusions to Oriental and Ameri-    195 can Indian lore, is not always readily available. Its title feelingly translates "ecology," a science that Paul Shepard and Daniel McKinley consider subversive—subversive, and urgent, in respect to the attitudes and ends of overly-technological civilization.[1] Its subtitle, "Technical Notes & Queries to Fellow Dharma Revolutionaries," suggests this revolutionary character, and as a manual for revolution, it offers a way (of thought and action) and indicates the studies and disciplines that, in the author's experience, lead us back to the back country where we may enjoy "Housekeeping on Earth." As "dharma" implies, this revolution turns on truth; it is what Emerson called a silent revolution of thought, and the thought, much of it, is Oriental, the "primal thought" spoken of in Whitman's "Passage to India." The revolutionaries are spiritual seekers whom Snyder, not without humor, now addresses as guerrillas. He once called them "Dharma-hobos" (in 1956) and Jack Kerouac, in the title of a novel relating his meeting and experience with Snyder, called them "Dharma-bums" (in 1958). Kerouac even prophesied a "rucksack revolution" and in his novel Japhy Ryder (Gary Snyder) says: "Think what a great world revolution will take place when East meets West finally, and it'll be guys like us that start the thing. Think of millions of guys all over the world with rucksacks on their backs tramping around the back country and hitchhiking and bringing the word down to everybody." The revolutionary here—in the 1950s—is one who withdraws from society; he "signs off," as Thoreau would say, and becomes a saunterer, a holy-lander. Bum, for Kerouac, translates *bhikkhu*, monk; hopping freights and hitch-hiking are in keeping with a free life of voluntary poverty. Or, in the phrase Snyder uses to characterize his friend Nanao Sakaki—a phrase that also characterizes him and reminds one of Bashō—the revolutionary may be a "wanderer and poet," whose only moral imperative "in this yuga," as Snyder declares for himself in the first journal, is to communicate. Now, at the end of the 1960s,

1 *The Subversive Science: Essays Toward an Ecology of Man* (Houghton Mifflin Co., New York, 1969).

as the subtitle indicates, this social passivity, so much in the grain of Eastern thought, is disclaimed; "revolutionary" has the meaning of the 1960s and the goal of revolution is represented for Snyder in the I. W. W. slogan, "Forming a new society within the shell of the old." Snyder's book begins where Kerouac's *The Dharma Bums*, a book about individual salvation, ends. It reflects the changing life-style, the increasing activism and communitarianism, of the past decade, and its quiet confidence and sense of vast tributary support (mostly out of the past—Snyder dates some essays and poems from the time of the earliest cave paintings) are noteworthy. It may be described briefly as a development from lookout to ashram.

The revolution Gary Snyder intends is vouched for by his life and work, by his poetry and by these journals and essays—this record of a life. Like Thoreau, he is a figure: he himself exemplifies his thought. This has much to do with his distinction and attractiveness. In the early days of the Beats, Kerouac paid him the tribute of *The Dharma Bums*, which, for all of its rapturous sentiment, is essentially sound portraiture. Robert Bly, the often testy Crunk of *The Sixties*, called him an "original man" and in treating his early work outlined a program for the American imagination. James Dickey acknowledged him by distinguishing his orientalism from "the mail order orientalism of the West Coast crowd." And Kenneth Rexroth, the senior West Coast poet to whom Snyder dedicated *The Back Country*, ranked him highest of the poets of his generation because of the range of his "real life" experience, his "life of eventfulness."

While partial, these assessments are substantial and accord with the reasons for Snyder's increasing reputation and recognition. His popularity among those whose response makes popularity a significant measure is almost as great as Allen Ginsberg's. Like Ginsberg, he stands for something not easily defined, especially by someone of another generation. To the young in search of an estimable way of being in the world (poetry is its correlative, one of its insignia but not necessarily its end), he is a hero, as Ginsberg, in the guise of a character in Kerouac's novel, once remarked ("Japhy Ryder is a great new hero of American culture"). An acceptable earnestness and moral seriousness have much to do with such popularity—certainly more than the poetry, which, as poetry, has not yet been sufficiently considered. The poetry is immediately interesting in an exotic way, like Snyder himself, for both tell us, as Thoreau said of the best poets, that here is someone who has gone beyond "the tame and civil side of nature" and has seen "the west side of [the] mountain." Snyder is learned, he has been to the academy, to Reed, Indiana, and Berkeley; but he is not an academic poet. His is not "white man's poetry" but the "Indian's report."

I remember my introduction to him in a televised reading on the National Educational Television Network: the poet in Japanese student uniform announcing his beliefs, reading his poems in a bare (empty, "oriental") room. How disciplined he was! How intensely attentive, every movement contributing to a ritual event, the speaking of the poem! Such economy and richness of spirit! (The portrait in A *Range of Poems* gives a similar impression.) I was immensely impressed by the self-possession and presence, the wonderful power of bringing one's full being to the present moment, much as I was later when attending the lectures of a Zen master. Other readings in this excellent series had prepared my surprise, for some of them were performances. Perhaps Snyder's was—a thought I entertained recently when I heard him read before a large audience and watched him create the situation he wanted by ritualizing the occasion (carefully untying and tying his bundle of books and papers—in his blue denim work clothes he might have just come in from the road—and using an oriental gesture of greeting) and by disciplining the audience's attention with his own (by eye contact, precise explanation, exact breathing and saying of the poem, and significant silence). The thought did not disturb me because I preferred these conditions to the more familiar vaudeville—the playing down by which older poets identify with the young. And these conditions were appropriate to Snyder's high conception of poetry and the poetry of love he was reading (from *Regarding Wave*, praise of the Goddess).

Perhaps they transcended performance by transforming it into ritual participation; as I told Snyder afterward, I felt that the reading had been one of the memorable meetings of my life. Yet I was disturbed, as one may be when subjected to so much spiritual power and so willingly gratifies it, by the possibility of arrogance, and I found myself wondering whether the portraits in *A Range of Poems*, *The Back Country*, and *Earth House Hold* might not be a form of spiritual self-advertisement.

Snyder, unquestionably, is a remarkable man: he has a center, is assured, and possesses a disciplined freedom that appeals to both young and old. (The young perhaps respond most to his moral permissiveness, the old to his moral toughness.) Though in these respects he is above or beyond the younger generation as a moral hero should be, he is also of them because his life still seems open to novelty ("we have nothing to fear," he says, "if we are willing to train ourselves to open up, explore and grow") and because he identifies with them in point of departure (after World War II, he explains, "the suspicion grew that perhaps the whole Western Tradition . . . is off the track") and in concern for what he calls "the Great Subculture" ("it transmits a community style of life, with an ecstatically positive vision of spiritual and physical love. . . . It has taught that man's natural being is to be trusted and followed").

As a personal account of our historical moment, "Why Tribe," the essay just quoted, comments after the fashion of other essays in *Earth House Hold* on the private experience recorded there. "At this point"—Snyder is referring to the observation on the Western Tradition—"many, myself included, found in the Buddha-Dharma a practical method for clearing one's mind of the trivia, prejudices and false values that our conditioning had laid on us. . . ." And this is where *Earth House Hold* begins, with a lookout on a mountain top clearing his mind and trying "to penetrate to the deepest non-self Self."

*Earth House Hold* begins in the back country which was also Snyder's boyhood world. Though he was born in San Francisco   199 (in 1930), his formative years were spent in the Pacific North-west. During the depression, his family tried dairy farming in Washington, and, after 1942, lived in Portland, Oregon, where he attended Reed College. The Northwest is his personal geography: the low country of "Nooksack Valley," where, sitting in "a berry-pickers cabin/At the edge of a wide muddy field/ Stretching to the woods and cloudy mountains," the smell of cedar reminds him of "our farm-house, half built in '35"; and the high country of the mountain wilderness of the North Cascades which he first entered in his youth. This landscape, especially the mountain wilderness, is aboriginal, like the "Fur Countries" that had early rejoiced Thoreau and the "*great west and northwest* stretching on infinitely far and grand and wild" that he later said qualified all of his thoughts—"That is the only America I know. . . . That is the road to new life and free-dom. . . . That great northwest where several of our shrubs, fruitless here, retain and mature their fruits properly." Wilder-ness of this kind, Snyder reminds us, as much from personal experience as from historical report, is what Americans con-fronted on the frontier. Here was "a vast wild ecology" that was "mind-shaking." For Americans, nature, he says, meant wilderness, an "untamed realm of total freedom—not brutish and nasty, but beautiful and terrible." And it meant the Indian, whose ways Snyder, like Thoreau, seriously studied (his bachelor's thesis, "The Dimensions of a Myth," treats the Haida)[2] and whose ghost, he says in the portentous manner of Lawrence, "will claim the next generation as its own."

Snyder possessed this primitive landscape in many ways, among them by learning woodcraft as a boy, mountain climbing as a youth, and working in the forest as a trail-maker, logger, and lookout in his early manhood. And while he was possessing it,

2  The range of inquiry of this important work in Snyder's development is suggested by his conclusion: "In its totality the study of a myth is the study of 'man and his works.' " In the course of considering the anthropological, folklorist, psychological, literary, and social aspects of myth, Snyder surveys much that is of consequence to his later writing and seems to be making a statement about his vocation as poet.

he was, as a student of folklore, mythology, religion, and Oriental languages, extending and deepening its meanings, transforming the back country into a spiritual domain. By the time he goes to Crater Mountain Lookout in 1952, the back country has become the "Buddha land," a place of spiritual enlightenment to which one ascends by means of the disciplines he practices there. Crater Mountain becomes "Crater Shan," another Cold Mountain, whose namesake Han-shan wrote the "Cold Mountain" poems that Snyder later translated, poems defining the back country as a condition of being: "Freely drifting, I prowl the woods and streams / And linger watching things themselves. / Men don't get this far into the mountains." [3] All high places become one and have this significance, as later, when climbing in the Glacier Peak Wilderness Area, Snyder recalls Cold Mountain and imagines himself a Tibetan mountaineer, a Japanese woodcutter, and an exiled Chinese traveler. The nature he enters is universal, like that Thoreau said he entered on his daily walk: "I walk out into a nature such as the old prophets and poets, Menu, Moses, Homer, Chaucer, walked in. You may name it America, but it is not America. . . . There is a truer account of it in mythology than in any history of America."

For the back country is *back*. It is reached by going back to what Peter Levi, in a recent review of Snyder's poetry, called the "sources" ("Snyder's work is a restoration of the sources, a defence of the springs," awakening in us a sense of a "lost dimension of life"). And back is *down*, a descent, as William Carlos Williams spoke of it, to the fertile chaos, the very "mother stuff" of our being, to the unconscious from which, Snyder believes, we can reconstruct, by means of meditation, whatever aspects of previous cultures we desire. Like the primitive wilderness—the "naked" world where both Thoreau and Snyder believe we are most alive—the sources are still there, a deeper down where love is rooted and creative forces play, the

---

3 *The Dharma Bums*, much of it about mountain climbing, is dedicated to Han-shan.

*nature* that is always woman ("no human man can belong to mountains except as they are nature, and nature is woman"). Here the mind is untamed and the "seeds of instinct," to use Thoreau's phrase, are nurtured (for a true culture, Thoreau remarked, does not "tame tigers"). It is a darkness, too, perhaps like the "back" where Coyote lives ("His house was back in the back of the hills") or the "Deep North" of Bashō's last journey, the "other shore," or the world after death, the back country of Snyder's "Journeys" that one enters only by dying. Finally, as wilderness and unconscious, outer and inner equivalents, the back country is *beyond*—beyond society, civilization and its discontents ("I did not mean to come this far," Snyder writes in "Twelve Hours out of New York,"—"baseball games on the radio / commercials that turn your hair—"). It is the "old, dirty countries," the backward countries he has wandered in, places where the old traditions are still living, and places like Suwa-no-Se Island where the primitive communal life he now advocates can be lived.

*Earth House Hold*—the very title declares it—records this deepening awareness of the significance of the back country. In it, one follows the random course of (a) life, sees it nurturing a poet, focusing and concentrating itself. The concluding essays, the most recent, comprise a platform or program, and are ardently didactic. But the early journals are exercises in recording one's life, part of a discipline of being. In this, they remind one of the journals of Emerson and Thoreau. The young man to whom they introduce us—they give us our first and earliest glimpse of Snyder—is already pursuing the way and is wholly intent on overseeing and shaping his perceptions; this, perhaps, accounts for the impersonal quality of the personal in Snyder's work and distinguishes him from the other autobiographical (confessional) poets of his generation. The journals are the work of a Zennist and a poet, a poet who has learned much about form from Pound but more, I think, from Chinese and Japanese poetry.

The first part of "Lookout's Journal," that covering the summer of 1952 on Crater Mountain, is the best of all the journals in *Earth House Hold*. In none of the others is the experiment in form and the experience so fully realized. It is, I think, a more daring work than any of the early poems collected in *Riprap* (1959)—larger, more open, able to contain, substantively and formally, more experience. The trajectory of experience it presents passes through *the* experience, which, unrecorded, is of the kind given in the carefully wrought Poundian-cadenced poem of purification, clarity, and serenity commemorating the following summer's lookout, "Mid-August at Sourdough Mountain Lookout," the initial poem of *Riprap*:

> Down valley a smoke haze
> Three days heat, after five days rain
> Pitch glows on the fir-cones
> Across rocks and meadows
> Swarms of new flies.
>
> I cannot remember things I once read
> A few friends, but they are in cities.
> Drinking cold snow-water from a tin cup
> Looking down for miles
> Through high still air.

This might be called a satori poem. It fulfills the need recorded in the first journal: "to look within and adjust the mechanism of perception." And it reminds one of Thoreau's realization at Walden ("Both place and time were changed, and I dwelt nearer to those parts of the universe and to those eras in history which had most attracted me") and of Emerson's reliance on the power of prospects.

The journal gives the essential particulars of experience that contributed to such attainment. It begins in late June, at the Ranger Station, with the following brief entry:

> Hitchhiked here, long valley of the Skagit. Old cars parked in weeds, little houses in fields of braken. A few cows, in stump-land.
>
> Ate at the "parkway cafe" real lemon in the pie
> "—why don't you get a jukebox in here"
> "—the man said we weren't important enough"

203

One probably notices first the abbreviated syntax—an expression of economy, one that tells us that the traditional syntax isn't essential enough and telegraphs a quick grasp of things, like sumi painting. We are given objective fragments, but even in this simplest entry they are arranged and placed on the empty space of the page. Like a haiku poem, they work by means of the art of omission, by what they suggest. They tell of arrival but indicate the journey (compare this entry with Kerouac's account in *The Dharma Bums*) and give the sense of increasing sparseness and emptiness. We are in the back country now, old cars in the weeds, little houses, a few cows in the stumpland, a place not important enough—frequented and commercial enough—for a jukebox but still backward enough, in its values, as Hemingway would have noted, to serve unadulterated lemon pie. As Snyder pointed out in reviewing a book of prose translations of Chinese poems, "any irregular line arrangement creates a manner of reading and a rhythm, which is poetical." So here. The entry is a poem. The balanced cadence of "Old cars parked in the weeds, little houses in fields of braken" is artful.

Each entry is a formal design, a field of experience, in which the poet intends the fragments (thoughts, perceptions, notations of objects) to relate, become whole. The unity of the entry is often the unspoken ground to which all refer, as in the following:

Granite creek Guard station    9 July

        the boulder in the creek never moves
          the water is always falling
       together!
A ramshackle little cabin built by Frank Beebe the miner.
Two days walk to here from roadhead.
           arts of the Japanese: moon-watching
               insect-hearing
Reading the sutra of Hui Nêng.
        one does not need universities and libraries
        one need be alive to what is about

    saying "I don't care"

The ground, here, is the resolve to pursue the way; the entry is really very intense and builds to the attitude of not caring about the "world" below. The poet is still struggling with—perhaps rehearsing—the "complete and total choice" he made about this time to relinquish a "professional scholar's career in anthropology" and set himself loose "to sink or swim as a poet." The entry begins with the poet's play (the rhythmic capitalization of the location) and with a haiku poem appropriate to resolute thought, and it moves associatively from the isolated little cabin of a miner to the meditative arts practiced in seclusion by the Japanese, to his own discipline (reading the sutra) and thoughts (the recognition of a Zen truth about learning), and determined statement of choice.

This principle of form applies to the journal as a whole and to many of the poems. Snyder observes in this journal that form is "leaving things out at the right spot / ellipse, is emptiness." This emptiness is not empty; it is the ultimate, the fullness of life of which a few carefully selected and carefully placed things may make us aware. The journal is not a diary or daybook. There are only sixteen dated entries for a period of two and a half months. While suggesting the distance between events, in an isolated place, these point to a fertile emptiness and not, as do the equally infrequent entries of the Sourdough Journal, to slackness and boredom. They also chart a complete event, the actual ascent and descent of "Crater Shan"—a pattern of experience that repetition, it seems, does not always recover in its original freshness and exhilaration.

On all accounts (we hear of it in *The Dharma Bums*), Snyder was an exemplary lookout. But this is not the primary work recorded in the journal. His work, he notes, is *"Zazen    non-life.    An art: mountain-watching."* It begins with his arrival— with his openness and attentiveness to persons, places, and things. The second entry, for example, is a characterization by speech of Blackie Burns, a forester, one of the roughs, to use Whitman's term, to whom Snyder dedicated *Riprap*. His speech, though strong, is not coarse, like some of the woods-

men's anecdotes of the Sourdough Journal, and its theme is significant. Burns announces the ecological concern of Snyder's
work: "GREEDY & SELFISH    NO RESPECT FOR THE LAND." The
capitalization, part of Snyder's design of Burns' speech, also
serves to emphasize what is most important, an attitude of mind
fostered by the Western Tradition (the Judeo-Christian tradition, according to Paul Shepard, which contributed to "the
hatred for this world carried by our whole culture"). Greed and
selfishness, Buddha said, were the principal causes of dissatisfaction and suffering and were to be overcome by disciplining
the mind, by changing one's point of view. Changing one's
point of view (adjusting the mechanism of perception) is the
revolutionary issue; only a discipline as radical as that undertaken by Snyder will, he believes, create an ecological conscience, prepare us to respect the land, the very ground of our
being. The ecological issue, therefore, is at the center of his
spiritual undertaking, as is poetry. A few entries later, he writes:
"—If one wished to write poetry of nature, where an audience?
Must come from the very conflict of an attempt to articulate
the vision    poetry & nature in our time." Snyder is preemi-
nently a poet of nature. And at the beginning of his career he
knows, as he says in the subtitle of a recent essay, that poetry
(requiring the highest discipline of the poet, and communi-
cating the "vision") is an "ecological survival technique."

The entries that follow his resolution on Zen enlightenment
record the strenuous and wayward pursuit. The entry of July 11,
somewhat in the nature of a Whitman catalog, conveys by its
randomness an eager readiness for new experiences other than
those recorded. The first entry from the mountain lookout gives
the elevation, which, honestly acknowledged, is only a matter of
feet ("8049 feet"). Everything goes wrong, he's dispirited ("Even
here, cold foggy rocky place, there's life—4 ptarmigan . . .") and
has only energy enough to read science-fiction. But the second
half of the entry, with the comparison of the light of the lookout
to that of a shoji, reports reviving spirits and resolve; and thereafter, with the entry of July 28 from "Crater Shan," the journal

gives an account—happy and contented, I think, when compared to the Sourdough Journal—of his discipline and its fruits.

Unlike the other lookouts whose radio conversations he enters in the journal as necessary fact, as ballast to his own experience, he is intensely occupied ("poor lonely lookouts," he remarks, "radioing back and forth"). He is not lonely, no more than Thoreau at Walden, who explained that "nearest to all things is that power which fashions their being." He has a close schedule of work and study, and, like Thoreau, metaphorically and literally, is transacting business with the "Celestial Empire":

> —first I turn on the radio
> —then make tea & eat breakfast
> —study Chinese until eleven
> —make lunch, go chop snow to melt water,
> read Chaucer in the early afternoon.

On August 10, he reports, "First wrote a haiku and painted a haiga for it; then repaired the Om Mani Padme Hum prayer flag, then constructed a stone platform, then shaved down a shake and painted a zenga on it, then studied the lesson." Transcriptions from the texts he is reading or recalls indicate his progress—most are from Oriental scripture, but Chaucer's line on "drasty ryming" is cited (perhaps he is reading *Paterson IV*) and an American Indian song is used to express his own feeling ("Is this real / Is this real / This life I am living?"). Sometimes a haiku poem marks his contentment—and the loneliness: "sitting in the sun in the doorway / picking my teeth with a broomstraw / listenin to the buzz of the flies."

By exposure, he comes to know his environment: "The rock alive, not barren. / flowers lichen pinus albicaulis chipmunks / mice even grass."

He meditates on the vastness of time, and the sufficiency of time for change in the lithosphere, and, as the syntax tells us ("When a storm blows in, covering the south wall with rain and blotting out the mountains.") he himself is caught up in the tremendous elemental action, the finality of it. And then, toward the end of his stay, he makes the crucial entry:

Almost had it last night: *no identity*. One thinks, "I emerged
from some general, non-differentiated thing, I return to it."
One has in reality never left it; there is no return.
    my language fades. Images of erosion.

Whether he ever has it is left in doubt, but the concluding entry
shows that whatever good to senses and spirit he has had has not
been lost on his return to San Francisco: "Boys on bicycles in the
asphalt playground wheeling and circling aimlessly like playful
gulls or swallows. Smell of a fresh-parked car."

This exceptional journal—a brief *Walden*—was the work of an
exceptional young man, only twenty-two, who already knew the
imperatives of art set forth in the poetic directive of "Riprap."
Like Roy Marchbanks, another of the roughs by whom he was
taught as a member of a trail crew in Yosemite National Park in
1955, he respects workmanship, in this instance the perfect
selection and placing of granite rocks in "tight cobble patterns on
hard slab." So he instructs himself in a poem that exemplifies
his skill and remains his test of art:

> Lay down these words
> Before your mind like rocks.
>     placed solid, by hands
> In choice of place, set
> Before the body of the mind
>     in space and time:
> Solidity of bark, leaf, or wall
>     riprap of things:
> Cobble of milky way,
>     straying planets,
> These poems, people,
>     lost ponies with
> Dragging saddles—
>     and rocky sure-foot trails.
> The worlds like an endless
>     four-dimensional
> Game of Go.
>     ants and pebbles
> In the thin loam, each rock a word
>     a creek-washed stone

Granite: ingrained
   with torment of fire and weight
Crystal and sediment linked hot
   all change, in thoughts,
As well as things.

The imperatives of composition are modernist: the unit of composition is the single word, like rock, a solid particular thing of weight and texture that exists in place and time and appeals to the senses ("body of the mind"); and the act of composition is architectural, a building by words, a deliberate handwork—the kind of labor with things that Thoreau said removed the palaver from the scholar's style and that, for Snyder, identifies him with workingmen. Poetry is his craft: "a riprap on the slick rock of metaphysics," as he says later in *Myths & Texts*. The "riprap of things" includes all things, the "cobble of milky way"—the phrase is wonderfully extravagant in Thoreau's sense, like his own metaphor of fishing in the upper air—and "ants and pebbles," the diminutive things that, one recalls in "Song of Myself," were the objects of Whitman's altered perception, the proofs of love. The substance of the *poetry*, what the art of poetry, the riprap of words, achieves is universal: a footing in the existential world, the granitic result of experience under pressure in a world of time and change that, carefully used, is the foundation of the way.

Tested by these standards none of the other journals is as good. The Sourdough Journal (1953) is written in rather loose paragraphs, is more routine, anecdotal, descriptive. The slackness is due to passivity, to awareness without an edge, the flatness of experience without subjectivity. Artiness and a feigned naïveté distress one immediately. The journal opens with, "The antique car managed it to Marblemount last week"—*antique*, used again in "patter from antique *Reader's Digests* he's found chez Lookout," puts one off, as does "managed" and the very cadence of the line. And one soon reads a Huck Finn-ish sort of entry: "in the bunkhouse found a magazine with an article about an eighteen-year-old girl who could dance and paint and sew and was good looking, too, with

209

lots of pictures." The journal is troubled—these are some of the indications—and, though it finally rises above this level, comes to neither resolution nor form.

The journal of Snyder's first stay in Japan, "Japan First Time Around" (1956–1957), is also in paragraphs, with little design. It is both impressionistic and meditative, recording the assimilation of Japan to his previous experience and the fluid movement of an open speculative mind. "Tanker Notes" (1957–1958) are the random jottings of the poet-seaman, the ebullient fireman of the *Sappa Creek*("—madly singing and laughing [the Han-shan of the boiler room], perched on pipes high on the shipside painting lower engine-room white—this is what I was born for—"). The poet is now one of the roughs and complements the austere training in Zen he has just undergone (see his essay, "Spring Sesshin at Shokoku-Ji") with its worldly, humble aspect. Much of this journal is given over to the conversation and folk-experience of the crew; and an occasional ungrammatical phrase, like that of the opening sentence ("was took on launch to this ship"), is the stylistic identification. Its longest entry, a high-spirited account of riotous shore leave in Samoa, depicts the rhythm of Snyder's way of being and is morally justified as a spontaneous act ("Everyone so beautiful") and perhaps as fulfilling a "higher sense of responsibility to holy ghosts and foolishness and mess." The last journal, that of a week's mountain climbing in the Glacier Peak Wilderness Area (1965), seems more like the first in design than any of the others, but the design is imposed and arty and the observation superficial, as in this portion of the second entry:

> descending to a previous pond for
> lunch over steep heather
> pick your way thru like a beast

Justine strips down and washes breasts and arms, tho all is chill; her jeans color of the lakeside sedge and hillside heather, hair color of the mountain wind.

> [Pugh creek goes into the Whitechuck
> the Whitechuck goes into the Sauk
> the Sauk goes into the Skagit
> the Skagit goes into the Sound.]

Rats, lambs, men, and whales
all drink milk.

```
┌─────────────────────────────┐
│ North Fork Sauk Trail       │
│ White Mt Shelter  5→         │
│ White Pass        9→         │
└─────────────────────────────┘
```

The ascent of Glacier Peak (in the company of Allen Ginsberg), though effectively given in short phrases, incomplete
sentences, and stage-by-stage entries, is good but not as good,
I think, as Kerouac's account of mountain climbing in *The
Dharma Bums.*

All of these journals lack the continuous intensity of the first,
but all are significant landmarks in Snyder's development and
valuable glosses on the poetry that accompanies it. The Sourdough Journal conveys the sense of some burden of crisis, of
waiting-out experience—"Chinese [*Hsiao-ching*]; plus Blake's
collected, *Walden* and sumi painting, pass the time." The only
entry approaching those of the first journal is a long meditation
on desire and discipline that ends with the following example of
awareness of relationship: "the desk is under the pencil." As the
poem on Dick Brewer's visit tells us, he is lonely and determined
to go to Japan ("Me back to my mountain    and far, far west").
The journal ends with an entry from Berkeley where he has gone
to prepare himself for Zen study there.

The period at Berkeley (1953–1956) was long and solitary. "I
was living in a little cottage," he recalls, "and studying Chinese
and Japanese . . . and going up to the woods and mountains in
the summer, writing and reading. Intellectually, and in every
way, that was a period of great excitement for me." (The last
months of this period are recorded in *The Dharma Bums.*) This
intellectual quickening and growth is apparent, I think, in the
journal of his first stay in Japan, for in this journal his thoughts
are coalescing and acquiring their subsequent direction. As in
the earlier journals, he is aware of the vastness and complex
processes of geological time; he meditates, he says, on "ecology,
food-chains and sex." The relation of sex to food-chains and
ecology is indicated in this entry: "Depth is the body. How does

211

one perceive internal physical states—yoga systems I guess—
well well. soil conservation / reforestation / birth control /
spelling reform: 'love the body.'" Sex has become a prominent
element in his thought, and he is working out a love ethic. He
approvingly cites Lawrence; he sees that "the Goddess is mother,
daughter, and wife at the same time" ("Looking at girls as
mothers or daughters or sisters for a change of view. Curious
switch"); and he begins to chart the connections between Zen,
Avatamsaka and Tantra:

> The giving of a love relationship is a Bodhisattva relaxation of
> personal fearful defenses and self-interest strivings—which
> communicates unverbal to the other and leaves *them* do the
> same. "Enlightenment" is this interior ease and freedom
> carried not only to persons but to all the universe. . . .
> So Zen, being founded on Avatamsaka, and the net-
> network of things; and Tantra being the application of the
> "interaction with no obstacles" vision on a personal-human
> level—the "other" becomes the lover, through whom the
> various links in the net can be perceived.

Poetry, too, is now defined as an act of love, and the poet of
nature is a poet of love: "POETRY is to give access to persons—
cutting away the fear and reserve and cramping of social life:
thus for Chinese poetry. Nature poetry too: 'this is what I've
seen.'"

This ethic is central, of revolutionary consequence. It contributes to ecological survival: "the organism alters itself rather
than continue fruitless competition." And it contributes to a
social vision which is set forth in two dreams:

> —dreamed of a new industrial-age dark ages: filthy narrow
> streets and dirty buildings with rickety walks over the streets
> from building to building—unwashed illiterate brutal
> cops—a motorcycle cop and sidecar drove up and over a fat
> workingman who got knocked down in a fight—tin cans and
> garbage and drooping electric wires everywhere—

> One night I dreamt I was with Miura Rōshi, or maybe an
> unheard of Polish revolutionary poet with a bald head—
> looking at Berkeley. But a new Berkeley—of the future—the
> Bay beach clean and white, the bay blue and pure; white

buildings and a lovely boulevard of tall Monterey pines that
stretched way back to the hills. We saw a girl from some ways
off walking toward us, long-legged, her hair bound loosely in
back.

The latter dream, one of the testimonies of intensive meditation, is a Joycean epiphany calling the poet to his work. It
answers the choice he puts himself earlier: "The poet must
choose: either to step deep in the stream of his people, history,
tradition, folding and folding himself in wealth of persons and
pasts; philosophy, humanity, to become richly foundationed
and great and sane and ordered. Or, to step beyond the bound
onto the way out, into horrors and angels, possible madness or
silly Faustian doom, possible utter transcendence, possible en-
lightened return, possible ignominious wormish perishing."

He has found a way-in, not a way-out, not Rimbaud's way;
and when he goes to the back country it is not to trade but, in the
phrase from this journal that defines the work of the later essays,
to "knit old dharma-trails." And, he says in "Tanker Notes," he
will rely as a poet on neither contrivance nor visionary derangement but only on the Muse, on reverential love, on the
cool water of inspiration, the "clear spring" of the mind, deeper
than the intellect and the unconscious, that "reflects all things
and feeds all things but is of itself transparent."

## II

*Riprap* (1959), Snyder's first book of poems, already fulfills
some of these ends. The title declares a humble yet exacting art
in the service of the things of experience; it names a back country
book that will be the foundation for others. The initial poem,
"Mid-August at Sourdough Mountain Lookout," establishes the
elevation he seeks, the "clear, attentive mind," spoken of in
"Piute Creek," that "Has no meaning but that / Which sees is
truly seen." Except for "T-2 Tanker Blues," none of the poems is
Beat, and this is Beat only by virtue of loosening an otherwise
tight form and adopting an explicitly oral instead of an inner,
meditatively spoken mode. Robert Sward's impression of the
poems as "restrained and relatively formal," quiet and "apart" in

tone, is just—these poems possess much stillness. All of them are autobiographical or confessional in the Whitmanian sense defined by Robert Bly: they embody "the pervading presence of the poet who simultaneously shares in the processes of life and reveals some of its meaning through his actions." They are arranged chronologically, and so follow the development recorded in the journals, and, like the journals, only with more concentration, they treat the first excursions into the back country and the attempt to truly inhabit it.

Nothing antedating the lookout period is included; only later will the poet remember the immediate past which these poems, especially the first, put behind him. There must have been earlier poems worthy of inclusion, for the poet of these poems is well-practiced in his art. But none is included because *Riprap*, like the journals, represents a decisive beginning. He is into the back country: beyond abstraction into sensation, as in "Water" and "Thin Ice"; beyond the timebound present into timeless primordial reaches of time, as in "Milton by Firelight" and "Above Pate Valley"; beyond Western romance into the mysteries of the Goddess, as in "Praise for Sick Women" and "For a Far-Out Friend." Beyond society, his poems are of the wilderness, the sea, the old countries. Beyond self, they need no reticence.

Some of the poems already mentioned are notable, especially "For a Far-Out Friend" and "Piute Creek," even though the former is marred by a weak ending and the latter by the phrase, "bubble of the heart." The central poem, and one of the best, along with the opening and closing poems, is "Nooksack Valley." Placed mid-way, it represents a turning-point toward the world of "A Stone Garden," a longer poem that may be said to answer it.

"Nooksack Valley" is a meditative poem that moves with the poet's thought and has the free form that typifies his work. The indented uncapitalized sentences are not unusual; they suggest the way thoughts, already in flow, enter the mind. Sentences, as 214 Charles Olson reminds us in defending nonsentences, represent completed thought. But the completed thought of this poem is the poem, all that happens in the mind during the short time it takes to heat the coffee.

At the far end of a trip north
In a berry-pickers cabin
At the edge of a wide muddy field
Stretching to the woods and cloudy mountains,
Feeding the stove all afternoon with cedar,
Watching the dark sky darken, a heron flap by,
A huge setter pup nap on the dusty cot.
High rotten stumps in the second-growth woods
Flat scattered farms in the bends of the Nooksack
River. Steelhead run now
         a week and I go back
Down 99, through towns, to San Francisco and Japan.
All America south and east,
Twenty-five years in it brought to a trip-stop
Mind-point, where I turn
Caught more on this land—rock tree and man,
Awake, than ever before, yet ready to leave.
         damned memories,
Whole wasted theories, failures and worse success,
Schools, girls, deals, try to get in
To make this poem a froth, a pity.
A dead fiddle for lost good jobs.
         the cedar walls
Smell of our farm-house, half built in '35.
Clouds sink down the hills
Coffee is hot again. The dog
Turns and turns about, stops and sleeps.

Having gone back to say goodbye to the north country, the poet finds himself in a landscape that confronts him with the experience and loyalties of his lifetime. Yet, as the form of the poem indicates, the very setting that awakens his agitation calms it. It does so—and this, I think, accounts for the poem's achievement—because the more deeply he enters it the more deeply it interpenetrates him. The trip north, presumably to fish for steelhead, has reached a "far end." (One thinks of Hemingway at Big Two-Hearted River.) The poet is not elated but depressed—passive, indoors, "Watching the dark sky darken." The landscape, so carefully described, corresponds with the poet's feelings of loneliness and heaviness, coldness and darkness; it contains his past and summons it to the turning, to the anguish, at the center of the poem, that is never fully admitted to mind because it remains in abstract terms. But the very land that calls up "damned memories" is the back country he loves ("Caught more on this land"), and knowing it, as he now knows it here, is what has awakened him and made him reject (again) the lures of civilization. What keeps the "Schools, girls, deals" from getting in and destroying the poem is the powerful objectivity of his present situation, the particular realizations he has of it, the smell of cedar at the end, pervasive, penetrant, that revives his earliest memory of home, of the child's unspoiled and sustaining world in which he began and to which, however far away he goes, he can in memory again return. The poem expresses his profoundest attachment to *this* back country even as he prepares to leave it for another.

The country to which he goes is Japan, "a great stone garden in the sea." And in the poem of that name, a stone garden of his own composed of four large blocks of poetry, he treats his discovery there of love, family, and home. Judged by the few poems on Japan, this is the wonderful reward of his experience. "Toji" tells of unusual acceptance ("Nobody bothers you in Toji") and "Kyoto: March" of the lovers beneath the roofs of frosty houses, who

> part, from tangle warm
> Of gentle bodies under quilt
> And crack the icy water to the face
> And wake and feed the children
> And grandchildren that they love.

Love of this kind, tendered in this way, is at the heart of "A Stone Garden."

In the first stanza the poet has a waking dream of the immemorially gardened land, a dream of past-in-present, while on a train carrying him from the countryside to the city—to Tokyo, where, "like a bear," he tracks "the human future / Of intelligence and despair." His awareness of culture, of form, of a mastered ecology achieved by centuries of care, contrasts with the urban jungle inhabited by "A horde of excess poets and unwed girls." Yet in the city, where he "walked a hundred nights" (this stanza begins with the recollection of "a girl I thought I knew," perhaps the "Robin" of later poems, and, like the first which bespeaks restlessness, bespeaks loneliness) he observes

> The thousand postures of all human fond
> Touches and gestures, glidings, nude,
> The oldest and nakedest women more the sweet,
> And saw there first old withered breasts
> Without an inward wail of sorrow and dismay
> Because impermanence and destructiveness of time
> In truth means only, lovely women age—
> But with the noble glance of I AM LOVED
> From children and from crones, time is destroyed.

Such love conquers time—his own rare insight into the beauty of old women convinces us of this. But it does this also because it venerates the fertile mystery upon which, in the poet's view, this culture is built and sustained through all vicissitudes, the mystery he associates with the "glittering smelly ricefields," the permanence of nature. His own invocation to this power—"O Muse, a goddess gone astray"—follows in the third stanza, where, in telling of the difficulties of *the* poem he would write ("one time true"), he confesses failure:

> The long-lost hawk of Yakamochi and Thoreau
> Flits over yonder hill, the hand is bare,
> The noise of living families fills the air.

Yet finally he writes that poem in the fourth stanza, which, like the others, follows from something he meditates on—"What became of the child we never had—":

> Delight binds man to birth, to death,
> —Let's gather in the home—for soon we part—

(The daughter is in school, the son's at work)
& silver fish-scales coat the hand, the board;
The charcoal glowing underneath the eaves,
Squatting and fanning til the rice is steamed,
All our friends and children come to eat.
This marriage never dies. Delight
Crushes it down and builds it all again
With flesh and wood and stone,
The woman there—she is not old or young.

The urge to transcend "the noise of living families," to grasp the hawk or turtle-dove of poetry, is what this poem subdues. Sometimes flawed in syntax, cadence, and rhyme, the poem is nevertheless of importance in Snyder's development: he would relinquish even the self-love of poetic ambition and willingly serve the Muse that so deeply inspires him and makes love, fulfilled in community and culture, a way of enlightenment.

Although it was published after *Riprap*, *Myths & Texts* (1960) was written concurrently, during the years 1952–1956. It is Snyder's most ambitious book, a work of forty-eight untitled poems in three closely related parts comprising a single design and developing the theme of destruction-creation-renewal. Only a few of the poems are made as well as the best poems of *Riprap*; they are generally looser, their Poundian form more obvious. But taken together, as one continuous poem, they are an impressive achievement. Their title, *Myths & Texts*— probably taken from such early ethnological reports as John R. Swanton's "Haida Texts and Myths" and "Tlingit Myths and Texts"—describes the kind of lore to which Snyder, sometimes himself a shaman, assimilates his poetry. In the first shaman song he speaks of his work: "I sit without thoughts by the log-road / Hatching a new myth." But if the myth is new it is so for these reasons: it is knitted now of old myths (Biblical, Greek, Oriental, and American Indian) and created anew in the poetry. To go back, to repossess, to know the materials and acquire the mind that made them, is Snyder's way to the newness. One thinks of Thoreau, at Walden, having an original relation to the universe, writing scripture.

And Thoreau, it appears, is a tutelary spirit of the book, having provided two of its thematic strands as well as his example. "Logging," the first section of the book, treats the destruction of the wilderness, which Snyder, by citing the text "But ye shall destroy their altars, break their images, and cut down their groves" (Exodus 34:13), attributes to Christian righteousness and rapacity. In the tenth poem of this section he says:

> What bothers me is all those stumps:
> What did they do with the wood?
> Those Xtians out to save souls and grab land

Thoreau expresses this theme of spoliation in *Walden* by asking, "How can you expect the birds to sing when their groves are cut down?" And the morning star, with which Snyder begins and ends the book, is explicitly Thoreau's ("The sun is but a morning star"), a promise of renewal, to be earned by the purificatory disciplines that Thoreau found in the East. (In "Dharma Queries," Snyder reminds us that Buddha "saw the *Morning Star* and had an enlightenment of which the content was a total comprehension of the nature of *interdependent co-creation.*")

Snyder begins the book in the present, with logging, the work he had done in the summer of 1954. He begins in the world of trees, with their violent quick destruction by machinery (see especially number 8), a terrible masculine force that also emasculates and can only be countervailed by feminine tenderness and love (see number 9). Having lost his job as a lookout because he had been considered a security risk, he turned to logging and had suffered through the lumber strike of 1954, as number 5 and "The Late Snow & Lumber Strike" (in *Riprap*) show. His politics may be said to begin here, in his association with loggers and with his intimate knowledge of their economic struggles (see number 7 and number 10)—with an awareness of the social fact that spoliation of nature contributes to spoliation of men. The concluding poems of the section (number 14 and number 15) contain his bitter anger and perhaps a Pound-like scorn. In both the text from Exodus is employed: in the first, as a refrain in a chronicle of destruction:

> The groves are down
> cut down
> Groves of Ahab, of Cybele
>
> . . .
> Pine of Seami, cedar of Haida
> Cut down by the prophets of Israel
> the fairies of Athens
> the thugs of Rome
> both ancient and modern;
> Cut down to make room for the suburbs

in the second, as sardonic comment:

> Men who hire men to cut groves
> Kill snakes, build cities, pave fields,
> Believe in God, but can't
> Believe their own senses.
> Let alone Gautama. Let them lie.

And since he has learned that the Marxian promise of permanent reform is a fairy tale ("O Karl would it were true / I'd put my saw to work for you / & the wicked social tree would fall right down"), he relies on the vast processes of destruction-creation spoken of in Hindu mythology. He is willing to wait out the Kalpa:

> Until the next blaze
> Of the world, the universe,
> Millions of worlds, burning

The second section, "Hunting," moves further back in time than the first. Hunting is an earlier wilderness occupation than logging and requires different skills and attitudes. By hunting we truly enter the wild and the world of animals. Snyder describes its virtue in "Poetry and the Primitive," in a section entitled "Making Love with Animals":

> To hunt means to use your body and senses to the fullest: to strain your consciousness to feel what the deer are thinking

today, this moment; to sit still and let yourself go into the birds and wind while waiting by a game trail. Hunting magic is designed to bring the game to you—the creature who has heard your song, witnessed your sincerity, and out of compassion comes within your range. Hunting magic is not only aimed at bringing beasts to their death, but to assist in their birth—to promote their fertility.

Hunting is a disciplined, reverential art, a ritual in a culture that knows its environment intimately. So here, as in collections of American Indian lore, are prayers *for* birds, bear, deer; poems listing the foods "we lived on then" and telling how to make a horn spoon. These poems belong to the shamanist world of Raven and Coyote, in which, as in the poem on the bear mating with a woman, little distinction is made between animals and people.[4]

But for the poet in the present, the shaman sitting by the log road, hunting is also a search for the sources of renewal, for the way back to this intimate, vital world. Hunting of this kind requires other disciplines: those of ecstatic vision, whether induced by drugs or solitary exposure and fasting, practiced by the American Indians, or those of Zen, which, Snyder associates with shamanism. (In "Japan First Time Around," he is reminded by a Zen chant of shamanism and plays with the possibility, somewhat realized in *Myths & Texts*, of "Buddhist lectures on Shoshone texts or *Shastra* / commentaries on Navajo creation myth.") In the search for vision—new awareness and renewal—he joins both; their common injunction, given in the third poem, is "See or go blind!" This discipline is arduous, an ascent out of the hell of the mind that delivers one

---

4 In a brief notice of *Myths & Texts* in the *Journal of American Folklore,* LXXIV (April–June, 1961), 184, the use of the oral literature of the American Indians, their motifs, songs, text translation, a Kwakiutl phrase, Coyote, etc., is pointed out—and also the fact of Snyder's competence in this area and his intention of dedicating the poems to Franz Boas. *Earth House Hold* contains two reviews of books on American Indian legends and tales; they represent there the particular focal interest of these poems. Animal-people and animal-marriage tales are emphasized in both. Their significance for ecological attitudes is commented on later in *Earth House Hold,* 122.

from the Karma of animal life. It figures in a concluding poem
on mountain climbing:

> First day of the world.
> White rock ridges
>               new born

and in the closing poem, which tells of the birth of a child:

> How rare to be born a human being!
> Wash him off with cedar-bark and milkweed
>               send the damned doctors home.
> Baby, baby, noble baby
> Noble-hearted baby.

and ends with girls nursing animals:

> Meaning: compassion.
> Agents: man and beast, beasts
> Got the buddha-nature
> All but
> Coyote.

The last section of the book relies more on Oriental scripture
than American Indian lore. Its title, "Burning," probably comes
from Buddha's fire sermon. The poems focus now on the
unconscious and on the need to "learn to love, horror accepted." The universe—"The Mother whose body is the
Universe / Whose breasts are Sun and Moon"—sustains us.
Like John Muir at impasse scaling Mt. Ritter, we can rely on
her. For we are "Balanced on the boundless compassion / Of
diatoms, lava, and chipmunks" and need only sacrifice our
self-love, the "clutchings," to realize it. We need to purify the
self, become the "pure bug" in the "dry, hard chrysalis," whose
hatching is rebirth and awakening. (The imagery is Thoreau's.)
And we need also to know that the "whole spinning show" is
"falling or burning"—that destruction, the burning, is the condition of creation and transformation; that, in a forest fire, "The
hot seeds steam underground / still alive."

This image (in number 15) brings forward again the theme of
renewal introduced in section one. There Snyder tells of the

lodgepole pine whose seed escapes destructive fire and thereby brings new birth. In the last poem of that section the "Lodgepole / cone / seed waits for fire" and we are enjoined to "wait / Until the next blaze." This is the blaze, the forest fire up Thunder Creek with whose cessation and the glimmer of the morning star and the new dawn the book apocalyptically ends.

Snyder's next volume of poetry, A Range of Poems, is his largest book to date. Published in London in 1966, it is, as the stamping on the spine indicates, a "Collected Poems"—here, in the following order, one finds Riprap, Cold Mountain, Myths & Texts, Miyazawa Kenji, and The Back Country. The translations in this volume are a notable part of his work and function in much the same way as the translation, "Record of the Life of the Ch'an Master Po-chang Huai-Hai," in Earth House Hold. The life of Master Po-chang is an example of Zen hagiography and, after "Tanker Notes," reestablishes the strict Zen discipline of "Spring Sesshin at Shokoku-ji" and serves as a foundation for the remaining essays. Cold Mountain, as we have seen, provides a model of Zen life and attainment—as Snyder says of Han-shan and his friend Shih-te, the original Dharma bums, "they became Immortals and you sometimes run on to them today in the skidrows, orchards, hobo jungles, and logging camps of America." It also provides a model of Chinese poetry just as the selection of poems from the work of Miyazawa Kenji (1896–1933) provides a model of recent Japanese poetry. These translations show us what Snyder has tried to assimilate and are as important in his work and in gauging his achievement as Lowell's translations in Imitations are to his. The selections from Miyazawa Kenji are in free verse and treat states of landscape-and-being, the Buddhist awareness of man in nature. They set a very high standard—only a few of Snyder's poems attain the excellence of Miyazawa Kenji's "Spring and the Ashura" and "Pine Needles." In A Range of Poems, they preface The Back Country; in the recent altered and enlarged edition of The Back Country (1968), they are placed at the end.

The development represented by The Back Country is not one

223

of kind so much as scope. The essential ground of the earlier poems is covered again only now there are some modifications in form, focus, tone, and theme. The design of "A Berry Feast," for example, is more complex, as perhaps it should be in a single poem resuming so many of the poet's previous themes. Williams' triadic variable foot is now employed, as in "A Heifer Clambers Up," and the use of space punctuation within the line is more frequent. There is even a calligramme—"Once Only." None of this is as significant as the poet's attempt to find a formal structure of sufficient openness for the full range of his work. The title itself serves this end of unity, and in the recent edition of the book, Snyder spelled it out by replacing the numbers of the previous edition with Far West, Far East (Japan), Kali (India), and Back (spelled ʞɔɐᗺ). This names the progress of his travels but also, in conjunction with an epigraph from Bashō, indicates the way of life exemplified by the poems. The epigraph announces the desire to wander, which requires an open form: "So—when was it—I, drawn like blown cloud, couldn't stop dreaming of roaming, roving the coast up and down." This is a free rendering and expresses a more youthful and carefree spirit than one finds in A Journey to the Deep North or in The Back Country itself. An adventurous spirit belongs more fittingly to a series of haiku published here under the punning title, "Hitch Haiku," and to what promises to be the poet's longest work, Mountains and Rivers Without End (six sections were published in 1956). The conception of this endless poem comes from scroll painting; in The Dharma Bums, Japhy Ryder describes it: "I'll do a new long poem called 'Rivers and Mountains Without End' and just write it on and on on a scroll and unfold on and on with new surprises and always what went before forgotten, see, like a river. . . . I'll spend three thousand years writing it, it'll be packed full of information on soil conservation, the Tennessee Valley Authority, astronomy, geology, Hsuan Tsung's travels, Chinese painting theory, reforestation, Oceanic ecology and food chains." The poems already published are often more "experimental" in form and more vernacular than the poems published elsewhere—and more uneven in quality. They are Snyder's version of an *open road* and their formal freedom and capaciousness sometimes reminds one of Pound's *Cantos*. There is yet no assurance that their unity may be of the kind declared in the following verse cited by Blyth (*Haiku*, I): "Mountains and rivers, the whole earth,— / All manifest forth the essence of being." Even though they are not placed in chronological order—perhaps because of it—they have the freshness of unfolding experiences. But they do not present experience as we now begin to find it in *The Back Country*, where the formal structure involves return, a turning back.

The unity of *Riprap* is essentially one of stillness, and that of *Myths & Texts* is thematic. The unity of *The Back Country* depends upon the notion of travel and the metaphoric force of the title, but neither secures it so much as the presence of memory which now begins to fill some of the poems. This is a third volume of poems, and so its ground is familiar to poet and reader and, in a sense, recovered. Now experience is compounded by remembering and deepening of life. Though the book, especially the opening section, "Far West," contains poems that might have been included in *Riprap*, its dominant tone is of another kind. There is agitation in *Riprap*, but it is resolved by a course of action, the journey to Japan. Now, much that the poet has carried with him on his travels is admitted, as in "Looking at Pictures to be Put Away":

> Who was this girl
> In her white night gown
> Clutching a pair of jeans
>
> On a foggy redwood deck.
> She looks up at me tender,
> Calm, surprised,
>
> What will we remember
> Bodies thick with food and lovers
> After twenty years.

And as he continues to travel, still by working aboard ship, he begins to ponder in "7.IV.64," and not with the levity the poem intends, his place in life:

all my friends have children
& I'm getting old.    at least enough to be
a First Mate or an Engineer.
now I know I'll never be a Ph.D.

What is now admitted in the poems, and we realize was hitherto almost wholly excluded, is the poet's experience of love. The more he travels the more he is possessed by thoughts of love and friendship, and by a sense of loss, by the memory of innocent desire with which he first knew them. Back, mirror-imaged, may be a reflection of this.

Friendship is a minor strain, best repeated by "August on Sourdough, a Visit from Dick Brewer" and "Rolling In at Twilight." The gesture of the poem itself, which names the friend and fixes forever an exemplary act, testifies to Snyder's feeling for the deep and open relationship of youth. In the first poem Dick Brewer "hitched a thousand miles" to see the poet, who, in turn, loaned him his poncho; in the second, Phil Whalen has laid in some groceries against the poet's probable arrival.

Love is the major strain and is first presented here in "After Work":

The shack and a few trees
float in the blowing fog
I pull out your blouse,
warm my cold hands
on your breasts.
you laugh and shudder
peeling garlic by the
hot iron stove
bring in the axe, the rake,
the wood
we'll lean on the wall
against each other
stew simmering on the fire
as it grows dark
drinking wine.

Love here is a prized part of a steady continuum of living whose 226 sensations the poet fully savors and deeply appreciates. It is depicted as a homecoming. And it is as simple and directly physical and without haste as the poem, for the poet who transfers the rhythm of his experience to the poem knows the values of relation and contrast, the care of the husbandman, and is as confident of the pleasures of love as of other goods of life, the food to come, the wine, the enveloping warmth and darkness.

This poem is among the new poems in the latest edition of *The Back Country*. Along with the concluding poem of section one, "For the Boy Who Was Dodger Point Lookout Fifteen Years Ago," it introduces the theme of loss and longing that before was not broached until the poems for Robin in section two. This concluding poem is explicitly retrospective. A head note tells us that the poet, now hiking alone in the Olympic mountains, remembers a trip in the same area many years before with his first wife (an experience treated in another poem, "Alysoun," which begins section three). The poem is for the boy-lookout and for the boy the poet had been. It describes the mountain meadows and, from the vantage of the lookout, to which the poet has climbed to talk with the lonely boy, the tableau of Alison (Robin) bathing naked in a pond. From this distance she is "Swan Maiden," a lovely icon as well as significant myth-motif. For what is important is the meeting of poet and lookout "in our / world of snow and flowers"—the representation of friendship as perhaps higher and purer than love. The concluding stanza, not without Hemingwayesque sentimentality, contrasts the pristine relations of love and friendship with the present desperate confusion of the poet:

> I don't know where she is now;
> I never asked your name.
> In this burning, muddy, lying,
> blood-drenched world
> that quiet meeting in the mountains
> cool and gentle as the muzzles of
> three elk, helps keep me sane.

In section two, "Four Poems for Robin" carry this theme. They tell of the lonely poet who remembers in his body ("I remember your cool body / Naked under a summer cotton dress") and now knows that in the "pointless wars of the heart" he lost the "grave, awed intensity" of young love:

> . . . what the others
> All crave and seek for;
> We left it behind at nineteen.

"December at Yase" tells of the wars of the will ("I was obsessed with a plan"; "I thought I must make it alone. I / Have done that")[5] but also acknowledges that he might have had another karma—something which his body also hints in "Siwashing it out once in Siuslaw National Forest" where he writes:

> I don't mind    living this way
> Green hills    the long blue beach
> But sometimes    sleeping in the open
> I think back    when I had you.

With section three, "Kali," the theme of love becomes more prominent. As a way of designating his travels, "Kali" stands for India; the section includes the poems on India that are counterparts of "A Journey to Rishikesh & Hardwar" in *Earth House Hold*. But Kali is the Mother Goddess, and many poems, variously, praise her. The opening poem to Alison acknowledges her as the first of many Kalis in the poet's experience. There are poems of the whorehouse and of erotic adventure and of marital celebration (Snyder married Joanne Kyger in 1960). But all—and this is invariably true of Snyder's treatment of love—are tender and reverential. Love for him, as other poems here on darkness and drunkenness suggest, is a dark ecstatic mystery. It is so in "The Manichaeans," where love is presented as a cosmic power, creating light, warmth, and life. This ambitious poem tries to assimilate myth to present experience and is less successful in doing this than "August Was Foggy," a simple poem of the last section that, in the concluding stanzas, achieves it:

5  Snyder was married to Alison Gass from 1950 to 1952. *Riprap* begins almost immediately afterward.

The first green shoots of grass.
   you
  like some slender
  fresh young plant
turn smooth and cool across me
   in the night.

touch, and taste, and interlace
  deep in the ground.  new rain.
as we begin our life.

This poem also conveys those aspects of Tantra, so important to the poet's love ethic, considered in "Nanao Knows" ("Each girl is real") and "How Many Times" ("open, / were I as open"). The poet's travels are a journey to love, a pursuit of the way.[6]

And as the other love poems of the last section show he has learned much on the way. "Across Lamarck Col" not only confesses his fault ("your black block mine") but the fact that all subsequent love affairs assert his loss, his fidelity to original feeling. And another fine poem, as good in its complexity as "August Was Foggy" is in its simplicity, realizes the equation of mountain=nature=woman. "Beneath My Hand and Eye the Distant Hills, Your Body" is a geography, geology, aesthetics, and metaphysics of love in which abstractions are used to deny themselves and yield the solvent feeling of experience. In this poem, Snyder shows as well as anywhere what it is that he has gone in search of and brought back from the East.

His most recent work, *Regarding Wave*, celebrates the world-as-woman and love as its ever-generative force, the spirit that moves him to poetry and now to marriage and fatherhood. The title and essential ideas of the book are glossed in "The Voice as a Girl," a part of the essay, "Poetry and the Primitive." He explains here what he tries to convey in the poems: that, for him, the universe is alive and enters his body as breath, thereby enabling him to sing out "the inner song of the self"; that poetry is such inspired speaking, a response of the self that is deeper than ego to the touch of the world. The attitude he wishes to

6 It should be noted that Snyder honestly acknowledges the correlative emotions in "To Hell with Your Fertility Cult" and "Tasting the Snow."

present is not that of the Western tradition of the Muse and
Romantic Love, though its notion of "woman as nature the field
for experiencing the universe as sacramental" is all of the
primitive tradition that is left to us. Not woman as nature but
nature as woman is what he sings—not a particular woman
divinized, as in the cult of Romantic Love, but the Goddess
herself. The Goddess Vāk. "Poetry is voice, and according to
Indian tradition, voice, vāk (vox)—is a Goddess. Vāk is also
called Sarasvati, she is the lover of Brahma and his actual
creative energy." Sarasvati means "the flowing one"; and "as Vāk
is wife to Brahma ('wife' means 'wave' means 'vibrator' in
Indo-European etymology) so the voice, in everyone, is a mirror
of his own deepest self." Such is the meaning of *Regarding
Wave*, the poet's reverential praise of the continual creation in
which he humbly and gratefully participates.

It is always difficult to write a poetry of praise. None of the
poems in this book is especially epiphanic. Snyder's achievement is not in single poems but in the sustained feeling and
quality of the book as a whole. The book is well unified by a
three-part structure that may be considered wavelike, by a
wavelike line and stanza, by the breath-phrasing of the line, not
unusual with Snyder, but emphasized here, and by its single-
ness of theme. The wave is to Snyder's apprehension of nature
what the leaf is to Goethe's—it is the ur-phenomenon. He
celebrates it variously: in ocean, river, sands, pebbles, clouds; in
flow and process and growth; in ecology and food chains. And
against this celebration of organic creation, he sets a counter-
theme of spoliation and violation of the female. The book
begins with an invocation to the wave

> Ah, trembling spreading radiating wyf
> racing zebra
> catch me and fling me wide
> To the dancing grain of things
> of my mind!

and ends with the prayerful awareness of the still flowing wave in
all things:

The Voice
is a wife
to
him still.[7]

From Lookout
to Ashram:
The Way of
Gary Snyder

And the book is especially well unified by its occasion, the fullness of the new life, a primitive, "archaic" life, he has found with Masa Uehara at the ashram on Suwa-no-Se Island, their marriage there (with which account the superb last essay of *Earth House Hold* ends), and the birth of their child out of the sea of the womb. In "It Was When," a catalog (or Whitmanian litany) of sexual consummations, he tells how "we caught"—and

>              Waves
>           and the
>                    prevalent easterly
>                       breeze
>                whispering into you
>                    through us,
>                         the grace.

In "The Bed in the Sky," he turns from the cold outdoors, where he feels he ought to stay to watch the moon, to the indoor warmth of bed and wife and the stirring child in her belly. "Kai, Today" announces the sea-birth of his son, and "Not Leaving the House" tells of the change this advent has brought:

>           From dawn til late at night
>              making a new world of ourselves
>              around this life.

This is not a book of travel nor of place, though the third section is largely devoted to the "burning island." Place is important but finally indifferent. What matters in this account of working in the elements of sea and land, of planting seeds and caring for new life, is that the current of the universal being has flowed through him and he has become, more selflessly, a

---

7 Snyder uses as space divider in this poem and "Rainbow Body," the *Vajra* device ( **✴** ) also used in "Dharma Queries." It is, he says, "an ancient wisdom / thunderbolt symbol."

231

servant of life. And something hitherto unattained has at last been attained: the wish of the lookout who long ago noted in his first journal, "Or having a wife and child, living close to the ocean, with skills for gathering food." This book commemorates the taking up housekeeping on earth.

From lookout to ashram. From Walden, we might say, to Fruitlands. The imperative throughout is Thoreau's: "Every man is tasked to make his life, even in its details, worthy of the contemplation of his most elevated and critical hour." But the direction is Alcott's: from solitude to society, from the individual to the family. Meditation is a seeing into the self that entails its acting out, and this action, Snyder says, in "Buddhism and the Coming Revolution," is "ultimately toward the true community (sangha) of 'all beings.'" The revolution—or transformation— he calls for is to be made in family life, for its agency is love and "love begins with the family and its network of erotic and responsible relationships." To change the form of family life is to alter society radically, at its root. And Snyder's Edenic vision of "ecological balance, classless society, social and economic freedom" is as radical for our society as the matri- lineal communal family that he believes enables it—the "family as part of the divine ecology."

The feelings to which this familial-social vision answers are neither unfamiliar nor radical. Literature, and the literature of youth, has always reported them. Snyder, whose writing tells nothing of his past family life, tells in "Passage to More Than India" of his own discovery, at eighteen, in a community house, of "harmony and community with fellow beings." This too, much later, is what he found ideally at the Banyan Ashram on Suwa-no-Se Island. Such feelings, like so much that is consid- ered radical, are conservative—conserving essential and full humanity—and Snyder is right to connect them with occult traditions and a persistent Great Subculture. What is radical now is not merely the repudiation of present social forms ("the modern family is the smallest and most barren that has ever existed"; "the traditional cultures are in any case doomed") but the search for social solutions in the past, the distance back being, perhaps, the measure of this. Snyder is radical because he holds, as he says, "the most archaic values on earth" and because he tries to advance them by realizing them anew in his life and his work. Yet there is nothing archaic in his appropriation of them: they are his (and ours) by right of modern psychology and anthropology as well as meditation. No more than Thoreau, can he be put down as a primitive: "I try to hold both history and wilderness in my mind," he says, "that my poems may approach the true measure of things and stand against the unbalance and ignorance of our times."

This declaration addresses our fearful centralizing technology and the sovereignty of the present that speeds it on; and it is noteworthy because it announces again, for still another generation, the great theme and major work of our time, the restoration of culture in its true measure. Like Lawrence and Williams before him, to cite only two of the pioneer modern writers with whom he stands, Snyder would redress our culture by restoring the vital and the feminine, by voyaging historically and psychically to Pagany, and by charting for us new contours of feeling.

We should not expect him by himself to work this great change. This is the mistake of those who confuse poetry with politics, critics like Peter Levi, who says that we need Snyder's poetry but adds that "his medicine is not going to cure anything." His work is political because it bears witness; on this account one respects the ways it combines autobiography and utopia. We should accept his optimism—can an ecological conscience be created in time to save a devastated universe?—as a condition of the work, as an act of faith founded on profound basic trust. It is not the register of social naïveté. The distance from lookout to ashram is long and difficult; it is not easy for us to enter the back country nor find the archaic springs. We cannot expect literature to cure us, only to hearten us by showing us new and true possibilities and how much may be achieved in life and art by conscious endeavor. Snyder's work, already a substan-

tial achievement, does this. And it may be especially heartening
to us because in it an American poet has finally turned to the
Orient and shown how much of America might yet be discovered in a passage to India.

This is an Iowa piece, as much the result of living in an
environment of poets as my study of Sullivan was of having the
Ricker Library of Architecture across the street. At Iowa, poetry
is a living art; it is widely practiced and deeply appreciated, and
its spirit pervades life and literature there. This is one of its
conspicuous attractions—and leavened, as it was when this
essay was written, by a vigorous counterculture, I found it
especially exhilarating. The *Iowa Review*, in which this essay
was published, was itself a product of this lively situation.

It is also a Minnesota piece. I wrote it in the woods, and it
should be dated *Taskodiak*, 1969, for that's the Indian name of
the small lake at the edge of the Chippewa National Forest
where we have a cabin on what once was—one buyer
removed—Indian land. We've gone up to Minnesota almost
every summer and for almost all of the summer ever since we
returned to the Middle West. That's one of the important facts
about our life, one of its redemptive features. We camped until
the vogue of camping overtook us. Then we bought some
burnt-over land in second growth, cleared the brush, and
began to build a homestead. Now we have a small cabin, a
barn-boathouse-garage, and a hut that I use for a study. The
woods at the end of the road have been cleared for a garden,
and the land behind us, mostly second growth, brush, and
pasturage, has been purchased—and posted—for the deer. It
was never really wilderness when we settled and it isn't arcadia
now. Others have moved in, realtors and developers have appeared, and the lake itself, clear enough ten years ago, has
begun to show signs of eutrophication. But it is still a good
place to be and a good place to work, and when, on the
publication of *Upstate*, I wrote Edmund Wilson about it, there

were more points of comparison to the old stone house than the latitude and the flora.

I intended to spend only a few weeks writing about Snyder. I wanted respite from work on Hart Carne. But the pleasure of this encounter was too great; the essay took over and took up much of the summer. It is easy to see why. Snyder is one of the exemplary figures of the counterculture. He enabled me to credit many of the things I valued in it—the open way of being, the concern with poetry and ecology, with Oriental and Amerindian thought, and, not the least, the continuity with the Transcendentalists, chiefly with Thoreau, but also with Whitman and Emerson.

**From Lookout to Ashram: The Way of Gary Snyder**

# ALFRED
# KAZIN

*I*

BY ITS very nature as autobiography, A *Walker in the City*,
Alfred Kazin's first installment in this form, serves a double
function. Its existential source—the occasion of its being written, its perspective on the past—tells us of the present, say,
1950; and its material, its riches of memory, tell us of the past,
of the period 1920–1932. The writer who undertakes this backward journey is thirty-five years old (too young, we wonder, to
be moved by the autobiographical impulse?). He has achieved
what he now recalls: escape from Brownsville, the ghetto, in
Brooklyn, at the end of the subway line. Like many Jews of his
generation, like the immigrant children of the Italians, Ger-
mans, and Irish who live nearby, like provincials everywhere,
from the small towns of the Midwest, for example, he has
reached the City and has made good in an alien and—he
thinks—superior culture. To appropriate a not unwarranted
phrase, he has, to some extent, found "the promise of American life"; he has "watched/the city from a distance," has believed it, as William Carlos Williams says, "ablaze" for him,
and has answered its call. By 1950, he is already famous—recognized in New York intellectual circles *and* in academia. At
the age of twenty-seven, in 1942, he published *On Native*
236  *Grounds*, a study of American literature from 1890 to 1940, a

tour de force whose spiritual necessity it is part of his autobio-
years as a reporter in England, had published the Viking *Porta-*
*ble Blake,* and—it is indicative of a notable aspect of his career—had begun to mediate the worlds of journalism (public
letters) and scholarship (the university). His achievement, his
success in what he had chosen to do, seems archetypal.

And it is archetypal in the telling in *A Walker in the City,* for
he knows that what he has done not only follows a social pattern
exemplified in the careers of others (there is a literature of this)
but the psychological pattern of growing up, discovering the
immediate environment and the distant world, and by various
rites of passage entering it. Yet the telling—the splendid remembering promoted by his return to the ghetto, by his hunger
for and delight in the sights, sounds, smells, taste, and touch of
the close world of childhood—this sensuous remembering is
nostalgic, intensely so, not out of sentimentality or wistfulness
so much as recognition of the fact that what was left behind, a
condition of spirit more than anything else, involved great loss,
that the world he entered had not fulfilled his deepest expectations.

We know the author's present situation primarily from the
way in which he gives us the past and from our own situation in
1950, a watershed time of postwar unsettlement and change, of
the cold war and the war in Korea, of the decision to make
H-bombs, of the investigations by Joseph McCarthy. We also
know it from a recent reference point—the farthest in
distance—that introduces the section on "The Kitchen," the
center, the nucleus, the smallest and most protected of the
spaces into which the narrative opens, a place associated with
the solidarity of home, of the Jews, of socialists, and with all that
comprises the warmth that is happiness: "The last time I saw our
kitchen this clearly was one afternoon in London at the end of
the war, when I waited out of the rain in the entrance to a music
store. A radio was playing into the street, and standing there I
heard a broadcast of the first Sabbath service from Belsen Con-

centration Camp." Not only the Sabbath reminds him of home, but the fate of the Jews in those camps (the terror, as Isaac Rosenfeld said, that was beyond evil, beyond moral comprehension). He remembers his "mother's fears from Dugschitz to Hamburg to London to Hester Street to Brownsville"; his memory is of the memory of pogroms, of his mother's profound anxiety, of the Jews' fate and never-relieved insecurity.

The period in London is recalled again in *Starting Out in the Thirties*, an autobiographical sequel published in 1965. Here a recollection of Belsen in the epilogue closes out the account of the political hopes of the 1930s and speaks for the diminished hope of the subsequent years.

> One day in the spring of 1945, when the war against Hitler was almost won, I sat in a newsreel theater in Piccadilly looking at the first films of newly liberated Belsen. On the screen, sticks in black-and-white prison garb leaned on a wire, staring dreamily at the camera; other sticks shuffled about, or sat vaguely on the ground, next to an enormous pile of bodies, piled up like cordwood, from which protruded legs, arms, heads. A few guards were collected sullenly in a corner, and for a moment a British Army bulldozer was shown digging an enormous hole in the ground. Then the sticks would come back on the screen, hanging on the wire, looking at us.
>
> It was unbearable. People coughed in embarrassment, and in embarrassment many laughed.

In these casual ways—how characteristic of modern life—he encountered history, the "unparalleled catastrophe," the war that he realized later "made many of us Jews again."

*The last time I saw our kitchen this clearly. . . .* He does not mean that he would never see it—remember it—so clearly again, but that never again would he trust its solidarity, its trust. As the temporality of the phrase indicates, it is impossible to trust now all that he trusted then. History, which it was once thought, in the 1930s, would redeem mankind, has betrayed it; and the distant world of his boyhood, his America, has failed him too. This is especially poignant because his mother's journey from Dugschitz to Brownsville, like his from Brownsville to Manhattan, was made in the hope and expectation of a brighter future. For him, America was what life opened into, something so glorious, so much desired, that even the Jew, for whom the Gentile world is suspect, identified with it and gladly became its American Scholar. The strength of his love of America is indicated by his allegiance, by everything in his early experience that prompted him to become the author of *On Native Grounds*—the title itself affirming for him a spiritual necessity similar to Williams' in *In the American Grain*. And the strength of his disillusionment is indicated by his need to work back, through reluctance, to that Jewish world, to accept his Jewishness and, with it, an inalienable alienation.

The story of his coming of age is the story of his desire to move beyond the marginal, alienated world of the ghetto. But the story told in telling it concerns the emotional deprivation beyonding required (we feel this especially in the evocation of the sensuous world). It concerns his willingness now to relive that time which, in respect to alienation, is similar to his present condition, and to find in it, as his parents and others had, and he had, the strength to survive. By turning back he discovers a fact of modernism and contemporary history of which he had not then been wholly aware: alienation. He learns what Joyce knew in making Leopold Bloom the "hero" of *Ulysses*, that the Jew is a type of modern man and that the Jew, who believes as Bloom does ("It's no use, says he. Force, hatred, history, all that. That's not life for men and women, insult and hatred"), is certain to remain alienated in the modern world.

In describing the general impression of the book, Allen Guttmann leaves us with its paradox: "How fiercely the young man sought to escape the world that the autobiographer lovingly reconstructs." The autobiographer reconstructs that world because he has need of it. He needs the refreshment of its sights and sounds—he needs to hear again the voices he sets in italics, he needs to remember intensely and render accurately his inner and outer world. By doing this, he creates a space that he fills, a space in which he can recreate the self. This is what it means—and feels like—to remember. Yes, under the psychological necessity of going backward in order to go forward, he would reclaim the past, not just its Jewishness but everything that made him, stirred him, that gave the boy he was such fierce hope and allegiance to America. He needs this imaginative act—the autobiographical act that itself awakens imagination and works to its source—to countervail a fact of history that even as he makes his way back he is painfully aware of in the eroded environment: that you can't go home again.

The way back is mediated by what he has learned in the course of leaving Brownsville: by the icons and epigraphs with which he also admits us—icons and epigraphs he uses now to create meanings he hadn't grasped then. The cover depicts Brooklyn Bridge, the frontispiece is Stieglitz's famous photograph, "The Steerage," and the epigraph is from Whitman's "Crossing Brooklyn Ferry" ("The glories strung like beads on my smallest sights and hearings, on the walk in the street, and the passage over the river"). Allen Guttmann says that "in the contrast between the photograph and the poem lies the tension of the book. The memoir is about those anonymous immigrants whom Stieglitz fixed forever at the moment of their arrival in the Promised Land and about Kazin's own passage from the Brownsville of the immigrants to the 'great world' beyond the ghetto, the world that he, like Whitman, was to claim as native ground." This perception is limited, for these touchstones are incomparably rich and do not create tension so much as accord. All relate to passage, to crossings; and all celebrate artists (two of immigrant origin, the other an outsider) who dealt in a direct organic or functional way with American life, who, by means of art, confronted, transformed, and vindicated it. These artists —with Blake, an epigraph from whom introduces Part I— are, in Pasternak's phrase, "beloved predecessors." To use them is not an act of convenience but of allegiance, a declaration of similar intent. By means of art, Kazin, in the very act of

going back and taking up his slightest sights and hearings, would
again create a passage.

Of course, Stieglitz's photograph is significant for its content. But it is significant for Stieglitz too. It recalls for us the preeminent modern photographer, the man who did so much to introduce and adapt modern art to America, who in this very picture, as Picasso confirmed, rendered in cubist form an everyday, commonplace event.[1] And by way of Stieglitz it reminds us of Paul Rosenfeld, whose *Port of New York* honors the artists of the Stieglitz circle and proclaims their faith in the "American Moment"—whose very epilogue on the harbor may be said to comment optimistically on Stieglitz's picture because, at the time of immigration restriction, it offered the promise of art. Though Kazin does not mention Rosenfeld, he undoubtedly had him in mind. In reviewing a memorial volume to Rosenfeld in 1948, he acknowledged that "from the day his *Port of New York* first introduced me to certain modern American painters and composers, I knew how much I owed him and even how much I would continue to rely on him." But this debt is not so great in respect to the writing of *A Walker in the City* as the realization he had, on reading about Rosenfeld, of what "the life of an independent critic of Rosenfeld's seriousness means in our present literary culture, and how peculiarly isolated, to the point of the deepest distress, a writer with his particular gifts could become." Among his particular gifts was the impressionistic style with which he rendered the tribute of close personal response to the artists whose work he served—a style that Kazin says once put him off but now, placed in the context of his awareness of the dominance of T. S. Eliot and his unchallenged "reactionary social-religious doctrine," acquires the utmost significance for him. "The revolt against 'softness' and 'romanticism' in literature," he writes, "has carried with it a fear of the humanistic moral passion that is still the great heritage of our romantic and democratic past. And to this, in an age of increas-

---

1 For the record, it should be noted that Stieglitz took "The Steerage" on a ship bound for Europe.

ing depersonalization and the outward hardness that conceals personal anxiety, has been joined the peculiarly contemporary fear of 'mere' personal expressiveness." The criticism of impersonal experts may be necessary in "a time when an overwhelming sense of having come to the end of a period in man's total history put a premium on intellectual revaluation rather than on the literature of 'real' experience." But Kazin, in upholding Rosenfeld, now reaffirms the literature of real experience and confirms the humanistic moral passion that has always moved him. By recalling Stieglitz, he declares these values and nullifies the subsequent period of Eliot's hegemony. All of his icons and epigraphs, in fact, point back to the great heritage of our romantic and democratic past, to the time when that heritage had not been denied.

In choosing an epigraph from Whitman, Kazin also affirms the values of the Stieglitz-Rosenfeld circle, for Whitman was its patron-poet, heralded in *The Seven Arts* and proclaimed by Hart Crane in *The Bridge*, the great *American* poem of the era, which, in turn, compounded associations with the Brooklyn Bridge. The epigraph is appropriate, as Guttmann notes, because it addresses Kazin's passage from Brooklyn to Manhattan—addresses, too, his posture of walker and his concern with the glories of perception. (Whitman's "the glories strung like beads on my smallest sights and hearings" reminds us of Emerson's "Experience," where, in a brilliant paragraph developing the notion that "life is a train of moods like a string of beads," he asks, "Of what use is genius, if the organ . . . cannot find a focal distance within the actual horizon of human life?" And it reminds us of Crane, who used the image of beads in "Legend" and "Proem: To Brooklyn Bridge.") But Whitman's confidence in "the impalpable sustenance of me from all things" is only part of Kazin's debt. He uses the epigraph—it comes from the stanza introduced by the line just cited—in the critical way Crane used Whitman's poetry in "Cape Hatteras." For though he concurs with Whitman's statement on "glories," "walk," and "passage," he does not concur with the statement preceding it, a statement expressing the faith necessary to Whitman's poem: "The similitudes of the past and those of the future." Whitman celebrates the continuity of experience, but faith in this continuity is not easily held at the "end of a period in man's total history"—or even in the presence of the gratuitous change we accept in the name of progress. Yet this is the faith that the autobiographical passage from present to past awakens. The successful passage back underwrites a successful passage forward. And this is corroborated by the dedication of the book to his son Michael, Kazin's "Kaddish," as he was his father's.

This reminds us that in Whitman's poem passage ("cross from shore to shore") is associated with death and that Kazin, who associates the Brooklyn Bridge with freedom and in the epiphanic episode of crossing it pays wonderful tribute to Crane's "Atlantis," also recognizes that darker meaning. At the close of the book, where he tells of his "strange quest for the American past," of his love of the dusky world of the *fin de siècle*, he places the Bridge, about which he reads in Lewis Mumford's *The Brown Decades*, in that "forgotten time . . . in which I, too, I thought, would someday find the source of my unrest." But why that time? "The present was mean, the eighteenth century too Anglo-Saxon, too far away. Between them, in the light from the steerage ships waiting to discharge my parents onto the final shore, was the world of dusk, of rust, of iron, of gaslight, where, I thought, I would find my way back to that fork in the road where all American lives cross. The past was deep, deep." Then, as now in going back, Kazin sought, in an underworld, the ancestors, the dead, who would prepare him for a new life. "Onto the final shore" reverberates with Virgil's description of the unburied dead whom Charon would not ferry across ("And they stretched forth their hands, through love of the farther shore") and with Thoreau's reference to the Atlantic as the Lethean stream "in our passage over which we . . . forget the Old World and its institutions." And "fork in the road," especially in the context of discovering the secret of American history, calls up not Frost so much as Oedipus meeting Laius on the road between Delphi and Daulis. There is nothing explicitly Oedipal here, only the association of a certain mysterious historical time with his parents; yet the resonance is strong and suggests itself as a measure of the depth and force of Kazin's motive.[2]

These devices help us make our way into the book, and one more, the epigraph from Blake that stands at its portal, shows us how much Kazin has invested in them. In the introduction to the *Portable Blake*, Kazin cites all of "London," the poem from which he took the stanza on "the mind-forg'd manacles," and devotes several pages of analysis to it. He tells us here that "Blake paints the modern city under the sign of man's slavery" and that his presence in the poem is that of "a walker in the modern inhuman city, one isolated man in the net which men have created." "For him," he says, "man is always the wanderer in the oppressive and sterile world of materialism which only his imagination and love can render human. . . . In the modern city man has lost his real being, as he has already lost his gift of vision." Of the "mind-forg'd manacles," which he notes is at the center of Blake's thought, he says earlier that for Blake "the only restrictions over man are always in his own mind" and that restriction is his enemy. The epigraph, accordingly, not only declares Kazin's passionate humanism, but suggests to us that the walker in the city is not the boy but the man who had arrived there, and that what he has learned of the city tallies with Blake's fact rather than the boy's vision. The walker is, as Veblen said of the Jew in a passage cited by Kazin in *On Native Grounds*, a man of divided (double) allegiance, "an intellectual wayfaring man, a wanderer in the intellectual no-man's-land, seeking another place to rest, farther along the road." Yet it is vision he wants. He would overcome the dualism of "the block [the ghetto] and beyond [the great world]," the geography of spirit

---

2 After I had noted this impression, I came on the following in Kazin's "The Jew as Modern Writer" (1966): "The real drama behind most Jewish novels and plays is the contrast between the hysterical tenderness of the Oedipal relation and the 'world'; in the beginning there was the Jewish mother and her son, but the son grew up, he went out into the world, he became a writer."

that so powerfully moved the boy; and he would close the **Alfred**
distance of past and present. The walker in the city knows that **Kazin**
Brownsville belongs to the city and the past is neither distant nor
dead but alive in the present—it is "in the inmost vital substance
of the present," as Crane (another Blakean) said. For him,
therefore, the writing of his book, which is the real excursion, is
an exercise in redemptive imagination and love. And its
achievement may recall not only Crane's and Whitman's, but
that of Sherwood Anderson in *Winesburg, Ohio,* because, like
Anderson, who looks from the city back to the town, he found
"the still unspent sources of love." F. O. Matthiessen, who said
this of Anderson in a lecture given in 1948 (not long before his
suicide), also said something equally applicable to Kazin's work:
that it was harder now than at the end of World War I to awaken
people to the fellowship of life and living; that if our writers
wished to do this, wished to overcome "their pervasive sense of
alienation," they would have to give themselves to economic
and social democracy and so repossess Whitman's "unshakeable
belief in solidarity with common life."

The walker with whom the book beings is not the boy who at the
end discovers that walking could take him back to the America
of the nineteenth century, though he is about to make good a
similar discovery in respect to his own past. The walker must
make—find—his way back, and Kazin is true to this difficulty
by beginning, in Part I, with his return to Brownsville. Then, in
the three remaining parts, in a movement that is both ever-
deepening in its descent into the boy's self and matched by his
growth, he tells of his boyhood passage out of the ghetto. What is
notable here is that the gap between present and past, which is so
wide at the beginning, progressively closes, and at the end the
past fills all the imaginative space, has become present, just as,
in consequence, the self of the writer merges with that of the
youth on the threshhold of his experience. The energy and
excitement of the book are generated by the difference in selves
and perspectives, and by the writer's overcoming them. It is not

so much the story of his passage that moves us, though we are always moved by such stories, as the telling of it. For that demonstrates the power of art—is the means by which he possesses his experience, has it for his possession. The journey Kazin undertakes is one of self-recovery, and it is made by imagination. The blurb on the back cover of the paperback edition (a good summary description: "This world [Brownsville] expands in time and space—and inwardly into the boy's soul— to become the whole city of New York . . . to become America, of the present and the past, to become the world of music and literature, metaphysics and religion")—the blurb suggests this journey when it says that the book is "the story of a soul awakening to the ecstasy of the senses, the power of language, and the meaning of existence." It is a journey of self-recovery because he recovers by means of imagination the resources of being that had originally empowered the imagination, because the imaginative action expresses his deepest loyalty to himself.

The journey back begins with something we recognize when we go home—that once we enter that world it is as if we had never been away. The self we've acquired by going away has not displaced but only covered an earlier, deeper self, one that is pervious to the sense impressions that call from it its store of memories. And then it's not the earlier world that has changed so much as we have, which is why, on returning to it, we become angry over the way *that* always seems to reduce us to what we were, to make us children again.

> Every time I go back to Brownsville it is as if I had never been away. From the moment I step off the train at Rockaway Avenue and smell the leak out of the men's room, then the pickles from the stand just below the subway steps, an instant rage comes over me, mixed with dread and some unexpected tenderness. It is over ten years since I left to live in "the city"—everything just out of Brownsville was always "the city." Actually I did not go very far; it was enough that I could leave Brownsville. Yet as I walk those familiarly chocked streets at dusk and see the old women sitting in front of the tenements, past and present become each other's faces; I am back where I began.

Kazin feels rage because coming back cancels the achievement of his going away. This feeling is compounded by shame for his dereliction and the dread he feels in seeing the world he has escaped ("I sense again the old foreboding that all my life would be like this")—seeing with the recognition of one who returns the poverty with which he was once familiar, smelling the "early hopelessness," the "damp out of rotten hallways." Yet there is something else we know from our experience of return: that "everything seems so small here now, old, mashed-in, more rundown even than I remembered it." And there is tenderness, a feeling aroused by the "heart-breaking familiarity" and by the fact that he is back where he began, that Brownsville is given back to him.

Besides this complex emotional response, what we notice most is his distance from the past even though he feels it belongs intimately to him. For the perceptions are those of the literary man: "In the last crazy afternoon light the neons over the delicatessens bathe all their wares in a cosmetic smile. . . . The torches over the pushcarts hold in a single breath of yellow flame the acid smell of half-sour pickles and herrings." Another line, *"You promis' me, didnja? Didnja promis', you lousy f...?,"* reminds us appropriately of the overheard conversation of the homeward-traveling poet of "The Tunnel"—the poet estranged, near mad, undertaking the night journey that earns the deliverance of "Atlantis." This line also initiates a minor motif concerning the Negro, provides a clue to the structure and theme of the book (sustained by *'promis' '* and fortune-telling), and confirms the vague suggestion that the old women we meet at the start are the Fates. The few introductory paragraphs, like "Proem" in *The Bridge*, condense much of thematic importance, notably the dusk ("The sudden uprooting I always feel at dusk"—the displacement in time that makes Brownsville now what the nineties were for the boy), the "old battle cries" (Zionism and Communism), and the road ("Brownsville is that road which every other road in my life has had to cross").

We begin with the consciousness of the literary man. This measures his distance from the old familiar world, accounts for

the doubleness (and richness) of his impressions, and renders
the fact that he is an outsider. Almost before we enter the five
blocks within which so much of his early life was spent, we are
led out again on a long subway ride to the city (with the
prefigurative "then, that great summer at sixteen, my discovery
in the Brooklyn Museum of Albert Pinkham Ryder's cracked
oily fishing boats drifting under the moon") and made to see its
connection with the liberation of culture as well as with success,
since the ride also provides a geography of social mobility, of
"making it." We are made to realize what the child thought in
terms of the adult's survey of the metropolitan landscape—that
*Brunzvil* was outside, at the end of the line and of the world, an
enclave of Jews in Gentile America.

With this geography in mind, the impressions that comprise
the short sections or episodes—the incremental units of the
book—fall into place. Most of them adumbrate release (from
the "long pent-up subway ride"). Some concern the identification of the literary interests of the boy, as, for example, the
recollection of the tough guys stealing his violin for a joke,
which evokes Odets' *Golden Boy*, and the account of his devotion to Deborah, to whom he bears the gift of volumes of *The
World's Greatest Selected Short Stories*—a charming episode,
important for bringing together eros, imagination, and religion,
profound intertwined elements of his being. Other impressions,
awakened by the fact that he now stands outside, concern his
memories of being an outsider. Of these, the primary memories
are of related institutions: the little clapboard Protestant church,
a Gentile survival, an outpost, feared by the boy and associated
by him with the English language; and the public school, a
WASP citadel, where one of the trials of his Americanization
and "success"—all the more difficult because he was a stam-
merer—was the "'refined,' 'correct,' 'nice' English . . . that we
did not naturally speak." The episodes on school are the most
numerous and focal, since the school (as the experience of
other minorities again reminds us) is the institution which
cruelly defines the child's exclusion ("accusing us of everything

we apparently were not") while at the same time providing the way to confirmation (*"Alfred Kazin, having shown proficiency"*) and inclusion. Kazin's recollection conveys both present and past anger over a "system" that plants and perpetuates self-doubt; it is, with Bourne's essay on Transnational America, one of the truly eloquent denunciations of Americanization. Here the present and past self unite in anger, and we begin to grasp one element of the continuity of being between the boy and the man who endorses Faulkner's fury and Blake's hatred of "mind-forg'd manacles." We also discover one of the sources of his infatua- tion with the nineties in the epiphanic episode in the empty assembly hall—the space of his loneliness—where the boy associates the "new land," the "real America," not with the present but with Theodore Roosevelt and Oyster Bay. And we are reminded by the genteel attitude toward sex that he en- counters at school ("Sex was the opposite of books, of pic- tures. . . . They would not let you have both") of an opposition, a prohibition, that he found unnatural and would try to over- come.

This is suggested almost immediately by the way restriction yields to openness in the recollection of the street market. Here are the cries of life and erotic appeals to its good things; here is a bazaar, a rich world of delight, of hearty women, of food. And so, for man as well as boy, coming on the market "told me I was truly home." The market anticipates the kitchen in Part II; it is the public representative of the mother, whose solicitude, in Jewish humor, is chiefly demonstrated in terms of food (*"Eat! Eat!"*). But placed where it is, it offsets the school—offsets, in sensuousness and satisfaction, a cold and denying discipline, our residual puritanism.

In keeping with the public nature of Part I, Kazin recalls his father, a house painter, as he turns down Pitkin Avenue, "Brownsville's show street." His memories of the street he says he "secretly hated" are merely memories, not evocations; their power is negative, like the ghostly presences they are, and chiefly because they concern politics, labor unions, the depres-

sion years. They concern the ideological debates of the
1930s—and lost causes, as of course he knows now: "Standing
there I seemed to see two long processions of militant ghosts
passing down each side of me. Even as they flung at each other
the old catchwords, accusations, battle cries, they were united
in giving my despair of both a harsh, contemptuous and unbe-
lieving look. . . . Where now is Mendy . . . who went off from
the slums of Thatford Avenue to disappear on the Ebro, in
defense of 'Spain,' and before he left dismissed me forever in
rage and contempt?" Yet even though history has vindicated
him, he still feels the old misgivings, a matter of significance to
his literary identity.

This identity and its connection with his earlier self is the
burden of Part I, especially of the concluding section. Here, in
terms of movie house and synagogue, he depicts claims of his
being that seemed to him discordant. The movie house, associated with the Freudian notion of night and the pleasure-
principle and with guilt for daytime indulgence, is the place of
imagination, connected with "delicious reveries," with eros and
freedom (love, he tells us later, was for his parents "something
for the movies"), and with his mind's "proper concerns." It is the
dark place where the unconscious enjoys itself, begins to flower
("deep inside the darkness of the movies everything that was
good in life, everything that spoke straight to the imagination
began"), while the synagogue, another dark place, is, like
school, a place of trial, of duty and obligation. Yet the
synagogue, like the movie house, is an interior space, the place
where he discovers a dreadful and fascinating God, the God, he
says, who held the "solitary place I most often went back to" and
awakened a sense of depth that made him feel "right to myself at
last."

Both places are coeval aspects of the self that presses outward
toward release and liberation as well as inward to the deep
centrality and security of the self. They represent the necessary
energies that create the vital tension of his being—and his work.
250    And as the priority of the treatment of the synagogue suggests, he

not only did not relinquish all that the synagogue meant to **Alfred** him—religion, Jewishness, the Old World—but even accom- **Kazin** modated the imagination to the moral necessity of his being. The author we know is himself the witness of this resolution. He put away *The World's Greatest Selected Short Stories;* he would woo the world in other forms. He became a literary critic, one whose Jewish heritage contributed to his literary passage, made it easier for him to assume the responsibility of moral imagina- tion that Emerson had given the American Scholar. This is what the concluding section, much of it telling of his prepara- tion for Bar Mitzvah, confirms as an act of writing in the present.

The security, the self-approbation, achieved in Part I is neces- sary preparation for Kazin's return home. After all, he did vindicate his parents' sacrifice ("We were the only conceivable end to all their striving; we were their America"). He had succeeded in making the outward passage and in entering with distinction the great world. London, in fact, is the point from which his recollections in Part II begin. And he had done this without denying them, had succeeded in a way that was con- sonant with his heritage. This is also what he remembers as he stands out of the rain listening to the broadcast of the Sabbath service at Belsen. For this takes him back not only to the "healing quietness" of the Sabbath, to the "ancient still center" of Jewry, which is also the deep place of his own being, but to the kitchen, the center of his earliest world, which, like Jewry, is a heart, a place of love and torment, of security and fear: "Jewry had found its way past its tormented heart to some ancient still center of itself." Part II takes us back to the precious place of childhood; it fulfills the writer's deepest need of cosmicity as well as the need to find the origin of what he has become. The fulness of this return—and the art of the book—finds its measure in the restoration of the diminished and impoverished world he enters at the start to its original size and brightness, to its fitness to the boy's awakening soul.

The dominant figures of this childhood world are women, chiefly the mother, who, like other immigrant women, Dreiser's mother, for example, "held our lives together." Kazin's portrait of his mother is loving even as it depicts the anxious energy of the dressmaker who, in the fury of work, tried to alleviate her constant apprehension of "the hazardness of life and the nearness of death." The portrait also depicts his soul, the moods that became his because he was so emotionally responsive to her. Usually these moods, occasioned by thoughts of loneliness and death, approached dread, but the conclusive occasion he remembers is otherwise: "But between my mother's pent-up face at the window and the winter sun dying in the fabrics—'Alfred, see how beautiful!'—she has drawn for me one single line of sentience." *Has drawn for me.* Yes, now: "I see her now," he says, and so she gives him forever that gift of sentience. The tribute is as deep and powerful as the art and reminds us of Allen Ginsberg's evocation of his mother in "Kaddish," especially of the line that renders her tormented yet loving spirit: "The key is in the window, the key is in the sunlight at the window."

Kazin's account of the family accords with Gary Snyder's rediscovery that "Love begins with the family and its network of erotic and responsible relationships." The eros denied at school and expressed in the market is of the very atmosphere of home: in the talk of love and marriage, in the ample satisfaction of food (the Sabbath board rivals the market), in the three ripe unmarried women who, he says, "had a great flavor for me." Eros fills this world with its shapes, motion, sounds, fragrance—it quickens the senses and the imagination. It occasions the "togetherness" ("It was a quality that seemed to start in the prickly thickness of the cut-glass bowl laden with nuts and fruits"); it moves in—*is*—the talk, talk of music and literature and socialism, indistinguishable, finally, from culture, freedom, brotherhood, the great world. "Those three unmarried dressmakers . . . fully wrapped me in that spell," he says, "with the worldly clang of their agate beads and the musky fragrance of their face powder and their embroidered Russian blouses, with **Alfred** the great names of Russian writers ringing against the cut-glass **Kazin** bowl. . . . Never did the bowl look so laden, never did apples and tea smell so good." Like the bowl, the space of consciousness is full. And he is grateful for this fulness which, at the end of Part II, overflows his being.

One of these "enfranchised" women, his cousin who lives with them, provides him a private space that he can inhabit, chrysallis-like, and prepare his own enfranchisement. In her bedroom, with its books (among them *The World's Greatest Selected Short Stories*) and pictures ("a picture of two half-nude lovers fleeing from a storm... an oval-framed picture of Psyche"), with its exposed redolent clothing and memento of Russia, sex is not the opposite of books and pictures, and eros and imagination feed each other. Here, in the heat of the setting sun ("Happiness was warmth"), his spirit acquires wings and is freed like the pigeons he watches being sprung from their traps. In a quiet inward way, the moment is wonderfully delirious with possibility:

> Now the light begins to die. Twilight is also the mind's grazing time. Twilight is the bottom of that arc down which we had fallen the whole long day, but where I now sit at our cousin's window in some strange silence of attention, watching the pigeons go round and round to the leafy smell of soup greens from the stove. In the cool of that first evening hour, as I sit at the table waiting for supper and my father and the New York *World,* everything is so rich to overflowing, I hardly know where to begin.

This concluding paragraph is in the suspended present tense of memory. He has found his origins and the themes of his work.

For the Sabbath recalls not only a fairly common Jewish source but a source unique to him and, as he explains, necessary to him because of his Jewish background. The theme of his own "new-found freedom on the Sabbath" happens, in this instance, to be "*Among the discoverers of the New World,*" a phrase prompted by reading in school of the voyages of Henry Hudson.     253

And undercover of the Sabbath talk, especially when it turns to the oppressive European past, he reads about Theodore Roosevelt and thinks of Oyster Bay, entering it finally to speak up for homesteading in the West. He wished, he says, "to get at some past nearer my own New York life"; and he wished, without having to be alone ("The most terrible word was *aleyn*, alone"), to find a passage out. His father, he remembers, "brought the outside straight into our house with each day's copy of the *World*," and he associated the *World* with Brooklyn Bridge, which "somehow stood for freedom." And now, as he sits in his cousin's room awaiting his father's return, he is overflowing with everything that, in time, will enable him to make good his escape. That begins in Part III, but only because the security of home provided the purchase of risk and growth.

The movements of the remaining sections of the book are similar, an oscillation which, in its outward swing, affords the taste of freedom and fulfillment but not their full possession. It is the motion of the exploring self. The memories of the boy in Part III belong to his thirteenth to fifteenth years (1928–1930), those of Part IV chiefly to his sixteenth year. The horizon of his life widens, but, like the pigeons, the symbol of his spirit, he is still captive, at home on the "block." In both parts the organization of episodes fits his spiritual development: in Part III, the impressions, at first diffuse, acquire focus; in Part IV, the randomness of events belongs to a fulness of experience that gathers to the realization of vocation.

The foci of Part III are sex, old New York, and religion. The "block," which the boy now enters as he leaves the warmth and security of home, is apprehended for us by the writer who finds that many of the old landmarks have been replaced by second-hand furniture stores. The image of the tarnished—and its reiteration in disgust ("The whole block is now thick with second-hand furniture stores")—is the clue to the nature of his nostalgia, which is here the bond between man and boy. The block had always been rough and vulgar. His immediate memories of it involve the prohibited: "That 'coffee pot' was the first restaurant I ever sat in, trembling—they served ham and bacon there—over a swiss cheese on rye and coffee in a thick mug without a saucer as I watched the truck drivers kidding the heavily lipsticked girl behind the counter." Orality here, unlike that at the market and kitchen, is connected with curiosity; it disturbs him, and so does all the sex he discovers on the block—and in the cellar. In his recollection of the barbership, it is associated with the barbarity of World War I; in the recollection of some iron grillwork, with a frightful anecdote of circumcision. The absence of the chicken woman calls up an almost surreal memory of her hands in the guts and her calling out to him " 'Hey, studént! My Alfred! Come give me a big kiss!' " And of similar intensity is his memory of the madwoman who "would smile and smile at me with a fixed and shameless grin." To enter the world is an erotic adventure, sometimes an unpleasant one in which the spirit is assailed, and perhaps this is why he urgently seeks his mother when his fullest, most imaginative and spiritually rewarding erotic experience ends in death.

This shocking introduction to the block is explained in the opening words of Part III ("The old drugstore on our corner has been replaced"), for the old drugstore, as he tells us later, is what he misses most and treats most extensively. That he defers this treatment to the concluding section is justified by the fact that the various depths and currents of spirit he discovers in exploring the "old and American" (for him the significant content of the "beyond") and in studying the prayer book (religion has now become for him a "fierce awareness of life to the depths") have their confluence in his feeling for Mrs. Solovey, the druggist's wife. In her image he gathers up all of his idealism; she fully represents the spirit within himself that he had early recognized in a painting in the Metropolitan ("most wonderful to me then [was] John Sloan's picture of a young girl standing in the wind on the deck of a New York ferryboat—surely to Staten Island, and just about the year of my birth?—looking out to water"). In the Russian druggist's pale, thin, blonde, unworldly yet cultivated wife, he finds an answer to his profound need "to bestow love that came from an idea" and for a companion in "the radiant brotherhood I joined in books." In her he finds the image of his defiance of Brownsville.

And she is the object of sexual fantasies, of reveries like those awakened at the movies, only she is for him also, as in the moment of meeting he describes, a character from literature, Anna of Tolstoy's novel, a representative of culture. So it is right that she appears in the kitchen and that their meeting, presented directly, is transacted in French, is a language lesson and a lesson of language ("To speak a foreign language is to depart from yourself"). This is why their awkward conversation earns her gratitude and his curiosity about her residence in Browns- ville betrays her. His gaucherie dispels the spirit of romance— she belongs in the dusky world and is the spirit of what he seeks there—and though the boy doesn't understand "how much I had betrayed," the man, who immediately relates the details of Mrs. Solovey's suicide, does. Mrs. Solovey's death repre- sents the first death of the spirit, the first impasse of being, the subsidence of glory, of so much that here and elsewhere in the book is rendered epiphanically. The account of her death and funeral—it is the only death treated in the book—is the mourning labor that then, in his bewilderment, he had not fulfilled. Nothing will ever replace the old drugstore. The lamentation that closes Part III is for the loss of the pristine self, for the trials of the fine resilient spirit that, even as it is forged by, transcends the narrow, brutal life of the block.

Mrs. Solovey answers the boy's needs for a "beyond" beyond even New York. She belongs to a more distant great world, whose glory, like hers, he possesses inwardly, in imagination. His anima, she is his shield against the present, outer world. Never mentioned again, she nevertheless provides the aegis under which, in Part IV, he enters more fully and joyously the splendid inheritance of his manhood. She is the hovering pres- ence we feel surrounding the unnamed girl with whom he strays in the summer of his sixteenth year, the summer, he says at the outset, that was "the passage through" and that later he speaks of as an advent: "My summer's time had come; my own time had come at last." (Summer, here, is a Thoreauvian season of delight, not only because of its margin for experience but because the experience fills the craving for reality: "the silence of summer would fall on top of my head, cleaving me through and through.") Now the warmth that is happiness is found in the heat of the city street. "I was so happy," he recalls, "I could not tell what I felt apart from the evenness of the heat in which I walked. The sweat poured out of my body in relief. It was me, me, me, and it was summer."

Because of this oneness, this sense of being-in-the-world, "Summer was the great time." Kazin's memory of it, which moves into the present tense, is richly sensuous, a catalog (not unlike Whitman's) of pleasures that evoke the scene, his total boyhood world, and in addition, by means of recurrences—the pigeons, the Negroes singing on their way home to Livonia Avenue—stir our memory into movement with his. Now, once again over a geography familiar to us, we accompany him as he goes out—and grows—by way of politics (we are in the depression years): "The way anywhere those summer evenings led through the rival meetings [of Communists and Socialists] on Pitkin Avenue." And by way of art and literature, which he comes to now through his friendship with David Isrolik. "It was to the sound of *The Waste Land* being read aloud," he says, "that I met David"—and in the "naked house" of the Isroliks found united the intellectual's concern with radical politics and avant-garde art. And by way of another brief confirming friendship with a young teacher: "We used to go round and round it [the reservoir at Highland Park], reading in turns all I had suddenly begun to write that year. It was the summer of my graduation from high school, the beginning of that cardinal summer at sixteen when, day after day, wild with gratitude and surprise, I began to take in what I would live for."

The prose itself is tonic with that summer. For an identity crisis need not necessarily involve rough passage, but, to use the

phrase from Melville that Kazin used later, may be an inward
growth, the unfolding within (and of) the self that brings one,
and not with the fear Melville expressed, to "the inmost leaf."
Like almost all autobiography, A *Walker in the City* is a narrative of vocation, of the encounters that helped the boy discover
his "ministry," and for the writer who relives that time in writing
of it a present means of confirmation. And in this part it
confirms a radiance known earlier but in the shadow of dread
and death, and without sufficient certainty.

In this book of epiphanies, those of Part III lack something
that those of Part IV complete. The winter walk over the Brooklyn Bridge is one of the glorious episodes of the book, but it is
characterized by a freedom known in insecurity. "I felt lost and
happy," Kazin remembers. But toward the end of the walk,
apparently in conjunction with the "riot" experienced in the
ascent of the cables, the boy cries out, "Papa, where are they
taking me?" Similarly his realization of the marrow of divinity is
accompanied by dread, by the awareness that "there was no
gladness in it." Now, however, as he walks about the streets of
the city on the errands of his first regular job, he is not lost,
though he says he was "lost in them," because he is "swimming
in the weather," coextensive with the world. And now, in
keeping with the citation from 1 Corinthians, the perfect is
come and the fulness ("the pleasure is unbearable, it is so full")
and everywhere there is light. In reading the New Testament—
*in reading:* Vaughan, Sir Thomas Browne, Blake, Whitman,
Lawrence, Hemingway—he discovers words and images, their
power to fix his attention, to stir and release him, and he
discovers the great themes of divinity and eternity, redemption
and rebirth. In the word he comes at last into the joy of religion,
and in Yeshua (Jesus) finds the deepest, most fully answering
image of himself:

> I had known him instantly. Surely I had been waiting for him
> all my life—our own Yeshua, misunderstood by his own, like
> me . . . the very embodiment of everything I had waited so
> long to hear from a Jew—a great contempt for the minute
> daily business of the world; a deep and joyful turning back

into our own spirit. It was *he*, I thought, who would resolve at last the ambiguity and the long ache of being a Jew—Yeshua, our own long-lost Jesus, speaking straight to mind and heart at once. For that voice, that exultantly fiery and tender voice, there were no gaps between images and things, for constantly walking before the Lord, he remained all energy and mind, thrust his soul into every corner of the world, and passing gaily under every yoke, remained free to seek our God in His expected place.

**Alfred Kazin**

Past and present merge in the exultation of which this is only one expression—in this possession, this summons to the vocation of spiritual life. "And now," he says, watching the pigeons in their flight, "there is time. This light will not go out until I have lodged it in every crack and corner of me first."

In this section, the writer reaffirms his faith, the personal religion he serves by means of literature ("Religion," he had written at this time in a *Partisan Review* symposium, "is essentially an occurrence within, a personal experience, especially among the most personal beings in the world, artists"). And it is instructive to note in this regard that Kazin, writing in the *Contemporary Jewish Record* in 1944, said that long ago he had accepted "the fact that I was Jewish without being part of any meaningful Jewish life or culture" and acknowledged that "the writing I have been deeply influenced by—Blake, Melville, Emerson, the seventeenth-century English poets, and the Russian novelists—has no direct associations in my mind with Jewish culture." As the autobiography declares with the authenticity of the deepest self, he would be Jewish without being part of contemporary Jewish life and culture; his passage would be away from that culture. But, as he realized in writing his autobiography, that passage could not have been made, in the way he made it, without it. In fact, the autobiography realigns him with it and prepares for his subsequent interest in it. For what, after all, does it mean to be Jewish without being part of any meaningful Jewish life and culture? Only that one finds other ways to fulfill one's heritage. What moved Kazin to disdain American Jewish "culture" (in the *Contemporary Jewish Record*) is the impoverishment of Jewish culture. In the au-

259

tobiography, he rejects the necessity of success demanded of the children of the ghetto and, in Yeshua, embraces the "furious old Jewish impatience with *Success*, with comfort, with eating, with the rich, with the whole shabby superficial fashionable world itself."

This is why the "deep and joyful turning back into our own spirit" finds its immediate cultural and literary verification in a dusky time before the meanness of the present. The brown decades become the boy's chosen historical moment, not only because he connects them with his parents' arrival in America, but because they are a past, as he finds by walking, still within reach, visible in the streets, at hand in books and museums—a past that is indeed "deep, deep," correlative with the self. The passage out, enacted in the closing sections, is a literary excursion, a walk to the library. It is comparable to his reading of the New Testament on the fire escape, for it provides a similarly intense and deep experience, and the possession of the one is linked with the possession of the other: Ryder and Eakins, Dickinson and Whitman, yes, "my beloved Blake, my Yeshua, my Beethoven, my Newman," all together. But even as the writer recreates this wonderful moment and makes it affirm him, he conveys the uncertainty that the very fulfillment of the boy's quest has taught him. When he says that "I [the boy] had at last opened the great trunk of forgotten time in New York in which I, too, I thought, would someday find the source of my unrest," the *I thought* casts the doubt of the adult. So does the *as if* in "I read as if books would fill my every gap . . . let me in at last into the great world." There is no question here of the profound motive that compelled him in his "strange quest for the American past." Instead what strikes one is the extent to which the account seems to evoke the writer's rather than the boy's sense of alienation. As he speaks of those decades, a cemetery of "solitary Americans," and of the title (" 'lonely Americans' ") he had already thought of for a book, the somberness overweighs the brightness and joy which we have come to believe are so much a part of the boy's spirit. Was he, as he suggests, attracted to the brown decades because its artists and writers were alienated and mirrored his own alienation? Or was the reason otherwise—that he hoped to find in images, like Theodore Roosevelt and Oyster Bay, an America agreeable to his imagination, if only there a homeland? He is moved by both, though Kazin gives more weight to the former because it has become for him the weightier reason. In the preface to *On Native Grounds* he characterizes American writing by "our writers' absorption in every last detail of their American world together with their deep and subtle alienation from it." He finds in American writing a "nameless yearning for a world no one ever really possessed," and says that "what interested me . . . was our alienation on native grounds—the interwoven story of our need to take up our life on our own grounds, and the irony of our possession." Did Kazin, wishing to account for the autobiographical source of *On Native Grounds*, impress this on his memory? Perhaps the answer is to be found both in, and in the fact of, the concluding section, which countervails loneliness by reenacting another walk, the boy hand in hand with his girl, in untended Highland Park, a remnant of Old America. Here, with the city aglow in the distance, everything unites, makes "a single background to my desire," and alienation is overcome by the lights themselves, no longer "something apart," reaching out to him—"they were searching out so many new things in me."

In an anthology of Emerson's writings that Kazin edited with Daniel Aaron, one finds the following comment of Emerson's on autobiography: "An autobiography should be a book of answers from one individual to the many questions of the time." Autobiography addresses the present. Accordingly, the "fork in the road where all American lives cross" is not located in past time only, in the nineties, when the emergence of modern urban industrial society threatened our democratic destiny. We, too, stand at the fork in the road. And this may remind us of what Edmund Wilson said in *Patriotic Gore*—that "the Republic . . . has had to be saved over and over again, and it continues to have to be saved"—and of what Kazin said in *On Native Grounds*—that our writers "have had to discover and chart the country in every generation, rewriting Emerson's *The American Scholar* in every generation... [and even so] must still cry America! America! as if we had never known America."

How does this autobiography answer the many questions of the time? It offers no answers but is itself an answer: it saves the Republic by rediscovering America, by repossessing a vision of it, and within the actual horizon of human life, finding again the sources of our humanistic moral passion. It saves the Republic after the fashion of Emerson and Whitman, Wilson and Crane, by recovering for us the exemplary power of individual expression. It is an example of what Kazin spoke of in the preface to *The Open Form* (1961), a personal form like the essay that he proposed for our time because of its openness to emotional and intellectual discovery ("the true issues are those we discover in our personal experience, upon which in some sense our lives depend. . . . Once we make such issues our own, we can connect them to the public questions"). In this textbook, Kazin addresses the student as Emerson had—and as his autobiography addresses us—in terms of self-trust. The essay is a form for self-thinking; it is self-consciously individual. Kazin commends personal witness, and this, as well as the repudiation of WASP culture, makes *A Walker in the City* one of the first examples of the open forms that, in the two decades since it was published, have become a conspicuous expression of our time. In this respect, the use of voice in it is notable—and notable also because it reminds us of another meaning of the title. "It troubled me," Kazin says of his stammering, "that I could speak in the fullness of my own voice only when I was alone on the streets, walking about."

## II

In its deepest aspects, *A Walker in the City* is glossed best by Kazin's comments on Blake. The book is his attempt to recover the lost child and the lost world, the "real man, the imagina-

tion," and thus the power, as Paul Goodman would say, to live
on a little. The movement enacted in the book may be described
as a return from experience to innocence, or, in the correlative
terms of Kazin's explanation of Blake's contraries, from doubt to
belief, from lovelessness to love. He says of Blakean innocence
that in it "there is a poignant foretelling of experience, which is
death without the return to confidence and vision." The return
to confidence and vision—their repossession and his
renewal—is what *A Walker in the City* achieves.

As a way back, the book afforded Kazin a way out of the
terrible insecurities of our time. But his way, unlike that of
others, even Blake (in his account), did not lead to an absolute
but only to the restoration of spirit needed to go forward again
into experience and the uncertainty of life. At the center of his
thought is Freud's injunction that "Man must learn to bear a
certain portion of uncertainty"—an injunction, he says, which
is "much harder [to follow] than the authoritarian faiths of our
time," but which may be followed with the help of the imagination. Wherever one turns in Kazin's work, one finds him upholding the liberating, life-sustaining power of the imagination
against the crippling certainties of ideology. Nothing is of
greater importance to him or so much certifies his allegiance to
modernism. He is a partisan of imagination, and imagination is
his invariable critical test—that, or where a work does not aspire
to imagination, the absence of ideology. It is the conspicuous
theme of his critical work and the theme exemplified in his own
imaginative work, in *A Walker in the City* and *Starting Out in
the Thirties*. These autobiographies vindicate the imagination
by demonstrating its power to strengthen and so enable one to
continue to live in times of panic and disorder.

All of Kazin's work has its origin in the crises of our time—in
the fact that "permanent crisis" has become the condition of our
lives. For him, contraction and hardening and darkness characterize our recent history. The modern movement in art, which
in the years before World War I had not "lost its connection with
revolutionary thinking in all social and ethical fields," was

eclipsed, according to him, by the "terrible slaughters" and the disappearance of the "last idealism and political hopefulness of Europe." The major point of literary historical interpretation in *On Native Grounds* is that the resurgence of art, the modernist movement in America in the war years and the 1920s, only briefly withstood the eclipse in Europe and the skepticism over culture that contributed to fascism and heralded the disasters of our time. *On Native Grounds* ends by bringing us to the present in which (and for which) it was written: to World War II, when "our whole democratic culture," and, with it, freedom of imagination from the imposition of "external unity," was being tried. It reminds us, especially the concluding section, "The Literature of Crisis (1930–1940)," which tells of the defeat of modernism, of what Kazin said later, in "The Background of Modern Literature"—that "only in 1929, 1933, 1939, did all men begin to see how dark it really was."

In both autobiographical works, as we noted, the recollection of the concentration camp at Belsen is focal. In *A Walker in the City* it bears witness to Jewish history and the Jews' sense of the precious-because-precarious nature of existence; in *Starting Out in the Thirties* it comments mordantly on the pragmatic social reform of the depression years and the war economy that ever since has underpropped "the more accomplished society in which we are now living." For Kazin, who included an essay on the concentration camps in *The Open Forum* and wrote about Anne Frank, the profoundest meanings of this recollection are expressed in a review of Eli Wiesel's *Night*. Here, he is deeply moved by the episode of the "young boy standing on a mound of corpses, accusing God of deserting His creation" and by François Mauriac's response, in the preface, to the trainloads of Jewish children being deported from France. "Mauriac," he says, "feels that the deportation of children touches upon 'the mystery of iniquity whose revelation was to mark the end of one era and the beginning of another. The dream which Western man conceived in the eighteenth century, whose dawn he thought he saw in 1789, and which, until August 2, 1914, had

grown stronger with the progress of enlightenment and the Alfred
discoveries of science—this dream vanished finally for me be- **Kazin**
fore those trainloads of little children.' " These passages—how
far they bring us from the Blake and Beethoven Kazin celebrates
in the *Portable Blake!*—confirm his belief that the crisis of our
time is fundamentally spiritual. He endorses Mauriac's view.
For him, too, World War II marked the end of one era and
the beginning of another. But for him the dream of man, of
Blake and Beethoven, though eclipsed, has not yet vanished
and, where men and women still possess imagination, cannot
wholly vanish.[3]

Kazin's eloquence, as well as fury and grimness—traits he
sympathetically studies in essays on Faulkner and Freud—
comes from his struggle to maintain the dream of man in the
face of his own disheartening awareness of the course of recent
history and of social and spiritual alienation. In *On Native
Grounds* (1942), where he is concerned with both, he is
confident and lyrical, very much the exuberant youth of *Starting Out in the Thirties*, who, even in that trying time of economic difficulty and political faiths, took up his vocation and
began to write his challenging first book. As autobiography,
*Starting Out in the Thirties* recovers *this* for the writer in a still
more trying time; like *A Walker in the City* it reaffirms for him
the allegiance and posture he needs to continue his work. (It
may also be read as moral fable for another younger generation:
one must make a start, take up life whatever the times.) And just
as the earlier autobiography informs us of the depth of Kazin's
concern with America, especially with the dusky *fin de siècle*
with which *On Native Grounds* begins, so the later autobiography informs us of what critics of *On Native Grounds*
overlooked—that for Kazin it was an important intellectual act,
a polemical work arising from and directed to the immediate
historical occasion.

---

3  Beethoven taught Kazin to "accept the idea of gratitude as the wellspring of
existence"—"Gratitude that we are here, that we are still here, and have a
man's work to do."

Size, scope, subject ("An Interpretation of Modern American
Prose Literature")—these, and the youth of the writer, are impressive. But more remarkable is the fact that in writing this
book, Kazin acquired a usable past and forged a critical self. The
energy of the book gathers in the concluding section where he
treats the literature of his own time (mostly in terms of the
"surrender of imagination") and, in "Criticism at the Poles,"
repudiates both the Marxist and New Critical schools ("criticism
became a totalitarianism in an age of totalitarianisms"). Though
the omission of drama and poetry troubled the critics, only a few
noted the inclusion of criticism, among them Howard Mumford Jones, who found the long discussion of Marxist criticism
"out of all relation to [Kazin's] own estimate of its importance,"
and Lionel Trilling, who, himself about to accommodate the
critical extremes in "the liberal imagination," suggested that a
consideration of poetry would have softened Kazin's attack on
the New Critics. Perhaps the occasional shrillness of "Criticism
at the Poles" went unnoticed in a fiercely intellectual time when
"criticism had become the crucial battleground of world values." In any case, no one seems to have remarked that here
Kazin not only establishes himself between the poles but aligns
himself with the earlier critics of *The Seven Arts*, chiefly with
Randolph Bourne and Van Wyck Brooks, and with Edmund
Wilson, the independent critic who has continued to mean
most to him.

This alignment does much to explain the book: its epigraph
from Emerson on the democratic source of vital culture, its
concern with the end of the modern movement and the need for
another resurgence, and its mode—moral history—which answered Kazin's demand for a criticism at once deeper than the
usual literary history and more complete and complex (not
narrow and doctrinaire) than the formal criticism of the New
Critics and the sociological criticism of the Marxists. That he
could appreciate both Henry James and Dreiser indicates his
depth as well as breadth but not any emphasis that identifies him
with either school. Kazin is not a formal critic, though he is

attentive to formal matters. In reading him, one feels that he has responded to the work, that even where formal considerations are not prominent, he has heeded his admonition to Marxist critics ("the significance of any art work begins with its immediate success and fulfillment as art, its fulfillment of esthetic need and pleasure"). But this statement also admonishes the New Critics who, he felt, made the beginning an end. Even in his later criticism, where attention to formal matters is greater, or highlighted, Kazin uses form only to provide an opening into what he always finds more compelling—the writer's "world," the universe of self, society, and cosmos that the work proposes.

Kazin's critical work builds on Van Wyck Brooks and Edmund Wilson and, to a lesser extent, on Vernon Parrington. (His later work, because its voice is more personal and its quality resistant, recalls Randolph Bourne.) Though considerably larger and sounder in its scholarship, *On Native Grounds* is a polemical work of the order of Brooks's *America's Coming-of-Age*. It, too, surveys a tradition, is concerned with a usable past and the present critical (cultural) situation. In its way, it also recovers the ground of *Letters and Leadership*, Brooks's subsequent book. Like the combative early Brooks, his purpose is diagnostic and declarative, to call attention to a decisive turning in the national life and to the important role of letters. He enters the dialectic of culture that Trilling, another critic he admires, said was the form of its existence, and he depicts it in the organization of the book. Though he follows Trilling in deprecating Parrington's conception of reality, Kazin himself is historian enough to be genuinely interested in and informed about the main currents that preoccupied Parrington. Still, his own preoccupation, like that of Brooks and Wilson, is with the life of literature, the literary life as the intersection of self and society, biography and history. What troubles him with the New Critic, apart from the fact that he considers literature a "game" and makes it an absolute, is that close criticism is a closed criticism, limited too much to sensibility, to imagination in its private aspect. He taxes the New Critic, but he tasks the Marxist critic

because the domain of the latter is his own. "No field of criticism," he reminds him, "makes so many demands on the active
imagination as the study of literature in its relation to society." It
is not enough that he treats art as an "'ideological' representation of class forces in society"; he must, of course, fight, as Kazin
does, "the reactionary ideologue, who holds that art is aristocratic and the property of a few exquisite sensibilities," but he must
also "admit (precisely because he is confident that it is only with
the advent of Socialism that human energy will be great enough, human fellowship broad enough, to make great works
possible again) that without individual talent and humility and
discipline, without its immediate origin in exceptional persons,
no art is possible."

Kazin's own book is an example of the kind of criticism he
advocates. He characterizes it when he says of Brooks and
Wilson that they have written "with such abundant sensibility of
literature in its relation to civilization [a category higher than
but inclusive of society, demanding that the critic concern
himself with tradition and history, with the entire human en-
terprise] that for the first time one really sees writers moving
through the stream of time, a view in which not only a new sense
of history is grasped, but also the pang of individual experience."
And he characterizes it further when he says, in measuring
Granville Hicks's *The Great Tradition*, that "a more imaginative
critic would have seen his problem as a series of discrete human
situations, a problem of personality and character and will
expressing themselves in form, a problem of talent moving
against the pressures of a particular age, a problem of the subtle
and multiform relations through which a writer moves in order
to write at all." But neither Brooks nor Wilson, any more than
Parrington, answers fully the requisites of criticism ("a great
human discipline") that the young critic, excusably because
heuristically, sets down in redressing them. Though he is so
much in Brooks's debt that the very manner of his prose declares
it, he finds Brooks's work "monstrously inexact" and too negative, serving too much his notion of victimization, "that whole

sentimental-pathetic conception of the artist in America which dominated the critical opinion of the time." (It seems that Kazin considered his own work positive, but Trilling, who concurred in his judgments, thought otherwise.) He specifies his debt when he compares him with Wilson: "A tougher and more adventurous mind than Van Wyck Brooks, he had none of Brooks's primary moral force, the spiritual conviction that has been so indispensable to the modern movement in America." Yet Wilson (too easily denied moral force) is the critic with whom Kazin concludes "Criticism at the Poles" and whose practice defines the "great human discipline," a critic exemplary, finally, in everything except "sympathy with the present"—a deficiency, one gathers, that Kazin himself makes good. "Few other critics of the time," he says, "could turn the mind to them [the "great springs of life"]; in no other critic was a fundamental remoteness from them something to be missed."

How much moral force and participant spirit figure in his book can be seen in the concluding chapters. That on Faulkner and Thomas Wolfe reverberates with feelings rendered later in *A Walker in the City*, and the discussion of the "idea of America" that engaged Wolfe prepares for "America! America!," the climactic close. Here Kazin reviews the "literature of nationhood" that accompanied the crisis of the 1930s, a literature of national self-discovery and scrutiny and, also, unfortunately, of national celebration. The very things that Kazin tried to do in *On Native Grounds*—"recover America *as an idea* . . . thus to build [as the Wobblies said] a better society in the shell of the old . . . thus to prepare a literature worthy of it"—this attempt to restore connection with the past and claim the "American inheritance" was compromised by nationalism and patriotism, by the denunciation as irresponsibles of the modern writers whose integrity and heroism he cherished. At the end of the book, Kazin stands up to Brooks, not the Brooks whose early work fired his own, but the Brooks who, in *The Opinions of Oliver Allston*, denounced the modernism for which he had once been spokesman. Kazin reminds us, by referring to Proust,

Joyce, and Eliot, of what Wilson had already claimed for them in *Axel's Castle*—he *is* at the center of controversy—and speaks for his own appreciation of Eliot's "extraordinary services in behalf of the continuity of the Western tradition," a devotion to tradition that he himself defined in treating Willa Cather's imaginative use of the pioneer tradition as an "image of order and . . . of humanism" in a time of dissolution. And he speaks again for his belief in the inextricable connection of literature and life and for what Brooks had once claimed for literary criticism when he said that it "is always impelled sooner or later to become social criticism . . . because the future of our literature and art depends upon the wholesale reconstruction of a social life all the elements of which are as if united in a sort of conspiracy against the growth and freedom of the spirit." Yet, even so, there is a correlative belief: "Literature lives by faith [in imagination] and *works.*" *On Native Grounds* ends with the reminder that in a time of crisis nothing programmatic avails literature, only the writer as writer and dedication to the work of the imagination.

In every way *The Inmost Leaf* (1955), a selection of essays covering nearly fifteen years' work, presses this view, a view undoubtedly strengthened by the study of Blake and the writing of *A Walker in the City.* For one thing, the title does more than indicate Kazin's esteem for Melville and his own sense of unfolding. Melville used the phrase to describe the rapid development that brought him to *Moby-Dick* and his presentiment, during its arduous composition, of his own completion and doom ("shortly the flower must fall to the mould"). But for Kazin whatever sense of doom the title conveys is not personal but public, and its meaning, as the essays define it, concerns "what is most deeply human in us" (as readers to whom the artist addresses his art) and the "deepest places" in the writer himself. The inmost leaf brings him to what Roland Barthès refers to as the "depths of the author's personal and secret mythology," or to that "angle of vision" which, Kazin explains in the case of

Faulkner, is more than a writer's opinions, sensibility, moral **Alfred** philosophy, psychology: "the angle of vision from which one **Kazin** recurringly sees the universe—that native disposition of mind which plants in us very early those particular words, those haunted stresses and inflections, those mysterious echolaic re- petitions, to which we most instinctively return." The inmost leaf describes that depth of self where religion is experienced and that depth of self which is the habitation of the imagination or, since its fundamental way of perceiving is involved, is perhaps the imagination itself. It is the core of being, the inalienable central creative self, which is also the "residue of human quality beyond the reach of cultural control" that Trilling believes makes possible an opposing self. And in Kazin's twentieth- century example of Lawrence as well as the eighteenth-century example of Blake, it declares an opposing self: "that painfulness [in Lawrence] is an unmistakable quality of twentieth-century genius, of genius as a force in itself—a genius that has learned to discomfort, to threaten, to shock, in order to assert the creative principle against the increasing awareness of how much inner freedom contemporary man has lost."

Almost all of the twenty-eight essays, which treat both Ameri- can and European writers of the present and the past, are studies of human depth and extremity, of "the human mind itself specifically in action." This, as Kazin reminds us in discussing the work of Walter Prescott Webb and Bernard DeVoto, is also a desideratum of the writing of history. He is concerned with spiritual desire, with its reach and depth, and in treating these writers, he wishes to awaken the "natural idealism" and "moral depth" that he misses now, to refresh our sense of life, of its spiritual striving, suffering, and joy. He relates everything to the present ("We live in a culture where the highest aim is not to live in the spirit"); and though he appreciates the artist's need for rage against the complacency of the bourgeois ("a being," Flaubert said, "whose mode of feeling is low"), his own response is somewhat gentler, sadder, more in accord with Chekhov's ad- monition, "You live badly, my friends. It is shameful to live like that." In keeping with this are the biographical approach, which relies on evocative quotation, the personal voice, now much more his own, and the writers themselves, who help him exemplify and explore reliance on "the real man, the imagination."

Beginning with a tribute to Joyce at the time of his death— Joyce is the unassailable heroic artist, "the last man in Europe who wrote as if art were worth a human life"—Kazin presents a pantheon of writer heroes. By way of Henry and William James, Proust, and Gorky (who permits him to treat Chekhov and Tolstoy), he brings us to Blake. His essay on Blake, originally the introduction to the *Portable Blake*, provides the historical framework of the collection as well as its inmost leaf. Like the essay on Faulkner that concludes the book, this essay is a set piece. It is the longest essay, and in it he most fully studies a modern artist and the pervasiveness of the imagination. Here, in explicating Blake, he expresses his own views, especially in regard to childhood ("the buried part"), sexuality and love ("the body is above all a person"), rationality and repression ("Blake is against everything that submits, mortifies, constricts and denies"), and naturalism ("a great and tragic way of looking at life" that, for him, is truer than Blake's view because, in stressing human limits, it acknowledges a reality other than the imagination, a reality which makes "struggle . . . the image of his [man's] true life in the world . . . one that he deepens by art, knowledge, and love"). This essay is a good example of taking possession of a writer—how, and how much so, we can see in Blake's presence in A *Walker in the City* and in the comparison of Kazin's Blake to Eliot's and Northrop Frye's. Eliot's treatment is unjust, denigrating, and Frye's, equally as engaged as Kazin's, is didactic and curiously remote. By contrast with both, Kazin's treatment is personal, that is, clearly the result of encounter. His relation to writers is neither magisterial nor pedagogical.

The subsequent essays graph artistic and critical achievement in respect to devotion to and depth of trust in imagination. The middle portion of the book describes smaller and larger waves in

whose troughs we find Turgenev, the Fitzgerald of *The Crack-*
*Up*, and the later E. E. Cummings, and we find Lawrence,
Flaubert, and Kafka at their peaks and near them, Gide,
Thoreau, Ellen Glasgow, and the critics Paul Rosenfeld and
Edmund Wilson. Then, with "On Melville as Scripture," an
essay on Richard Chase's *Herman Melville*, the book takes
another course, turning mostly to the practice of criticism, to
current examples like those of Webb and DeVoto, Peter Quen-
nell, Francis Steegmuller, and Robert Elias. More than before
the tone of these essays is stringent and combative.

In the essay on Chase, Kazin attacks the critic-as-ideologist,
the critic who fails to treat the artist and the art and tries instead,
by modish critical means that simplify the complexity of art and
history, to make Melville the "Messiah of the 'New Liberalism.'" To sacrifice "a unique experience to the abstracts of a
moral lesson or ideology" is the worst critical failure, reduc-
tionism at the expense of all the imagination offers—the common fault, he finds, of all the critics except Steegmuller. He
emphasizes this failure by following Chase with Simone Weil,
who "stood apart from all contemporary ideologies," and by
noting, in contrast to his own enthusiasm, Eliot's caution in
writing about her. Simone Weil is one of his contemporary
heroes, placed here because her commitment was both social
and religions ("She was a fanatically dedicated participant in the
most critical experiences of our time, who tried to live them
directly in contact with the supernatural"). Kazin values the
"direction of her work" and, with the shallow political endeavor
of the "New Liberalism" in mind, wants us to appreciate its
depth, its truth to our spiritual crisis, the condition of our lives,
of which he reminds us in amending Chase's version of Melville
and establishes as the frame of the book by treating Dostoevsky
and Faulkner at the end. Simone Weil's gift, he says, was her
remarkable openness "to all human experience at its most extreme, neglected, and uprooted" and her "loving attentiveness
to all the living world that would lift man above the natural
loneliness of existence."

In saying this, Kazin speaks for his own work, for the depth from which he feels criticism must speak, especially now, as he notes in introducing Dostoevsky, "in this season of deep human winter, when so much facile humanism lies frozen on the stalk of our science and ethics." He turns to Dostoevsky now for the homeopathic cure we may find in literature; we ourselves, he believes, are "all a little Russian these days" and "even more Russian in our growing approximation to that absolute spiritual crisis which Dostoevsky's heroes accept as the ground of their lives." And since this crisis, "however measured by political disorder . . . is not to be defined in political terms alone," Kazin's only solution is exemplification of the way the "noblest individuals" have lived in their historical situations—have, as he says of Faulkner's Negroes, whom he likens to the Jews, taken in "the whole of their situation precisely because they know it is the *human* situation, and so in some sense cannot be remedied." Insisting more than most critics—even New Critics—on the depth and complexity of human experience, Kazin also relies more on the imagination that enables us to know it and meet it, and not only to courageously will to endure it but, as he says of Sherwood Anderson, to "never let go that trembling vision of love which is all we ever offer to the great mystery around us."

Long after we have read *The Inmost Leaf*, we remember its consonance. It is a small book, every part ably made and carefully joined, that strikes us as critically right and valuable because it has the point of view promised by the title. "It is a writer's point of view," Kazin says, "that gives us our immediate experience of his mind in all its rich particularity. It is *in* his point of view, though not necessarily for his point of view, that we read him."

When we take up *Contemporaries* (1962), Kazin's next book and most recent collection of essays, we enter it with the familiarity which is one of the rewards of following a writer's work and with the pleasure of reading him for as well as in his point of view. Yet we may be troubled by size—*Contemporaries* con-

274

tains seventy-three essays—not because we dislike abundance but because its size suggests, as does the need to order the essays in various sections, the overwhelming task of the critic who has elected to keep up with contemporary literature and who has done so because he feels that we are living in a time of "constantly accelerating historical advance" when "the only check we have on events at all is contemporary literature." The book itself tells us something of the moral history of the seven-year interval between collections: the critic who believes that "contemporary literature somehow records our fate" is more vigilant.

The title is also declarative. It announces Kazin's rejection of what, especially since the end of World War II, had become of the modern movement. Not only, he believes, were its "essential ideals of freedom, spontaneity, individuality" dismissed by writers, it was institutionalized in the universities and became a fashion in society, emptied of its creative and political significance. And so, the modern, he bitterly remarks, "has become the enemy of the contemporary." Contemporary, of course, suggests the immediate, the now and the vital. It is approbatory, as in the characterization of Edmund Wilson in *On Native Grounds* as one who worked in "the foreground of contemporary literature." By dedicating *Contemporaries* to Wilson, Kazin stresses the value of this commitment even as, by evoking the critic with whom he now wishes to be compared, he may be reproving Wilson for no longer so fully undertaking this task.

Yet Kazin would have been able to appreciate Wilson's work in the postwar years because, like much of his own, it fulfilled another function of criticism occasioned by the acceleration of history. "Criticism takes place in society," he says in "The Useful Critic" (1965), "it is a dialogue with the past and one's contemporaries." *Contemporaries* is not wholly contemporary. It is most accurately described as a moral history, not exclusively American, that begins at the time of the French Revolution and ends in the present with the critic assessing criticism. Contemporary writers figure in it, but they are prepared for by essays on

earlier writers and are provided the context of the full range of
Kazin's concerns. In reading it, we realize that Kazin has something of the Proustian quality he attributes to Wilson as well as
the kind of "cultural imagination" that he said saved Wilson
from loss of perspective in the 1930s. We realize, too, that by
exemplifying the virtues of cultural imagination—notably
perspective and awareness of continuity—he is asking us now to
make it our own.

The disquiet of the present prompts this book, but the imagination in it turns to the past. The tone of *Contemporaries* is
harsher than that of the previous collection; there is desperation
in it, and its taste is sour. The present is shutting down. Kazin
finds nothing auspicious in it, neither the advent of a new poetry
(open, as he would have the essay), a poetry he does not treat
except in the case of Lowell, nor the Beat writers, whom he
merely notices hostilely. Instead—it is an old concern but a new
element in the book indicative of the times—he writes, as he
says in an essay on I. B. Singer, of "the immemorial Jewish
vision of the world." Now he takes up the Jewish writers (Bellow,
Malamud, Roth, Salinger, Mailer) whose emergence after the
war was a significant development in American literature; and
he takes up Sholom Aleichem and Freud, the former for the
sustenance of the Yiddish tradition and the latter for the "gift of
conviction" he believes he derived from his Jewish background.
Now he travels to Israel.

The book consolidates. The critic stands his ground. Having
provided a historical context in the initial essay on the modern
movement, he turns to some American writers of the nineteenth
century whose relevance to the present is their concern with
imagination and consciousness and the "modern" predicaments
of self and society; and, in an essay on the Civil War partly
indebted to the early installments of Wilson's *Patriotic Gore*, he
treats the issue of ideology and imagination and relates the
earlier crisis to the present agitation for civil rights. Melville is
the exemplary figure of this section, where Dreiser and Faulkner are the exemplary figures of the next, which is devoted to

early twentieth-century and long established writers. Here, Kazin depreciates Gertrude Stein, Ezra Pound, Graham Greene, and John O'Hara, and by way of Dreiser and Faulkner, who, with Melville, express his sense of life, upholds a view unpopular in a time when writers too much cultivate their sensibilities—that "literature grows out of a sense of abundant relationships with the world." When he proceeds to contemporary writers, he addresses the "alone generation" ("we get novels in which society is merely a backdrop to the aloneness of the hero") and condemns those, like Salinger, who are "reduced to 'personality,' even to the 'mystery of personality,' instead of the drama of our social existence." His position is not unlike Wilson's in respect to the Symbolists, and, like Wilson's it is political, connected for Kazin with all that the opposition of ideology and imagination stands for in his thought. It is the position implied in the 1955 Postscript to *On Native Grounds:* "Our early twentieth-century American fiction seemed to carry the whole weight of our society; now it has the effect of exquisitely studying personal problems alone—by which I mean that the characters in contemporary American novels do not criticize the world they live in and have no thought of changing it; they merely live in it . . . and keep their own counsel."

Of course there are exceptions, Saul Bellow, for example, whose novels, Kazin says, "offer the deepest commentary [imaginative criticism] I know on the social utopianism [ideology] of a generation which always presumed that it could pacify life, that it could control and guide it to an innocuous social end, but which is painfully learning . . . to celebrate life, to praise in it the divine strength which disposes of man's proposals."[4] Other writers of Bellow's generation provide instances of this painful learning, but Kazin gathers them in the

4  Like his friend Richard Hofstader, Kazin knew that the "political culture of progressivism . . . [had become] part of the modern crisis rather than its solution." See Christopher Lasch, "On Richard Hofstader," *New York Review of Books*, March 8, 1973, and especially Lasch's excellent comparison of *On Native Grounds* and *The American Political Tradition.*

subsequent sections on European writers, on his own travel reports from Germany, Puerto Rico, Russia, and Israel (again he follows the example of Wilson), and on Freud and the cultural consequences of psychoanalysis (an interest, it seems from the dates of the essays, stimulated by Trilling). And he points it up immediately in the next section, "The Puzzle of Modern Society," where contemporary works on the past, like those of Leslie Fiedler, Dwight Macdonald, Edmund Wilson, and Arthur Schlesinger, Jr., enable him to consider the 1930s, the period to which we owe our legacy of ideology. The placement of this section dramatizes Kazin's most important theme, for it sets the ideologists against the creators of the previous sections as well as against the critic with whose responsibilities he concludes in "The Function of Criticism Today."

The Arnoldian title is appropriate if only because it reminds us of Arnold's view of literature as a criticism of life—a view which has been, as Trilling says, "a gage thrown to all critics since." Kazin accepted that challenge from the outset, and his work exemplifies it. Now, however, he offers his own challenge in a time of crisis that might be fittingly described by Arnold's "darkling plain." He is not so much concerned as Arnold was with creating "a current of true and fresh ideas" as with using criticism to "enliven the imagination" and, since literature itself, according to some observers, is of less significance now, to uphold its necessity and the belief that life is sustained by the imagination. The kind of criticism he wants defines his own. Of *histoire morale* he says that it "sums up the spirit of the age in which we live and then asks us to transcend it . . . enables us to see things in the grand perspective, and . . . asks us—in the light not only of man's history but of his whole striving—to create a future in keeping with man's imagination."

It has been difficult for Kazin to fulfill these high demands of criticism in a time that, he said in 1966, offers "everything but hope." Only a few of the essays written in the 1960s—since the publication of *Contemporaries*—enliven the imagination.

Many seem to be written on demand, not out of vital need. Some cover old ground, others well-established figures; few treat contemporary writers ("we must learn to practice criticism on the newer writers," he had said in *Contemporaries*),[5] and those that do are among the short pieces in *Vogue* that lend credence to his remark in an interview that he earned his living as a professor and journalist "in order to support myself as a *writer.*" That he has been a writer ("not a reporter but a literary artist," as he said of Wilson) has been his distinction. But he has not been so distinguished a writer of criticism as Wilson nor so consistently fine. After *The Inmost Leaf* there is a falling off. The incidence of clichés rises in *Contemporaries*, and much of the work of the 1960s lacks vigor and is written loosely. It would not be possible for Kazin to make of these reviews and essays a collection of the quality and pertinence of the earlier ones— though such a collection would document the dislocation he felt at this time.

His interest is elsewhere. We feel in the essays on nineteenth-century writers that he wrote during the 1960s—he planned to do a book on the nineteenth-century imagination— that, as he said of John Jay Chapman, he is "excited by old ideas" and that he has turned back because it has become important to him "to revitalize the symbolic theme of our experience." The gauge of his sense of these years and of his response to them is the necessity he feels to retrieve (I cite an earlier phrase) "the great heritage of our romantic and democratic past." He would like, it seems, to follow Chapman who "recharged and uplifted—not by mere partisanship of old causes, such as professional liberals give us when they invoke the past as a slogan, but through imaginative reinvolvement." And this is what he does, not in a book on nineteenth-century writers, but in *Starting Out in the Thirties* (1965), which the interest in the nineteenth-century writers may have helped to precipitate. "I shared much of their belief in the ideal freedom and power of the self, in the political

5  He follows this counsel in *Bright Book of Life* (1973), where he moves from familiar to new writers, not however without considerable selectivity.

and social vision of radical democracy," he says in "The Useful Critic," where he tells of falling in love with American literature. "It was as if I started from the same human base and was accompanying them to the same imaginative goal."

Starting out in the "age of Hitler," the nineteen-year-old boy already has a literary tradition and notion of calling to which he is steadfast and which will see him through. Kazin tells us immediately that "I was a literary radical, indifferent to economics, suspicious of organization, planning, Marxist solemnity and intellectual system-building; it was the rebels of literature, the great wrestlers-with-God, Thor with his mighty hammer, the poets of unlimited spiritual freedom, whom I loved—Blake, Emerson, Whitman, Nietzsche, Lawrence." He explains that a literary radical is not an "ideologue." His resources are not political but literary: "the revolutionary yet wholly literary tradition in American writing to which I knew that I belonged." He looks "to literature for strong social argument, intellectual power, human liberation," and he awaits the salvation by the word that the "true writer," like Malraux in his account, may bring. At the start, Kazin identifies the literary radical with the sixteen-year-old in A *Walker in the City*—and with the writer who now needs to reaffirm his literary faith.

He does not tell us that he owes the phrase and much of the conception of literary radical to Randolph Bourne. Bourne's autobiographical chapter, "The History of a Literary Radical," is a prototype of his own book and a still-quickening summons to the work he set himself then and sets himself now: to create a usable past; to rescue American writers, Bourne said, "and try to tap through them a certain eternal human tradition of abounding vitality and moral freedom, and so build out the future." Bourne confessed that of the two elements that he tried to fuse in his conception of the literary radical, the radical (or sociological) in his case was predominant; in Kazin's case, it is the literary (or imaginative). For Bourne this was probably the result of early experiences of handicap and injustice; for Kazin, as A *Walker in the City* tells us, it was the result of the encounters of self, word,

280

and world whose convergence is conversion. And Bourne was sociological because he opposed gentility and, by using sociology to open new vistas, was able to advance the claims of democracy and modernism; while Kazin stands for the imagination not because he repudiates, as the New Critics did, a concern with society (social change), but because he opposes a sociology that no longer sustains the democratic and modernist spirit, a sociology that prohibits possibility because it has become ideological and doctrinaire. Opposition to such a sociology, or rather ideological habits of thought, has been the outstanding and longstanding issue in his work. It was the issue with which he contended at the start, and by telling us now, he would remind us that it is still the issue with which a liberating critic must contend.

Except for the absence of the erotic theme, which the epigraph from Odets' *Awake and Sing* advises us is central, chapter one is an epitome of the book. Kazin is not concerned with movements but with some of the literary people on the Left he himself knew—people whose political inclination he shared, who occasionally helped him in his career, but who, for reasons that show the complex entanglements of self and history, did not always have his approval. Though the book depicts various milieux—those of the Village, of mid- and upper Manhattan, of Brownsville, Brooklyn Heights, and Provincetown—its essential work is to provide a gallery of portraits that help Kazin place himself and chart his victory against what in most instances he considers defeat. He makes *his* way in a world of ideologues, ideologues whose representations embody the meaning of ideology.

The first of these is John Chamberlain, to whom Kazin owed the letter of introduction to the *New Republic* that launched his career. This portrait is excellent and like most of the others is nicely double in its rendering. For it evokes the brilliant young journalist of the New York *Times* and the boy's excitement in meeting him—the "poetry of remembered happenings," as Kazin says of the creative achievement of autobiography in

"Autobiography as Narrative" (1964)—evokes this as well as his disapproval of Chamberlain as a representative intellectual, "the golden boy of a generation of ideologues." The characterization is accurate yet not as neutral or laudatory as it seems, for the author of *Golden Boy*, whose work Kazin exuberantly treats later, stands for much that he opposes to Chamberlain's "abstract mind." Chamberlain, he says, "lived on ideas, 'notions' of things . . . completely missing the color and emotion of the human crisis behind them"; "one could never talk to Chamberlain about imaginative literature, music, painting, women." But Odets "worked with human samples, not abstractions," as Kazin himself is doing; and just as important, he had not gone to Yale, was a plebe, one of the writers of the immigrant and working class to which Kazin belonged, whose advent, he says, was the real and lasting achievement of the 1930s: "The real excitement of the period was in the explosion of personal liberation which such writers brought in from the slums, farms and factories." The age of Hitler was also "the age of the plebes," an age whose political failure is designated by Hitler and whose success, enabled by the revolutionary ferment of the time, is designated by the plebes. "What the young writers of the Thirties wanted," Kazin says, and his own writing now carries it forward as an act in the present, "was to prove the literary value of our experience, to recognize the possibility of art in our own lives, to feel that we had moved the streets, the stockyards, the hiring halls into literature—to show that our radical strength could carry on the experimental impulse of modern literature."

Though Malcolm Cowley, literary editor of the *New Republic*, fostered this and was a partisan of literature more than of ideology, Kazin places him with the ideologues because, like Chamberlain and even Otis Ferguson, one of the "real roughs," Cowley was a "have," an Anglo-Saxon (WASP, we say now) in a position of power. He explains later that he felt that literary men from the business and professional classes were "outsiders," that "they could only interpret in an abstract and literary way the daily struggle that was so real to me in Brownsville" and "would have been puzzled by anything personal that was outside their literary categories." Chamberlain's letter to Cowley opened Kazin's "path to the outside world"—the phrase also calls up Hawthorne's need of literature. But even though it helped him make good the passage from Brownsville, bringing him to the brownstone house on Twenty-first Street occupied by the *New Republic* and still evocative for him of Brooks's literary radicalism, the world remained outside, more sharply so than he imagined it would because, with his "violent class prejudice," the depression drove him back to his own world. Now, he tells us, the subway ride to Brownsville excited him: "I was leaving the stiff world behind. . . . I was coming home to my own."

The vantage of Kazin's vivid impressions of Cowley is the bench in the waiting room of the *New Republic*, where with other "hungry faces" he waited for the weekly handout of books to review. But the portrait that emerges is again mediated by subsequent awareness and skillfully touched. For those who know Cowley's career—know, for example, that he wrote *The Literary Situation*—Kazin's later remark that he liked Cowley "as little as ever" is not unexpected. Strokes such as "he was unable to lift his pipe to his mouth, or to make a crack, without making one feel that he recognized the literary situation involved" are deflationary and spiteful. After all that Kazin says to Cowley's credit, we remember the literary bellwether ("Wherever Cowley moved or ate, wherever he lived, he heard the bell of literary history sounding the moment and his own voice calling possibly another change in the literary weather")—we remember that, beneficial as his leadership was to the plebes, "it was this feeling for movements that made Cowley redirect the literary side of the *New Republic* in the direction of a sophisticated literary Stalinism, since for Cowley 'revolution' was now a new stage of development."

How much this statement judges! Cowley's revolutionary commitment led him at the time of the Moscow Trials to support "the Stalinists with whom he identified the future." This commitment, Kazin believed, was both misplaced and shallow. It lacked the ardor and sacrificial heroism of Katov in Malraux's *Man's Fate* and the compassion and love of Berado Viola in Silone's *Fontamara*, books of revolutionary example that Cowley's reviews had kindled for him—books that he uses now to recapture the special quality of 1934 and the pitch of his own passion, and to pit the writer, the bona fide literary radical, against the ideologue.

The portraits are the brilliant foci of the book. Moving from one to the next, we find ourselves in the widening circle of Kazin's literary life—a literary life so inextricably political that we find ourselves also in the deepening crisis of history. There are portraits of plebe writers: James T. Farrell on the day he finished the last volume of the *Studs Lonigan* trilogy ("For the first time," Kazin says, "I felt that I was in my own world, and that it had expanded into the creative life") and William Saroyan, whose freedom from "Anglo Saxon convention" and belief that "with a book he would create his own life at last" he found exhilarating. There are bright miniatures, like those of Nathaniel West and of Mark Van Doren at his teaching; and there are portraits of intellectuals, the fullest that of V. F. Calverton, the independent socialist editor of the *Modern Monthly*, who did not accept the official verdict in the Moscow Trials. This warm and generous tribute is in keeping with Calverton's own remarkable openness and overrides Kazin's disdain for the intellectual systematizer. The Calverton who matters to him is the believer in liberation, who in his own life, Kazin discovered, was liberated. Not Cowley, not Otis Ferguson, who came to dinner in Brownsville, but Calverton "brought my two worlds together": "He put me at my ease, he took me up, he brought me directly into his office-home in the house always shadowed by the great tree on Morton Street, at a time when I had no human connection with the people I wrote for." And Calverton brought him directly to an ideological forum, where independent Marxists like Max Eastman and

Sidney Hook argued mightily and a survivor of other ideological wars, Max Nomad (unnamed), taught him that power corrupts everyone, even revolutionary idealists.

There are portraits of types of his generation also starting out, among them Francis, "the pedant as Communist," who became a repentant Communist after the Hitler-Stalin Pact, and Harriet, who like many radicals at the time—Chamberlain was eventually one of them—worked for Henry Luce; and portraits of Malraux and Ralph Bates rallying support for the Spanish Loyalists, the one "the writer as the conscience of intellectual and fraternal humanity, the writer as the master of men's souls," the other "a political commissar." (Their manners of speech tell the propagandist from the artist: Bates is "dangerously fluent," where Malraux speaks with "such fire that his body itself seemed to be speaking"—speaks in the passionate way of Kazin himself. Though Kazin places Malraux in Harriet's perspective, he expresses by such means his own identification.) And at the end, in 1940, when the United Front had been destroyed by the Hitler-Stalin Pact and World War II had begun, there are portraits of other intellectuals who, like Kazin, are summering at Provincetown. The most striking are those of Bertram Wolfe, an old professional revolutionary who "had lived a dangerous and exhausting life in the Communist opposition to Stalin," and Mary McCarthy whom he had met at the Wolfes' and against whose kindly spirits he etches her destructive, censorious intellect. That she is the young wife of the Edmund Wilson we glimpse riding his bicycle to the bakery is not mentioned. Nothing mitigates the portrait, which distills all the bitterness of general disillusionment as well as his own resentment of those, like her colleagues on *Partisan Review*, who "did not value imagination"—and of "cocksure" women like Harriet, who, he says, "could never forgive me for not regarding her as an artist." His portraiture is not unlike that of his subject's: Mary McCarthy is one of those young radical intellectuals "who had already passed through the radical movement as if it were a bohemian experience"; she is "the first writer of my generation," Kazin says, "who made me realize that it would now be possible to be a radical without any idealism whatsoever." With her, Kazin closes out the age and prefigures another when criticism would supplant creative imagination and intellectuals who "had failed at revolution [would] succeed as intellectual arbiters." At the end of the gallery is a portrait, in chiaroscuro, of Philip Rahv, "the Doctor Johnson of his small group of radical intellectuals [on *Partisan Review*]," an avant garde that "gnawed on each other, lived on each other," yet in the person of Rahv, an old-style Russian intellectual, commanded Kazin's respect because they at least understood the relation of literature to society and still believed in it as a force for social change.

One of the remarkable things about Kazin's gallery is that it contains, as conspicuously present and as much a part of the time, portraits of people whose claim to attention is not historical but personal. These portraits—of his cousin Sophie and his mother, of Nora, with whom he played marriage, and Natasha, whom he married in 1938—bear much of the weight of the book because for Kazin love and the liberation it brings stands to history as literature and imagination stand to ideology. When Kazin brings Otis Ferguson home, he opens a space in the narrative where he can again depict the women to whom he owes his emotional nurture and erotic awakening. Cousin Sophie, he says in a headnote to the passages concerning her reprinted in *The Open Form* (third edition), "was at once a mother figure and a love object," for him "the embodiment of Woman"; from being near her, he says that he guessed "all that a man would experience in loving women." But in Sophie's determination to have love, he also learns that one is justified in rebelling in behalf of a full and joyous life, that liberation is a necessity of spirit, that there are depths deeper than those of politics, existential abysses, and a moving power in love that may be greater than that of politics ("Mom," Ralph says in *Awake and Sing*, "I love this girl"). Unlike Kazin's mother, whose sense of the "grimness of life" dominates her portrait, Sophie makes demands on life and finally risks herself for love. "The world is made to be risked . . . our fate is not always to be deliberated"—this is what she teaches him; and this, too, is what Cot's *The Storm*, a picture foretelling Sophie's fate and his own marriage in a time of historical crisis, teaches him.

Sophie's abandonment and tragedy provide a background for the abandon of his marriage and the "happy time" when he and Natasha pursue their vocations and enjoy a simple life of high thinking and cultural pleasure untroubled, it seems, by political weather. The liberation of love and work are coincident, but the love that preempts his memory is of work ("I had fallen in love with the Eighties and Nineties, with the dark seedtime of modern writers and modern art"). The glory that fills these pages is not so much that of the kind of purified life that he believed justified revolution as it is of his coming, finally, to the source he had hoped to find in *A Walker in the City*. Living in a dusky old Brooklyn near the Bridge, working daily on his book in the New York Public Library, he was, he says, "living in the turn of the century . . . the dark revolutionary time." And he was discovering the tradition of literary radicalism to which his own work was an act of allegiance. "When I read Randolph Bourne and the young Van Wyck Brooks," he recalls, "I could not feel that 1938 was so far from 1912." He felt connected to them, and to Wilson; their literary and social aspirations were his, and working on his book, he felt "radicalism as a spiritual passion" and that he was helping "to direct a new impulse into the future." This, of course, is what recollection now exemplifies: with him, we feel that 1965 is not so far from 1912, that the connection, even with all the history that follows 1938, has not been broken. The stirring quality belongs also to the present. When Kazin recalls his response to Brooks's belief that literary criticism must become social criticism because our social life needs to be reconstructed ("*There* was the voice I recognized, the vocation I loved"), he reaffirms a deep impulse of his own criticism and declares—it is what the autobiographical work performs—a victory over ideology by showing an indomitable "insurgency of spirit."

The measure of the present victory is the disillusionment with history that provides the lasting impression of the book. Against the exultation of his happy time, Kazin places an account of his disbelief when first hearing of the Hitler-Stalin Pact. For he, too, believed in history, in the "historical destiny so clearly foreseen by liberals and socialists in the nineteenth century," and history had sustained him as a Jew and as a writer. Once he had believed that "even in Hitler Germany, to be outside of society and to be Jewish was to be at the heart of things" because "History was preparing, in its Jewish victims and through them, some tremendous deliverance and revelation." Writers like Odets had convinced him that "History was going our way" and that as a writer the "surging march of history might yet pass through me." For a time, he read the enormities of France, of Mussolini and Hitler as signs of challenge, not defeat. "I trusted," he says, "to the righteousness of history"—"Just as I was trying to break through, so history was seeking its appointed consummation. My interest and the genius of history simply had to coincide." But on August 22, 1939, he learned that the appointed consummation was neither righteous nor coincident, that he had been betrayed. "All my life," he writes, still moved by the rancor of that time, "I had lived among people who seemed to me beautiful because they were the dust of the earth; I had taken literally the claim that they identified their suffering with the liberation of humanity. I now saw that the ideologues among these people had no moral imagination whatever, and no interest in politics. They were merely the slaves of an idea, fetishists of an ideology; the real world did not exist for them, and they would never understand it."

As he told us at the start, the age was Hitler's, and it would end—or would it end?—with the concentration camp at Belsen, whose "liberation" he witnessed at a newsreel theater in London in 1945. By concluding the book with that episode, Kazin gives us a perverse image of the redemption promised by History, an image still unbearable because we respond to it now knowing what Kazin has taught us: that History neither redeems nor progresses but recurs; that it is neither orderly nor simple like
his chronological headings, but capricious and complex (he

became a critic by chance and achieved personal success in a time of public failure); that the heart may prepare us better than the head to endure it, but that love—Sophie's, even his own, which he realizes now was not reciprocated—cannot outrun the storm.

In "The Jew as Modern Writer" (1966), one of several codas to *Starting Out in the Thirties*, Kazin sketches a history of the Jewish writer that begins with Veblen's observations on the intellectual advantage of the Jew's divided cultural allegiance and goes on to explore his own awareness of the Jew's resources. Of most importance is the resistant power that derives from long experience of disaster and from a sense of history as purposive and able to reassert itself against repeated horrors. (In an introduction to the *Selected Stories of Sholom Aleichem*, Kazin cites Tevye's aside on the part of the evening prayer that petitions the healing power of the Lord: "Send us the cure, we have the ailment already.") Whether as vaudevillian or black humorist, the Jew, he believes, upholds life. He feels that the emergence of the Jewish writers and intellectuals in the 1930s, and more prominently after World War II, was the result of the need in times of extreme situations and accelerating history to witness and explain and that, having also been responsive to modernism, they were prepared to do this. "What these writers all had in common," he says, "was the ascendancy of 'modern literature,' which has been more destructive of bourgeois standards than Marxism, was naturally international-minded, and in a culture bored with middle-class rhetoric, upheld the primacy of intelligence and the freedom of the imagination." Their task, accordingly, was to be "the instructors and illuminati of the modern spirit."

In another coda, "Autobiography as Narrative" (1964), Kazin obliquely comments on his own autobiographies and addresses an important issue in his criticism. His finest work is autobiographical,[6] and yet he maintains that self and imagination must

6 A *Walker in the City* is not a memoir, as Allen Guttmann says, and is superior, I think, to *Starting Out in the Thirties*, which is still a work of

go beyond themselves, that work so exclusively of the self is creatively inferior to drama and fiction. But when he comes to the conclusion of the essay, the pressure of present history provokes this justification: "Autobiography as narrative can serve to create the effect of a world that in the city jungle, in the concentration camps, in the barracks, is the form we must learn to express even when we have no hope of mastering it. We are all, as Camus showed . . . strangers in our present-day world— and as strangers, we have things to say about our experience that no one else can say for us. In a society where so many values have been overturned without our admitting it, where there is an obvious gap between the culture we profess and the dangers among which we really live, the autobiographical mode can be an authentic way of establishing the truth of our experience. The individual is real even when the culture around him is not."

*Strangers.* When Kazin uses this word in a review of *Growing Up Absurd* (1960), he has Camus in mind but, perhaps because the context is youth, it stands for all that "walker" did: "To be young is often to find oneself in the position of the 'barbarian' in the classic sense of the word—the stranger, the man from without, who does not know the ways of the capital but who longs for its prizes." When he comes to know the ways of the capital and has secured some of its prizes, he is still a stranger, not solely for the reasons Veblen considered the Jew a wayfaring man but for others connected with recent history. The great human symbol of contemporary literature, Kazin said in 1958, was not the rebel but the stranger because "there is no authoritative moral tradition that he can honestly feel limits and hinders his humanity." And so "it is the stranger . . . who seeks not to destroy the moral order, but to create one that will give back to him the idea of humanity."

The incentive here is conserving. "When there is a break in tradition—too injurious a sense of 'strangeness'—the critic

autobiographical impulse, though in some respects a memoir. It is too early to judge the autobiographical necessity of Kazin's forthcoming volume of recollections, but the installments already published suggest to me that it will be a memoir, not an autobiography.

wants to restore consciousness of it," Kazin said in an interview following the publication of *Contemporaries*. He speaks for a major element of his work, of the book on the nineteenth-century imagination that he put aside and of *Bright Book of Life* (1973), his most recent book. This swift-moving narrative of "American Novelists and Storytellers"—the subtitle is accurate: the writer is central, writing is peripheral—is substantively less weighty than his other books, though the moral burden it carries is as great. The writing is exuberant because Kazin is confident, full of his subject, and eager to write about it. *And eager to be writing:* more than anything the prose suggests that he finds this salutary, for the prose expresses his need better than the somber story it is asked to tell. This disproportion marks the book. The subject, which provides the evidence, is somehow unworthy of the moral demands Kazin makes on (against) it. The devotion to literature, a virtue of this inquiry, and literature itself which merits such devotion are sapped by the need to reprove, by the evident dissatisfaction with so much of the writing of our time.

The book turns, as all of Kazin's work does, on the moral shock of World War II, an enormity to the nth power, as yet unassimilated by the imagination. The difference between World War I and World War II is incommensurable, and the faith in literature to master violence—Hemingway's work is the example—was destroyed by the second war and by its aftermath. "World War II," Kazin writes, "turned into a very different war [impossible to think of as an 'old-fashioned war,' a war contained within a civilization] over the twenty-five years in which we have been forced to think of Hiroshima, Auschwitz, Dresden, the thirty million dead . . . the threat of universal nuclear destruction." [7] This war—that literature has not been able to tell it tells its horror—has become the "War that . . . never ended, War as the continued experience of twentieth-century man"— yes, and though Kazin says it otherwise, the health of the state, as Bourne learned in World War I.

Kazin's sense of contemporary disorder and of the failure of

7  And Belsen, which Kazin mentions again.

the liberal imagination pervades this pathology of writers. The discontinuity of past and present that he momentarily overcame in writing *Starting Out in the Thirties* is the most apparent cause of all that disturbs him. And faced with it, his recourse is not that of his novelists and storytellers, which is for the most part to experiment as best they can in however limited ways, but to fall back on the past in order to remain true to himself. History, denied by the outcome of the 1930s, is once more a reliance; and the novel, "the one bright book of life," as Lawrence said when proclaiming the superiority of the novel and of the novelist, is still, whatever the failure of contemporary writers (they are judged in terms of the conventional social novel and very few have written bright books of life), the immense resource it had always been.[8] Kazin's gusto for literature, especially for the novel, is irrepressible and expresses a gusto for life, a desire for intimacy with the broadest range of experience, and, always, social experience. What is continuous in his work, which now faces less easily addressed moral crises than at its beginning (this is one measure of the difference between *On Native Grounds* and *Bright Book of Life*), is passionate moral engagement, concern for our social condition and the condition of the creative consciousness upon whose triumphs he believes we depend. Though the evidence of the moral history of our time is dismaying, he refuses, as perhaps all creators must, to believe that life is meaningless and human endeavor worthless.

It was in Cambridge, in 1950, I think, that I first heard Alfred Kazin speak. Nearly twenty years passed before I heard him again, this time on an academic program I had helped to

---

8 Lawrence's praise of the novelist as getting all of "man alive" and making "the whole man alive tremble" is probably sound and certainly understandable as a personal declaration. But should this view be taken over by the critic, however much he loves the novel, without acknowledging that the forms Lawrence dismissed—poetry, philosophy, science (and why not add theology, even criticism?)—have on occasion made "the whole man alive tremble"?

arrange. The text of his speech is in print, but not the furious utterance prompted by an earlier speaker who alluded offensively to Jews from Brownsville. That night, we talked for several hours in the hotel coffee shop; I met him then, when his public speech had released him, still in the excitement of the occasion. I wrote this essay by the time of our next meeting, in the spring of 1973, when he came to Iowa City to give an intensive course on the contemporary novel. Now, six weeks later, I have finished revising it—up here in the woods, where besides rereading Homer I have been working through the pile of late copies of the New York *Times* for all the news of Watergate.

How constant Alfred Kazin's criticism has been! Every afternoon he talked for two hours about one or another of the authors he had just written about in *Bright Book of Life*. He spoke without notes, quietly but impassionately. (Had he learned to teach from the example of Mark Van Doren or Lionel Trilling? I thought of both). For pedagogical reasons, perhaps, he set his lectures in the perspective of modern history. Students now, he believes with some justice, do not know history, and some responded to the iterance of wartime enormities—the holocaust is obsessively present to him—in the way they respond to their parents' stories of hardship in the Great Depression. They were impatient and disapproving. They had not come to be instructed in moral history but to learn about the novel, and they were not, I found, especially pleased with the kind of criticism that brought them together. The critics they knew were formalist, phenomenological, structuralist, were critics of criticism and theorists of the novel, poetry, language. Kazin was none of these. His moral vision, moreover, had not been altered as theirs had been formed by the counterculture.

I understood their dissatisfaction, but I heard him in the recognition of what I owed him. I had followed his work since 1947, when I read *On Native Grounds* and the *Portable Blake*, and that time I had for reasons of history caught up with him. I was now able to appreciate what in national terms might be called the New England Transcendentalist and Southern Calvinist aspects of his nature. I was heartened now by the way he sustained himself on a tradition and so sustained the tradition itself: when I heard Kazin, I also heard Brooks and Bourne, Rosenfeld and Wilson. And when I reread the autobiographies, especially *A Walker in the City*, I was deeply stirred and understood better the sources upon which I relied, the vocation I had chosen, and the way autobiographical impulse may become a correlative of tradition.